TRACKING

THE
CHARLATANS

TRACKING

THE CHARLATANS

An Environmental Columnist's Refutational Handbook

for the
Propaganda Wars

Edward Flattau

Global Horizons Press
Washington, D.C.

PRINTED IN THE UNITED STATES OF AMERICA

Cover design by Arne Lewis
Text design by Renee Winfield
Production management by Publication Creation Co.

First printing 1998

Library of Congress Catalog Number 97-94082

CONTENTS

PREFACE

Since June 1972, I have been writing a twice-weekly nationally syndicated environmental advocacy column, which at the height of its circulation appeared in more than 100 daily newspapers. Such longevity makes me something of a patriarch (some would say relic) among environmental journalists. For most of that period, I was the only columnist who regularly championed environmental causes and ethics on newspaper op-ed pages across the land.

This protracted labor of love has given me a unique overview of environmental issues. I may not be an expert on any one subject, but I know enough about all of them to recognize when someone is taking atrocious liberties with established facts. Moreover, my intense involvement with environmental concerns has acquainted me with renowned specialists who can clarify matters when a topic's technical complexity is beyond my expertise.

I have had only abject contempt for most of the eco-bashing that has been occurring in recent years. Along with the vast majority of environmental activists, I've made it a point to ignore as much as possible this ideologically motivated witch's brew of half-truths, specious innuendo, and outright falsehoods for fear of dignifying them with a response. Since President Clinton's 1992 election, however, the denigrators' campaign to discredit the degree, and in many instances the existence, of environmental concerns has benefited from an unprecedented surge of publicity through the publication of numerous books as well as increased coverage in the print and electronic mass media.

Why?

Nothing quickens the pulse of editors more than an opportunity to present, even emblazon, confrontational and contrarian views. Overnight, on the heels of the Clinton-Gore victory, an especially tempting target was created with the elevation of environmentalists into the Washington inner circle. I say "especially" because most mass media executives have never cared much for the environmental movement's condemnation of the cultural imperative on which they have long relied for the bulk of their enormous revenues — namely, conspicuous consumption. Those disgruntled executives simply had to repress their antipathy and provide a platform for pro-environmental crusading when public censure of the Reagan administration's abusive policies, and to a lesser extent those of President Bush, became too widespread to ignore.

With foes of the environmental movement abruptly out of political favor and thus acquiring an "underdog" status, many publishers and editors reversed field with relish.

Although I don't believe the environmental bashers' newfound publicity has won them many converts, assertions repeated often enough in highly visible forums of supposed authority begin to acquire credibility, no matter how preposterous they might be.

This book will provide ammunition for those who are skeptical of laissez-faire, libertarian-oriented environmental bashing and who yearn for succinct, straightforward rebuttals. Once you possess an elemental understanding of the principles and facts underlying the issues in dispute, the bogus nature of the anti-environmental tirades begins to crystallize.

The vulnerability of those who engage in these tirades is staggering. Under pressure to keep their impassioned groupies from bolting to the next bombastic ideologue, prominent bashers find themselves in the untenable position of not being able to admit they are ever wrong or their adversaries right, even when it is embarrassingly evident. The constant demand to appear omniscient and maintain their disciples' morale in upholding a distinctly minority view thus forces the high-profile detractors to create straw men and red herrings when reality begins to intrude on their flimsy hypotheses. They put words in environmentalists' mouth to create radical caricatures repugnant to the general public.

It's inconceivable that the bashers are not frequently aware that they are disseminating calumny. But they evidently consider their cause—discrediting the environmental movement for allegedly strangling the nation with centralized government and overregulation—sufficient justification to stretch the truth. One can only conclude they are operating from the premise that the end justifies the means, in a paradoxical recycling of the Marxist doctrine they so despise.

By viewing every environmental controversy in stark black and white, the leading spokespersons for the bashers—most of whom are media personalities, ideological policy wonks, politicians, academicians, business leaders, or scientists—remove themselves from reality's pervasive shades of gray and become even more vulnerable to refutation. Seemingly unconcerned about maintaining the integrity of the written (or spoken) word, they behave as though all they need do to prove their point is buttress their arguments with official-sounding facts, figures, citations, and endorsements. That someone might not accept such presentations at face value and actually check the accuracy of their sources doesn't seem to have occurred, or perhaps mattered, to them.

Hence, they go blithely about, rehashing the same flawed themes, out-of-context quotes, and factual manipulations, even after their deceits have been exposed. That is not exactly a for-mula for establishing lasting credibility in the eyes of an informed public.

You will find an overview of the book's themes in Part One. Distortion of general environmental principles, misrepresentation of specific issues, and shameless downplaying of highly publicized environmental mishaps are dealt with in Part Two. Character assassination of leading environmental activists and bashers' commonly used propaganda techniques are examined in Part Three. The bashers' godfather, Ronald Reagan, as well as their chief scientific guru, the late Dixy Lee Ray, and one of their most visible contemporary practitioners, radio talk show host Rush Limbaugh, are the focus of Part Four. Finally, the positive nature of the mainstream environmental movement's vision is the subject of Part Five.

ACKNOWLEDGEMENTS

I owe a debt of gratitude to my wife, Pamela, for her patience in guiding an old-fashioned journalist into the modern era of the computer. I am also extremely grateful to my talented editor, Roger Williams, for helping me make the formidable transition from column-writing to book-writing. My thanks to Brent Blackwelder, Brock Evans, Diane MacEchern, and Debbie Sease—all veteran and highly expert professionals in the national environmental movement—who reviewed individual chapters and came up with many useful suggestions. An important contribution to this book was made by Laura Gillies and Lisa Gerrard, who provided research and secretarial assistance. Thanks also to Merideth Menken, who guided the book through publication.

Last, but certainly not least, *Tracking the Charlatans* could not have been written without the many conscientious and knowledgeable environmental activists from all walks of life who have been a constant source of inspiration as well as information over the past quarter century.

PART 1

AN INSIDER'S
PERSPECTIVE

1

FIGHTING BACK

Personal resentment was a catalyst for my writing of this volume. It took a while, but the recent spate of grossly slanted books, newspaper articles and broadcasts that typecast activists such as myself as environmental wackos waging war against God and country finally got under my skin. Most columnists expect their viewpoints to come under attack from various quarters, and there can be honest disagreement over issues. But no self-respecting journalist can remain indifferent when his or her professional integrity is being constantly maligned.

In response to the critics, I would point out that every writer is going to make some mistakes over a 25-year span, and I am no exception. Nonetheless, I am proud of the overall accuracy and numerous prophetic insights that have characterized my more than one and a half million words of environmental commentary.

Of course, the environmental denigrators are entitled to their opinion. Unfortunately for them, the rationales they employ to peddle their competing global vision usually collapse under objective scrutiny. The bashers are for the most part perennial "feel-gooders" who preach that all's right with the world; the more people on earth, the merrier; pollution should be considered an inevitable as well as acceptable consequence of progress. Environmental leaders and commentators are dismissed as doomsdayers who conjure up phony crises to attract new followers.

While environmentalists warn that some problems could turn cataclysmic if left unattended, they emphasize that viable solutions exist, solutions that may entail sacrifices but are ultimately dwarfed by the societal benefits that accrue. Environmentalists don't reject capitalism, individual rights or reverence for human beings' special status on the planet. They do promote quality over quantity, health over profit, reasoned conservation over profligate consumption, and substance over style. That is a value system with which few Americans would quarrel and most seem eager to experiment—and one which many individuals have already integrated into their daily routine.

As evidence of environmentalists' fallibility, the bashers triumphantly point to some dire predictions that have failed to materialize. But don't be put off by environmentalists' prophetic shortcomings. When all the pluses and minuses are added up, the environmental movement has compiled an enviable record of accuracy. True, an anemic economy has caused conservation-oriented public interest groups to scramble at times for additional financial support. And typical of such cause-oriented organizations, they have solicited in the most dramatic manner possible—by sounding the alarm against potential ecological devastation. Note, however, that the operative word is "potential." The environmental groups stress there's no inevitability here, often not even imminence. "Prudence" would more aptly describe the thematic rallying cry.

It should also be pointed out that some of the enviros' forecasts of adversity have failed to occur because of successful implementation of the preventive measures they advocated. Other unrealized predictions of environmental slippage might just turn out to be late bloomers.

The bashers are trying to build a case against more stringent environmental protection by exploiting the fact that the most visible environmental insults have been eliminated. That's especialy pernicious because what remain are mostly insidious forms of degradation that can often progress unnoticed until they are irreversible. Such subtle threats, which rarely lend themselves to simplistic solutions, further complicate the mission of environmetal activists. Without readily discernible incriminating evidence, it's more difficult to sell the public on reforms that would require modifications of daily routines at possibly a higher initial cost than is currently the norm.

Thus, the bashers' specious, rose-colored appeal tends to be very alluring to the uninformed and indifferent. Recognizing the importance of pocketbook issues, the cornucopian crowd seeks whenever possible to blame economic downturns and inflationary spurts on the environmental movement. Indeed, they regularly portray environmental activists as anti-capitalism, anti-people, and, for good measure, anti-God. The first epithet is an effort to separate environmentalists from society's mainstream by depicting eco-activists as promoters of a hidden agenda for transforming the nation into a socialist state. The last two are attempts to discourage populists and devout individuals from casting their lot with the "Greens." All I can say is that in 25 years of covering the national environmental scene, I have never encountered a single shred of evidence suggesting the existence of a clandestine plot to replace our current political system, nor have I ever heard of any journalist who has.

As for the defamatory accusation that "green" individuals as a class care more about butterflies and dandelions than they do about people, why would environmentalists risk societal rejection by adopting such a misanthropic posture? And regarding the allegation by the bashers' Christian fundamentalist wing that environmentalists commit sacrilege through their "deification" of nature, you will learn in this book (if you don't already know) that Judeo-Christian religious leaders as a rule do not perceive the sanctity of their faith to be threatened by treating nature as a manifestation of God's work. Indeed, many of them are in the forefront of the environmental movement.

Riding the Backlash

When the first anti-environmental tract to receive more than cursory attention surfaced in the late 1970s, it was repudiated by an overwhelming majority of the scientific community. Herman Kahn and Julian Simon's anthology, *The Resourceful Earth*, attempted to refute the validity of Carter administration warnings that serious global environmental problems lay ahead if corrective conservation strategies were not undertaken without delay. Then along came Ronald Reagan, who parroted Kahn and Simon's ideas both prior to and during his presidency and gave those views more exposure than they had ever had before. Although President Reagan enjoyed considerable popularity among the American electorate, his snide anti-environmental aspersions evoked little support and a great deal of scorn throughout the 1980s, leaving the bashers to sink into relative anonymity.

How then did they manage to regain media attention? Certainly, their papering over of many of the problems at hand appealed to those in the press who had grown weary of reporting on one environmental crisis after another during Reagan's reign. The backlash even spread to the electronic media. A case in point: the *CBS Evening News* solicited Julian Simon to comment on the environmental significance (or lack thereof) of a dolphin dieoff along a pollution-plagued section of the Mid-Atlantic coast. Whatever you might think of Simon, he is an economist, not a marine biologist, and it showed. Instead of speculating on the scientific explanation for the dolphins' plight, he delivered an ideological harangue that shed no light on the high seas mystery but delighted those who view nightly television news as an instrument of titillation, rather than edification.

Another egregious example of miscast roles occurred on ABC's *Nightline*. Ted Koppel presided over an environmental debate between Vice President Al Gore and conservative radio personality Rush Limbaugh. Given the topic, the arrangement was akin to pitting the president of Harvard against a grammar school dropout in a freewheeling discussion of the nuances of higher education. One may not agree with some or any of Gore's views. But there is no dispute that the vice president is extraordinarily knowledgeable on environmental subjects, having studied them extensively and spent many hours over the years in congressional committee rooms listening to experts testify on the major environmental controversies of our time. He has also demonstrated broad understanding of the biosphere in his best-selling *Earth in the Balance*.

An ideal adversary for the vice president would have been any one of a number of respected scientists who don't buy his positions on various environmental matters. Instead, viewers were subjected to an opponent who, lacking even rudimentary environmental knowledge, responded to the vice president's substantive remarks with extraneous ideological nostrums. If I were the producer of *Nightline*, I would have been greatly embarrassed at this pathetic excuse for a colloquy.

Hot Properties

For at least some in the media, environment bashers suddenly were hot properties when Bill Clinton's election transformed the national environmental movement from an out-of-the-loop gadfly to an ostensibly integral part of the establishment. Overnight, the movement became a tempting target for contrarian criticism as a manifestation of the widely despised "inside the Beltway" crowd and culture.

But that was only the beginning. The bashers were convinced that in the person of Vice President Gore they had a highly visible "environmental extremist," who would rally public support to their cause, much the way fanatical Interior Secretary James Watt drove the country into the arms of the conservation movement in the Reagan years. As has been noted, media types invariably find the contrarian point of view attractive because of its sensationalist overtones. A confrontational stance against conventional wisdom and/or officialdom is seen as a surefire way to boost circulation. If publishers and editors happen to empathize philosophically with the contrarians, as they often have in the case of the bashers, so much the better. Many newspaper executives have always been hostile towards environmental activism, due to its promotion of conservation at the expense of a "shop 'til you drop" mentality. Frugality can force cutbacks in companies' advertising revenue, adversely affecting the main source of income for the newspaper industry and other media. Rare is the publisher who doesn't link his or her business's financial success to how enthusiastically the American people engage in conspicuous consumption. Fearful of being dislodged from a comfortable status quo, many newspaper entrepreneurs are resistant to even the hint of change. Thus, stories that refer to any potential negative aspects of strengthened environmental regulation are often blown way out of proportion, while the benefits are glossed over or, more likely, totally ignored.

Yet the environmental movement isn't waging a vendetta against consumption and advertising. It only advocates a shift to more efficient, less wasteful manufacturing and purchasing practices. In an environmentally sustainable society, the emphasis is on qualitative rather than quantitative values, creating a marketplace in which recycling prospers and planned obsolescence becomes anachronistic. Many corporate chieftains won't entertain that scenario, whether out of ignorance or myopic design. Heartened by the media's newfound receptivity to the bashers, these captains of industry have eagerly funneled money to the publication of books and production of programs aimed at discrediting the national environmental movement.

Free-Market Fantasy

The most outspoken of the new wave of bashers are libertarians and ultra-conservative elements of the political right. They believe the workings of the free market will solve virtually any problem, and they oppose all but a token federal regulatory presence. The bashers have added modestly to their numbers of late by fanning people's fears that private property rights will be increasingly abrogated by government in the name of environmental protection. It is argued that the Endangered Species Act will enable Washington to restrict an owner's use of his or her property if a rare animal or plant is on the premises, thereby "taking" the land without just compensation as required by the U.S. Constitution. That phony argument is the mainstay of a nationwide "Wise Use" movement, which emerged in the late 1980s and regards most natural resource protection laws as breaches of private property rights. By playing on emotions associated with proprietorship, Wise Use advocates have been able to enlist the sympathies of non-ideological Americans who are concerned they will be unable to profit from their property at some future date.

Denigrators of the national environmental movement distrust natural resource protection because they consider it merely an instrument for legitimizing an extensive network of federal regulation. They view centralized authority as a threat to individual freedom, even though the individual in a democracy must operate within boundaries demarcated by a central government. And they ignore the fact that many environmental concerns transcend local jurisdictions and can only be resolved through a centralized approach. There is no recognition on their part that complex environmental problems demand a disciplined response that rarely is forthcoming without the catalyst of regulation.

Last but not least, the bashers pay no heed to the greed factor in the marketplace. It's naive to think that competitive pricing alone will compel entrepreneurs to worry about the long-term societal consequences of their actions, especially if lucrative short-term gains are within reach.

Yet, consistent with their conviction that the United States' stature as a nation rests primarily on how well its free-market economy functions, environment bashers view any but the most minimal restraints on commerce as un-American. It is an outlook that dominated our nineteenth century industrial revolution, when environmental degradation was scarcely noted and even less understood. The bashers are simply throwbacks to those who dismissed pollution as the inevitable price of doing business. As environmental abuses became more intrusive in the twentieth century and pervasive corporate malfeasance was exposed, public sentiment developed for riding herd on laissez-faire practices. That is why the bashers have such difficulty recruiting disciples today.

The detractors of environmentalism regard humans' cognitive superiority to all other life on earth as a license from the Almighty to plunder the planet's natural resources. To ease any pangs of guilt, they express confidence in the capability of our technology to neutralize whatever human excesses are perpetrated against Mother Nature. The quick "technological fix" implants a false sense of security in the ignorant. So does the failure to integrate the environmental costs of doing business into the bottom line.

One objective of this book, therefore, is to challenge the belief that the earth can indefinitely withstand—and we can indefinitely redress, through technological proficiency—any despoilation of the planet's natural resources.

The Origins

The original author of the newspaper column I currently write was Stewart Udall, interior secretary in the Kennedy administration. He began the column shortly after April 22, 1970, the nation's first Earth Day. Udall had concluded that the national awakening to pollution's menace created an urgent need for environmental advocacy in American journalism. Abetted by his celebrity status, formidable writing skills, and the wave of environmental consciousness sweeping the country, Udall was able to convince 40 or so newspaper editors to subscribe to his pioneering environmental column.

Many newspaper publishers had no use for an environmental movement whose target so often seemed to be their corporate advertisers. Yet in the early and mid-1970s, in the true pack-journalism tradition, they dared not risk negating coverage of a social movement obviously taking the country by storm. Unpalatable as it was, they felt obliged to hop on the bandwagon and provide space for an environmental advocacy column.

As the 1970s drew to a close, however, and the excitement engendered by the first Earth Day tapered off, many of these publishers seized the moment. They began to scale down environmental coverage and, in some instances, felt bold enough to dismiss the environmental revolution as a narrowly focused passing fad. Just as their wishful thinking appeared to be gathering momentum, along came the Reagan administration, with such a venomous anti-environmental stance that it evoked a broad-based negative public reaction that could not be ignored.

The historical pendulum once again swung in environmental journalism's favor, although the reprieve was short-lived.

When the Republican environmental ogres were chased by white knights Clinton and Gore, publishers were handed a contrarian role much more to their liking. Sensing the electorate's complacency from having placed a regime perceived as environmentally friendly in the White House, those publishers who were so inclined realized they could display their true colors without fear of provoking what was generally a passive audience to begin with. (Many readers look only at the sports pages, comics or classifieds.) The bashers were rushed onto center stage with a vengeance.

Many of the best and brightest environmental journalists quit in disgust, were fired, or were reassigned as their beat shriveled and sometimes took on the appearance of an anti-environmental jihad.

What's It All About?

At the column's inception, Udall defined "environment" in the broadest possible sense, and I continue that approach to this day. That means I consider any issue relating to human beings' inter-action with the world around them germane. Controversies involving public health, nutrition, energy, occupational safety and urban decay fall within my bailiwick as much as air pollution, endangered species and wilderness preservation.

Stewart Udall was associated with the column for two years, and was the sole author during the first 12 months. When other responsibilities cut into his schedule, he enlisted the assistance of a gifted Washington-based writer and demographer, Jeff Stansbury, and the column acquired a double byline.

In the spring of 1972, Udall joined Senator George McGovern's presidential campaign as an advisor. At the same time, Stansbury contracted to write a book on the recycling of sewage sludge into the soil. Both men realized they no longer could devote their energies to the column, yet they were reluctant to see it killed just as the environmental revolution was beginning to gather steam. They also knew that while a newspaper column can be terminated on a moment's notice, such an enterprise is enormously difficult to launch, with hundreds of different columnists competing for extremely limited space.

I came to Udall's attention through some of my freelance environmental magazine pieces. Stansbury and I hit it off particularly well, which was fortunate since he was going to remain involved with the column until a successor was comfortable enough to proceed on his own. The first column with the double byline of Stansbury and Flattau appeared in early June 1972.

Three years later, Stansbury went to work for a labor union and severed his ties with the column. Though I missed his input, I was well prepared by that time to go it alone, and have carried on in that fashion ever since. In the ensuing years, I have filed columns from five continents, won nine national journalism awards, and had professional contact with virtually every environmental leader of consequence.

Tracking the Charlatans is grounded in my newspaper commentaries, a few of which in recent years have been expressly devoted to rebutting the particularly outrageous anti-environmental polemics of would-be luminaries intent on projecting an unrelenting, attention-getting, contrarian image in a cynical pursuit of fame and fortune.

A Final Observation

The bashers' most persistent refrain (indicating they think it's the most compelling) has been that environmental activists are professional doomsdayers who can only justify their existence by fermenting a perpetual state of crisis.

Suffice it to say here that the bashers' characterization is a scurrilous misrepresentation. The environmental movement in fact exudes optimism. Its principal tenet is that we can obtain more with less, a notion very much in sync with the proclivities of human nature.

PART 2

DISTORTION AND

MISREPRESENTATION

2

ABSURD PROPOSITIONS

Bashers are fond of portraying environmental activists as individuals who consider nature a benign force and humanity the epitome of evil. The bashers want you to typecast environmentalists as painfully naive and repugnantly misanthropic. If they can sell you such character assassination, they know the odds increase that you will pay greater heed to their free-market-oriented propaganda in which nature is depicted as far more destructive than mankind.

Identifying the human race as the lesser of two evils also conveniently serves as rationalization (and absolution) for environmental damage inflicted by the engines of free enterprise. The portrayal of environmentalists as misanthropes is designed to jumpstart us into asking why we should hold in high esteem anybody who sees only the worst in everyone else.

Of course, this is all sheer slander. Green activists recognize the ferocity inherent in nature. They simply maintain that if society operates in as close concert as possible with the natural order, human beings will sustain less damage when the elements go on a rampage. Nature, after all, makes no secret of where it is likely to strike hardest. To anyone not blinded by the moment, human vulnerability is obvious in flood plains, valleys in the shadows of active volcanoes, the unprotected beaches of barrier islands, and acreage above a fault line.

The precise degree and timing of nature's violent outbursts are unpredictable. But if we are prudent enough to profit from the painful experience of previous generations, we can usually provide ourselves with some advance notice and a buffer.

Far from being misanthropes, environmentalists pin their hopes for the future on the human race, which is clearly the only life form possessing the intellectual capacity to halt and ultimately repair the widespread ecological damage it has inflicted. They are confident that mankind can meet the challenge, as long as the response (even when delivered through technology) is crafted in harmony with nature.

And what of the claim that humanity's environmental abuse pales before injuries resulting from the wrath of nature? With the advent of thermonuclear weaponry, the assertion that nature's destructive force exceeds that of man is certainly open to question. Nonetheless, let's assume for the sake of argument that nature exhibits greater ferocity and is more of a polluter. Do these characteristics make it a villain?

It's tortured logic to judge nature in human terms. For example, benevolence and cruelty as we know them are difficult—some would say impossible—to detect in natural law. Ultimately, the awesome force and powerful impulses of nature seem directed towards one primary objective: perpetuation of life. And nature goes about its complex business in such an extraordinarily efficient manner that only the most jaded among us aren't at some point smitten with a sense of wonderment.

In achieving its goal, nature often lacks compassion in the sense that we commonly use the term. "Survival of the fittest," which reigns supreme virtually across the board, is a concept inconsistent with the humane moral imperative that most cultures attach to the treatment of the less fortunate in their ranks. Nature sometimes even discards survival of the fittest for random selection, using massive regeneration to assure succession. Certain species of fish, for example, hatch in such vast numbers that predators could never consume enough prey to threaten the population's viability.

If nature often does not seem particularly merciful, can it be considered cruel? And if so, does it deal with us more harshly than we at our worst behave towards each other?

Death in the wild is often violent, but plenty of killing occurs in civilization as well. Furthermore, nature may not be as unremittingly callous as it sometimes seems. There are those who regard shock and coma as nature's way of tranquilizing us (and lesser species) to ease the trauma accompanying painful injury and death.

Every species is equipped with some trait, weapon, or defense that maximizes the chances of optimum longevity for the most robust among them in a danger-filled world. In most species, the maternal instinct is crucial to survival. Yet in those instances where the young are on their own from the moment of birth, nature compensates by endowing them with instant maturity.

Natural phenomena that are routinely regarded in a negative light have their silver linings. Blight assures that only the healthiest trees survive in our woodlands. Forest fires are agents of renewal that clear out weak trees, recycle nutrients, create new habitats and often eliminate alien species. Even nature's cataclysmic events turn out to have some redemptive value. Hurricanes replenish the water table. The ash from volcanic eruptions regenerates soil fertility. Though the restorative effects of earthquakes' and tidal waves' culling activity arrive by a more circuitous route, the end result is renewal nonetheless.

Conversely, the destruction human beings inflict on the landscape rarely has any positive effects, delayed or otherwise. When people raze a forest and transform the site into desert, when they draw down their groundwater supplies to zero, when they pave over a wetland that is highly productive biologically, the damage is long term, perhaps even irreparable.

Injudicious human intervention can also greatly exacerbate the devastation caused by natural catastrophes. When people build on flood plains, drain wetlands and rechannel winding rivers, they eliminate natural catchments that minimize the destructive impact of overflows. Constructing beachfront homes in traditional hurricane alleys enhances the odds of obliteration, just as relocation to a less vulnerable site improves the chances of emerging relatively unscathed.

All of this doesn't convince the bashers. Their vision of the world exculpates industrial polluters by classifying nature as a far more lethal degrader of the environment than the human race.

Typical is the following passage from a recent contrarian tome, *Eco-sanity, a Common-sense Guide to Environmentalism.*[1] "Every person on earth is exposed to natural radiation coming from the ground, from space, and even from the food we eat. Compared to all this background radiation, exposure to man-made radiation is very slight." Other examples include trees being worse polluters than factories, volcanic eruptions releasing more ozone-depleting chlorine molecules into the atmosphere than manmade sources, and crops containing more natural toxins than poisonous residues left over from the application of synthetic pesticides.

Keep in mind that nature somehow achieved a highly effective modus vivendi before modern civilization came on the scene. Witness the potability 200 years ago of American rivers and streams, whose waters are undrinkable today without extensive purification treatment.

Hence, nature's frequent edge in sheer volume of contamination needs to be put in proper perspective. Every species on earth has had millennia to adapt to the vagaries of nature. With the help of natural selection, the passage of time enables creatures and plants to develop highly effective defense mechanisms against even the most lethal manifestations of the natural world. Although human contributions to the pollution mix are often relatively small, they may be just enough to make a critical difference. There could well be a saturation point beyond which any additional increments would throw the whole system into disarray. Scientists have already discovered that the cumulative effects of pollution exposure are not necessarily linear, suggesting that an organism's capacity to withstand the rigors of such exposures may eventually reach a breaking point.

It should also be noted that nature usually releases pollutants in a more gradual, less concentrated form than humans do, thereby giving the environment far more opportunity to adjust. That is why the comparison between trees and factories as sources of pollution is a fallacious one.

What of the contention that volcanic eruptions are the real culprits behind the ozone-depleting chlorine molecules in the stratosphere? Bashers would love to see volcanoes rescue corporate engines of free enterprise from blame so the latter could proceed unencumbered by the compliance costs that regulatory restraints impose. But the volcanoes are innocent as charged. According to a consensus of the world's leading atmospheric scientists, "volcanoes can emit large quantities of hydrogen chloride, but this gas is rapidly converted to hydrochloric acid in rain water, ice, and snow, and does not reach the stratosphere. Even in explosive volcanic plumes that rise in the atmosphere, nearly all of the hydrogen chloride is scrubbed out in precipitation before reaching stratospheric altitudes."[2]

While many toxins are native to the natural world, they are not as threatening to human health as the synthetic poisons introduced into the environment. Taking the opposite tack is one of the bashers' leading gurus (and an outspoken apologist for corporate America), Bruce N. Ames, a professor of biochemistry at the University of California in Berkeley. Dr. Ames maintains that natural pesticides in our crops' genetic makeup are thousands of times more numerous and potent than the residues of man-made pesticides found in our food.

If you accept his premise, the concerns expressed by environmentalists regarding synthetic pesticide use are unjustified, and the government's regulatory energy should be directed elsewhere. It's an analysis that warms the cockles of the chemical industry's heart and gives much aid and comfort to those who believe the marketplace is far better suited to protect the public than government regulations.

Ames' problem is that most scientists don't buy his thesis that natural pesticides are a greater threat than synthetic ones — and the research leans persuasively in their favor. Dr. Devra Lee Davis, a senior adviser at the U.S. Department of Health and Human Services, points out that poisons existing naturally in our fruits and vegetables are part of a chemical mix that also contains some powerful natural antioxidants. Aflatoxin, for example, is a potent cancer-producing agent, but its presence in peanuts is offset by anti-carcinogenic ingredients, including zinc, iron, fiber, and selenium.

Furthermore, the evidence suggests that human beings have evolved a genetic resistance to natural toxins as a result of exposure over the span of millennia.[3] By contrast, synthetic pesticides lack a "natural" countervailing influence and subject human beings to contact with unadulterated "new" toxic substances to which no resistance has been developed.

Dr. Davis cites convincing epidemiological evidence that nature protects us from naturally occurring carcinogens in our food. She points to data showing that vegetarians have the lowest cancer rates despite ingesting an abundance of food with Ames' "killer carcinogens." Even smokers who are vegetarians, she notes, have a lower cancer incidence than smokers who are meat-eaters. By contrast, Davis says, the epidemiological data cast suspicion on synthetic chemicals in the environment. There have been recent increases in different types of cancers and respiratory disease that cannot be statistically explained by cigarette smoking, early diagnostic testing, or aging. "There is something out there," Davis declares, adding that manmade toxic chemicals, frequently in the form of pesticide residues, are prime suspects.

We Can Do Better

Bashers are not content to stand pat on their position that nature is a worse polluter than mankind. Even when nature is on its good behavior, they believe human beings are capable of doing a better job.

Few would dispute that the human race can sometimes improve on nature—but, paradoxically, only within the framework of the natural system. Even modern technology cannot fulfill its enormous potential if innovation is employed to replace rather than complement natural processes. Ingenious as the human mind is, it has not yet shown itself capable of consistently replicating the complexity of nature on any sustainable basis. Nowhere has this been more graphically dramatized than in the recent experiment with the closed-environment facility, Biosphere 2. Researchers found that despite the hundreds of millions of dollars spent on the construction and operation of the eco-project, "it has proved impossible to create a system that could support eight human beings with adequate food, water, and air for two years."[4]

It thus behooves us not to buy into the belief that natural resources can be destroyed with impunity because we have the capability to recreate them. A wiser course would be to piggyback on natural processes, a technique that has already paid big dividends, with the promise of much more to come. That is why drip irrigation has had such success, why mimicking nature through sustainable agricultural practices raises the prospect of an infinite food supply with infinite resilience to the elements, and why gene therapy possesses such potential.

Troublemakers

Where humanity gets in trouble is when it tries to go nature one better without obtaining her cooperation. A perfect example: the introduction of exotic species. Engineers of this exercise are often intent on correcting an ecological imbalance that they created in the first place. If humans' overriding purpose is to outsmart nature, they are bound to fail. Only when they work in concert with the ecosystem and introduce a species that research suggests would adapt to and not disrupt the existing environment do they stand a chance of success.

Modern mechanized agriculture is supposed to improve on nature's bounty, but heavy applications of fossil fuel-based synthetic fertilizer and pesticide are in some instances depleting the natural fertility of the soil. And the drive to concentrate solely on the strains with the highest yields has resulted in shrinkage of the gene pool for various types of crops, increasing their vulnerability to blight and pest destruction.

Used in a highly selective manner that does not contaminate the surrounding environment, pesticides can be beneficial. But employed injudiciously, they become their own and our worst enemy. Excessive applications become less and less effective as the target pests build up immunity. At the same time, desperate pesticide users feel compelled to apply even more poison, an action that often eventually harms non-target species, including some predators which are natural inhibitors of pest populations.

The late Dixy Lee Ray was a leading exponent of the thesis that mankind excels over natural processes when it comes to managing the environment. One of her favorite illustrations was the aftermath of the 1980 volcanic eruption of Mount St. Helens in her home state of Washington, where she was once governor. "Within a year or two," she wrote, "the return of life, both plant and animal, was remarkable" on adjacent tracts of public and private land.

More than a decade later, Ray continued, "the differences between the 'natural' and the managed areas are dramatic. Both are recovering, but the undisturbed public lands lag far behind. ... The same species of plants, flowers, and grasses have occurred on both tracts, as have a number of trees, but the growth has been far slower and the trees more sparse on the undeveloped land (designated a national monument in the wake of the eruption) than on the land managed [by Weyerhaeuser] for timber harvesting purposes." As for the future, Ray asserted that both forests will have "approximately the same complex of tree species and varied undergrowth, and the same wildlife, birds, and insects. Deciding which forest surpasses the other is a value judgment heavily influenced by what one believes a forest is for."[5]

Ray prided herself on her scientific expertise, yet here was a case in which her bias apparently drove her to ignore the unalterable truth of evolution. Even as she was writing the aforementioned passage, the 110,000-acre National Volcanic Monument already possessed a greater variety of animal and plant species than the Weyerhaeuser monoculture; and as time passes, the disparity is bound to grow even more pronounced.[6] It's simple: the more different natural habitats that exist, the more opportunities biodiversity has to manifest itself.

But there is more to the comparison of manmade and natural forests than the difference in biodiversity. After World War II, Japanese bureaucrats decided to replace their country's diverse hardwood forests with what seemed to be a more commercially lucrative alternative, a cedar tree monoculture.

As *The New York Times* pointed out in 1995, "The aim was to make the country self-sufficient in wood products, but the widespread human sensitivities to cedar pollen are just one indication of how this single-minded strategy went awry. It is becoming increasingly apparent, experts say, that the superabundance of a single specie of tree is threatening wildlife, causing heavy soil erosion, reducing the water table, and creating the potential for disastrous landslides."[7]

In our own country, too, when we don't operate in a manner that respects the natural processes, the penalties are harsh. Witness what reckless exploitation of the Pacific Northwest (through indiscriminate agriculture, logging, and dam and road construction) has done to the salmon population and the water quality of the spawning streams on which fish depend.

Beware of those who contend that human beings need not worry about accommodating nature because any damage can be easily repaired. Examine the claims of individuals who maintain they can restore natural wetlands that have been destroyed, or people who boast that the submerged sections of oil rigs can serve nicely as surrogate coral reefs. Studies indicate that it's virtually impossible to duplicate the rich biodiversity of natural wetlands. There are just too many variables in complex combinations of relationships. Any reasonable facsimile that is somehow created appears to be the product of blind luck.

As for those oilmen who brag about how their rigs serve as artificial reefs, don't let them sell you on the idea that their equipment is interchangeable with natural coral reefs and that the latter are therefore expendable (especially if their existence interferes with hydrocarbon exploration). Scientists have found that while fish in tropical waters eventually do flock to the shelter of oil rig pilings, the diversity of species is far narrower than it is around a natural reef. That is not surprising when you realize that some species have little or no tolerance for any level of petroleum residues.

An admission that nature inherently can do a better job than humans is no denigration of the latter. Our intellect makes us the sole life form qualified to serve as nature's special custodian, providing us with the capability to build on its accomplishments—if we are astute enough to manipulate the natural processes without disrupting them.

As slaves to emotions fueled by their anthropocentric ideology, environmental contrarians view any subservience to nature as a threat to the unique human identity. Sad to say, this feverish reaction often triggers an irrational response. Take the environmental-bashing writer Alston Chase. In his passion to make the point that nature revolves around human beings, he defended a proposed intrusion of the timber industry into a national forest by exclaiming that "without logging, trees die."[8]

Negative Thoughts

In *Science under Siege*, enviro-basher Michael Fumento writes that "nature worshipers often approach environmental issues with the unreasoning zeal of crusaders in a holy war."[9] He vilifies enviros for "erring on the side of caution," maintaining that such a course would dictate banning all products that are not risk-free. Thus Fumento sets up the ultimate straw man.[10] Since no product is absolutely risk-free, he declares, it's impossible for a manufacturer to prove the negative and justify distribution of the merchandise.

Of course, such a ridiculous burden of proof is not imposed on industry by environmentalists or anyone else. To require companies to demonstrate that products were absolutely safe before being allowed to enter the market would do away with commerce as we know it. Once again, the bashers attempt to paint the environmentalists into an untenable position that would alienate the general public.

What the law does require when a product's safety is challenged is that the manufacturers show that the risks associated with use are reasonable in light of potential benefits. If, in weighing the merits of the product, the risk equals or even marginally exceeds the benefits, regulators are obliged at least to alert the public that a more benign alternative exists, and if it doesn't, to warn consumers that they proceed at their own peril. If the threat to health is found to far outweigh any possible benefit, the regulator has little choice but to ban the product outright.

Contemptuous of this judicious process, the bashers persist in depicting environmentalists as a cadre of fanatics demanding a risk-free society and willing to sacrifice our economic prosperity in pursuit of that goal. As evidence of this alleged perversity, the former cite the zero discharge of pollutants provisions inserted into some major federal statutes at the insistence of environmentalists. Ignored is the statutes' legislative history, which makes clear that zero discharge was not a literal objective. Lawmakers explained that they inserted the language out of concern that if goals did not spell out the ideal, compliance performance would underachieve.

Moreover, zero discharge *is* attainable when the polluting substance can be eliminated entirely without disrupting the production process or when it can be replaced by an environmentally benign alternative.[11]

Another reason for the statutory inclusion of zero discharge is that it creates pressure for the added protection needed by particular groups: the young, the old, the infirm, and other highly vulnerable individuals who might otherwise be doomed by chronic exposure to low levels of highly toxic substances.

The Devil is in the Details

Bashers seek to construct a no-lose situation for themselves. They disparage environmentalists for caring too much, and when circumstances permit, for caring too little. After complaining about environmentalists being overly protective of the human race, bashers have no qualms about denouncing them for dismissing humanity as a menace to the survival of life on earth.

This misanthropic characterization is the lead-in to a stereotypical portrayal of environmentalists as individuals who care more about animals and plants than people—again, an image designed to isolate the Greens from the mainstream. In truth, the environmental movement operates on the premise that human beings are as much victims of their own pollution as the plants and animals lower down the food chain. Indeed, this rationale was the impetus for the creation of the U.S. Environmental Protection Agency (EPA), whose primary focus throughout the years has been safeguarding public health. Only secondarily is the EPA concerned with conserving natural resources. That mission belongs more to a land management agency such as the Interior Department.

The same rationale also explains why many environmentalists devote enormous energy to the alleviation of human suffering, especially among the economically disadvantaged. The latter's shortage of political and financial clout inevitably subjects them to society's most severe public health threats, since they are unable to fend off questionable industrial siting decisions and other exploitative actions by corporate polluters.

Nazi Ad Absurdum

Not content with maligning the beliefs of ecology-minded activists, detractors routinely launch scurrilous attacks on the moral character of members of the national environmental movement. One extraordinarily malicious allegation, originally limited to wild-eyed fringe groups, has begun to creep into denunciations by supposedly respectable contrarian types. I am talking about drawing a parallel between American environmentalism and Adolf Hitler's Third Reich. Even Rush Limbaugh picks up on this. He attempts to assign guilt by association, archly noting that Lili Reifenstal, the famed German filmmaker who chronicled Hitler's triumphs, not only was the Fuehrer's mistress (false, though she clearly was a sympathizer) but today is a card-carrying member of Greenpeace.

A more "sophisticated" analogy to the Third Reich has been conjured up in the halls of academia and become the chief frame of reference for those looking for the slightest excuse to subscribe to the theory. Originally hesitant to chime in with this sort of environmentalist-baiting, the "mainstream" detractors have been emboldened by publication of a seemingly credentialed scholarly work linking bird watchers and stormtroopers.

The "authority" who purportedly confers legitimacy on a Nazi-environmental connection is one Ana Bramwell, a historian who laid out her convoluted thesis in a tract written in 1989 while she was a research fellow at Oxford, England's Trinity College.[12]

Bramwell finds great significance in the fact that some top Nazis—Rudolf Hess and Heinrich Himmler being cases in point—were vociferous advocates of organic farming. She notes that Himmler, a onetime chicken farmer, ordered the enactment of anti-vivisection laws and that "SS training included a respect for animal life of near Buddhist proportions."[13] In addition, some members of Hitler's entourage convinced the Fuehrer that the Third Reich should not drain German wetlands, and a faction of the Nazi Party led by Rudolf Hess "worshipped the simple life of the peasant farmer and promoted it as a preferred alternative to industrialized society."

Bramwell asserts that "Nazi Germany was the first country in Europe to form nature reserves," and that the oak leaf (representing a deep-rooted love of nature) became the insignia of the dreaded SS Corps. In conclusion, she explicitly links environmentalists and Hitler's minions by declaring that, "like ecologists today, the Nazis opposed capitalism and the consumer-oriented market mechanism."

Where to begin in exposing the sham of this construct? With its lack of accuracy or lack of logic? We might as well start with the latter, because Bramwell's attempts to establish guilt by association are ludicrous. If Hitler were crazy about ice cream, would Americans who fancied Ben and Jerry's fudge ripple therefore be neo-Nazis? Environmentalists' advocacy of organic farming and animal protection is a far cry from engaging in genocide.

Bramwell maintains that the Nazis idolized the small farmer and embraced a back-to-nature philosophy. Maybe so, but they left a trail of horrendous death and devastation in the rural regions of the nations they invaded. She describes the Nazis' contempt for the western industrialized world, allegedly in conjunction with their supposedly romantic, pastoral vision of peasant farming. Yet even a superficial examination of history reveals that Hitler relentlessly courted German manufacturers to engineer his massive rearmament in what was surely one of the most frenzied spurts of industrialization in modern times. In addition, the Nazis rose to power by using an armaments-driven industrial boom to engineer a transition from a deep recession to consumer-friendly prosperity.

Quality and Quantity

In advocating their theory that environmentalists are engaged in a socialist conspiracy, the bashers assert that the Greens unalterably oppose the economic growth necessary to meet the needs of an expanding population. Again, the bashers distort facts to place environmentalists in an indefensible position. No rational person can oppose growth, because growth is the engine of life. We only stop growing when we stop breathing.

Hence, accusations notwithstanding, environmentalists are very much in favor of growth. It's just that the type of growth they champion is qualitative rather than quantitative. The former minimizes adverse environmental impacts while giving rise to a lifestyle that wins over almost everyone who adopts it, despite the de-emphasis of materialistic values. If quantitative values are replaced with qualitative ones, people are bound to derive more from less. Having fewer but more durable possessions and gaining more satisfaction from the development of ideas and personal relationships than ownership of material goods have proven gratifying choices for most who have attempted such a course.

As for the bashers' claims that environmental activists are overzealous elitists who refuse to compromise, how did the conservation lobby register so many victories on Capitol Hill and in the courts over the past two decades? These institutions aren't exactly hotbeds of extremism.

I'll tell you the secret of environmental lobbyists' and lawyers' successes. They have not relied on emotional appeals as the means of making their case to save butterflies and redwoods. Instead, when they have entered a congressional office or courtroom, they have been armed with a passel of facts, figures, and other documentation that their opposition could not refute. Whether it was setting tough air pollution standards, establishing the regulation of strip mining, or blocking the construction of an airport in the Florida Everglades, the environmentalists carried the day with powerful economic and scientifically based arguments.

Prior to 1970, science had been used to win legislative protection for wildlife, especially in the creation of the National Wildlife Refuge system. But it was during the 1970s that environmental activists began to marshal the technical data that led to the passage of the nation's landmark anti-pollution statutes.

There was another key to their success. These activists were not wild-eyed radicals. They were cool, often dispassionate negotiators who were always willing to strike a reasonable compromise. Furthermore, the research of such pioneering organizations as the Washington-based Environmental Policy Center and the Natural Resources Defense Council was so original and far-ranging that it revolutionized the field.

Bashers portray environmental activists as an affluent, self-absorbed segment of society, a hypocritical stance for critics who often seem to place profits ahead of public health concerns. Yet, as noted earlier, *Homo sapiens* has been at the center of environmentalists' concern from the start. The poorest among us find themselves most susceptible to environmental harm, usually because they lack the financial and political clout to prevent heavily polluting industrial facilities from moving into their neighborhoods. Hence, we should not be surprised that members of Congress representing districts with large percentages of the economically disadvantaged invariably have superior environmental voting records.

3

FALSE ASSUMPTIONS

Bashers invariably portray environmentalists as self-serving crisis mongers raging against a world that pretty much has ecological problems under control.

The feel-gooders' sanguine view of the state of the environment places many of them in the awkward position of having to attribute their present comfort level to the same federal anti-pollution statutes they relish denouncing as ineffectual and oppressive. The only way they can reconcile their love-hate relationship with the nation's major environmental laws is to maintain that we have squeezed all the benefits we can out of these statutes. The last remnants of pollution, they argue, are either of negligible risk to society or, if still a threat, can only be cost-effectively purged through marketplace incentives. Bashers warn that any attempts to make current laws more restrictive will simply circumscribe John Q. Citizen's freedom for no appreciable gain.

Some of these Pollyannaish critics won't even concede that any substantial benefits ever resulted from landmark environmental regulations. Typical of this school of thought are the authors of *Taking the Environment Seriously*, who assert that "the Clean Water Act has produced hardly any real progress since 1972."

Since such bashers also contend that the environment is now in pretty good shape, we can only surmise that they consider the nation's waters to have been as clean from the start as they are now, or to have undergone improvement without the benefit of regulatory pressure. Either way, those are preposterous notions.

The Real Optimists

Environmentalists are not allergic to good news. They are the first to point out that the national environmental statutes enacted in the 1970s are responsible for impressive gains over the past two decades. They point with pride to emissions of major air pollutants dropping nearly 60 percent between 1970 and 1993, the percentage of waterways meeting Clean Water Act standards rising from 36 percent in 1972 to 60 percent today, and millions of acres being added to our national parks, refuges and wilderness systems.[1] But they caution that these triumphs must not obscure how much work remains to be done.

No such sobering qualifications are forthcoming from the unabashed bashers. They boast of cancer rates on the decline and remind us that the United States is a healthier place in which to live than at any time in recorded history.[2] They assert that current levels of air pollution are too low to pose health threats, our drinking water is safe, use of pesticides is falling, the supply of American farmland is remaining constant despite urbanization, and there is more forest cover today than two centuries ago.[3]

Some of these allegations are accurate. Others are not. Equally important, although anyone can call a glass half empty or half full, it's a mistake to stand pat with either interpretation when a full glass is necessary to assure that the quality of our lives improves.

Detractors try to characterize environmentalists' caution as pessimism. Yet, if anything, the Greens are more upbeat than their critics. Though environmentalists warn of chaos should the root causes of ecological degradation not be addressed, they are confident that humanity can meet the challenge.

By contrast, what could be more defeatist than preaching "all's right with the world" when it clearly is not and time is of the essence?

Unapologetic Cornucopians

One of the more outspoken cornucopian denigrators of the environmental movement is University of Maryland economist Julian Simon. He dismisses environmentalists' dire warnings as disingenuously alarmist, noting that people throughout the world are on average living longer and eating better, and that severe air and water pollution have been decreasing in advanced countries.

From a global perspective, living conditions may be relatively better now than at the beginning of this century. But the situation is hardly cause for rejoicing when more than 700 million of the five billion-plus souls on earth are malnourished, two billion suffer vitamin deficiencies and one billion earn less than $200 annually.[4]

Nor are conditions in our own country grounds for euphoria. If you have any doubts, check out EPA Administrator Carol Browner's inventory of unfinished business:

- 40 percent of our rivers are not fishable or swimmable.

- 30 million people get drinking water from systems that violate public health standards.

- Two out of five Americans still reside in cities where air quality standards are breached.

- Asthma has risen 40 percent in little more than a decade, with air pollution widely suspected of being a culprit.

- One in four Americans lives within four miles of a toxic dump site.

- The amount of pesticides released into the environment has increased dramatically.

- Lead remains at dangerous levels in the blood of approximately 10 million kids.

Let's Get It Straight

The bashers' claims that the war on cancer is being won are seriously flawed. They mislead from the start by highlighting cancer morbidity rates (which in some instances have declined) while ignoring incidence rates (which in most instances have not).

If the critics had provided the full picture, they would have disclosed that prostate cancer has increased at a rate of four percent annually and breast cancer at two percent, with one out of nine American women currently projected to develop the disease.[5] That's not all. Between 1973 and 1991, the incidence of melanoma, the most serious form of skin cancer, increased approximately four percent annually, and during that same period the overall mortality rate jumped 34 percent.[6]

Bashers have stock rebuttals for all this. If forced to confront their omission of rising incidence rates, they discount the statistics as insignificant, arguing that the greater numbers are due to improved detection and don't reflect a spread of the disease. If that explanation doesn't suffice, you may hear some assert that cancer is only increasing in people over age 65. That trend is normal and has nothing to do with environmental factors, they say, because cancer is primarily a malady of old age, and more of us are reaching that stage of life.

The only trouble with this theory is that children, too, have suffered an increase in cancer—17 percent between 1973 and 1990.[7]

As for melanoma, the bashers argue that its increase results from people spending more time in the sun and doesn't stem at all from environmental conditions. Perhaps there is some truth in that. No one really knows.

But what about the rise in the incidence of and death rates from brain, kidney, lymph node, and testicular cancers at levels above and beyond the degree that can be attributed to better detection? Many scientists consider environmental factors to be prime suspects in these instances.[8]

Hooray for the Good Times

Here are some other comforting claims frequently made by bashers to embellish their cornucopian vision and assuage our concerns:

- "The United States is safer today than at any
  time in recorded history."[9]

In many respects, this is true, but certainly not in all. Just ask
city dwellers old enough to remember when it was no big deal to
leave the front door unlocked, much less venture outside after
dark. Well and good, you might interject, but what does that have
to do with the environment?

Right you are. I wandered off on a tangent. Let's return to comparisons such as Americans being able to drink directly from
streams and eat fish from the Great Lakes several centuries ago
without fear of being fatally poisoned.

- Current levels of air pollution are too low to
  be health threats, so don't bother fretting
  about them.[10]

Tell that to persons suffering from asthma, chronic bronchitis,
emphysema, and other respiratory diseases scientists have linked
with air quality. Perhaps the debunkers of environmental concerns are unaware of the findings culled from an extensive 1995
epidemiological study conducted by the American Cancer Society
and Harvard Medical School. The data from that study strongly
suggest that many thousands of people in major urban centers die
prematurely every year from cardiopulmonary causes linked to
particulate air matter.[11]

- There is more tree cover in the United States
  now than there was in colonial times, so stow
  all the talk about overcutting forests.

Before celebrating this arboreal triumph, one should take note
of a 1994 Department of Agriculture (USDA) survey.[12] It found
that "forests today cover about 70 percent of the area that was
forested in 1600." And that doesn't take into account the loss of
invaluable biodiversity as old-growth forest has been leveled and

often replaced by relatively homogeneous, severely fragmented tree plantations.

- Farmland acreage in this county is not decreasing, despite the advance of urbanization.[13]

Again, USDA researchers constitute the opposition. According to their latest data, the period between 1987 and 1992 saw urbanization engulf a million acres of farmland, one-fourth of which possessed the highest soil quality. During that same period, how often did you hear of farmland being reclaimed from territory that was previously paved over?

- People throughout the world are eating better and living longer on average than ever before.

Reports of improved nutrition in industrialized nations are credible. But what of the one-third of all countries whose population growth is outstripping food production increases, with environmental degradation clearly a major contributing factor?

If food shortages are not already a reality in these places, they are soon likely to be. The situation is especially grave in sub-Saharan Africa, where demographic expansion has exceeded food production increases in recent years. Furthermore, it is projected that populations in that region will grow at three percent annually until the end of the century, while crop yields are forecast to increase by only two percent annually. If that happens, it's estimated that the number of malnourished people in the region will soar by 50 percent to 265 million during that five-year period.[14]

As for survival rates, it's true enough that two centuries ago, life expectancy in the United States was less than 30 years and now it is 75. Demographers point out, however, that this extended longevity is largely due to widespread success in reducing infant mortality, primarily through improved medical care and sanitary conditions. At the upper end of the scale, there is little difference in the life expectancy of a 65-year-old person now and two hundred years ago.

- How about the bashers' lament that preservation of wetlands is responsible for expanded numbers of mosquitoes and the spread of malaria?

Hold it! The last I heard, the increase in malaria was attributed to lax efforts to reduce exposure to mosquitoes, failure to eliminate repositories—such as rubber tires—for standing water in densely populated areas, and the inevitability of insects and malaria parasites building up immunity to the pesticides and drugs used to control them.

- There is little credence to the stratospheric ozone depletion threat stemming from a widening seasonal "ozone hole" over the Antarctic.

Bashers repeatedly refer to data showing that fewer of the sun's lethal ultraviolet rays are penetrating the earth's protective ozone shield and reaching the surface. What the bashers neglect to tell us is that the ultraviolet ray monitors are located primarily at airports, where airplane exhaust dilutes the ultraviolet rays, thereby producing artificially low readings.

As evidence of environmental recovery, Simon submits that "the Great Lakes are not dead" (true) and "offer better sport fishing than ever" (false).[15] This hardly squares with the view of those charged with nursing the Great Lakes back to health. For example, Gordon Durnil, the chief American representative to the U.S.-Canadian International Joint Commission for the Great Lakes, declared in early 1994 that "the Great Lakes pose a threat to the health of children as a result of their exposure to persistent toxic substances, even at very low ambient levels."[16]

Money Isn't Everything

We hear from Simon that "raw materials are less scarce," so let the good times roll. The economist's sanguine appraisal is tied to pricing in the marketplace and is typical basher methodology.[17]

He ignores that lower prices don't necessarily mean a resource isn't being depleted. Markets can be artificially propped up by shrewd, often unscrupulous entrepreneurs.

Sometimes, the abundance that drives down the prices is an illusion carved out of nature. For example, fishermen tend to deliver a big catch just before the population of a depleted species collapses, because they intensify their activity in a desperate effort to return home with a respectable harvest. The sea is swept clean of everything that moves.

It's Not Worth It?

In their exuberance to make the case that the fiscal demands of many environmental regulations—particularly new ones—are prohibitive, some bashers will confuse (dare we say purposely) the compliance costs of all regulations with the costs of environmental measures alone. While both figures are no small change, there is a huge gap between the two. Total expense of all regulations amounts to more than $600 billion annually, as opposed to environmental rules which produce outlays in the vicinity of $140 billion.

When bashers do acknowledge the lesser sum, they are quick to point out that it represents more than two percent of the gross national product (GNP), or roughly a sum equal to $500 per person a year—still an onerous liability in their minds. What they don't say is that compliance costs are not spread evenly across the nation. Potential industrial polluters bear the brunt of the burden since competition (and sometimes regulation) limits how much of the cost they can pass on to their customers. And of course not all of us are their customers.

Still, it's true that frequently the vast sums spent in the name of regulatory compliance to protect large populations against chronic low-level exposure to various pollutants end up saving only thousands—perhaps just hundreds—of lives.

Does that make environmental protection initiatives poor investments? Not when amortized over the vast numbers of people that could conceivably benefit. Millions of dollars of pollution abatement costs can translate into anywhere from a few cents to a few dollars a month for an individual—less than the average person spends on a single foray to a fast-food restaurant.

Most individuals would undoubtedly view this sum as a bargain price to pay to enhance the odds they wouldn't end up among the unlucky few.

Fiscal Oppression

Environmental detractors maintain that anti-pollution regulations have an even more repressive effect on society. Their spiel is that compliance costs have risen to the point where they stifle the nation's economic growth, eliminate jobs, and in general create an enormous amount of human misery.[18] This is an astonishing allegation, especially the reference to "human misery." Most Americans, after all, credit environmental regulation with reducing the pollution that has long created health problems, and ample documentation confirms that their gratitude is not misplaced.

Bashers can provide plenty of details about costs of regulation, but when it comes to benefits they are vague or fall silent altogether. One cannot deny benefits are far more difficult to quan-tify than costs, which typically are line items on company balance sheets. This more concrete documentation leads detractors such as Michael Fumento to claim that, without environmental regulation, real GNP would be 2.6 percent higher than it currently is.[19] How such a figure was compiled remains a mystery, because no mention is made of the offsetting regulatory benefits such as decreased medical expenses, increased worker productivity, and net job creation. These positives are absent from corporate balance sheets. So is the windfall companies experience from passing along to their customers part of the expense of meeting pollution abatement standards. It's tanta-mount to receiving a subsidy to pollute. (An EPA economic analysis of the Clean Air Act—released in October 1997—pegs the amount spent on pollution abatement equipment between 1970 and 1990 at $523 billion, and estimates a minimum of $6 trillion in reduced medical costs as a result, not a shabby quid pro quo.)

What can be computed in reasonably precise fashion is the net job gain in the United States resulting from the imposition of environmental regulation. E.B. Goodstein of the Economic Policy Institute found that while environmental protection has displaced some workers, it is a labor-intensive activity that has generated 4 million jobs. The result is slightly increased net employment for the U.S. economy.[20]

But that's only part of the refutation of the allegation that environmental protection breeds unemployment. Nowhere are the bashers more vocal about environmentally induced adverse economic impacts than in the Pacific Northwest. Yet a Wilderness Society study analyzing the economy of the Columbia River basin (i.e., eastern Oregon and Washington, most of Idaho, western Montana and parts of Nevada, Utah, and Wyoming) contradicts the bashers' dire picture.

The Washington, D.C.-headquartered Wilderness Society found that the growth of new industries—often attracted by favorable environmental conditions—more than offset declining natural resource extraction in the region. Personal income from logging, mining, and other resource extraction enterprises dropped from seven percent to five percent of the region's total between 1969 and 1993. During that period, personal income from high-tech industries and service occupations rose by 100 percent ($28 billion to $56 billion). More than half the wages in the Columbia River basin are now earned in service industries.[21]

In Oregon, the hue and cry was that the Northern Spotted Owl would drive the state into bankruptcy because of an ESA prohibition on timber harvesting, imposed in the bird's behalf. In fact, Oregon's economy is one of the most robust in the nation, thanks to an influx of light industry, tourist-oriented enterprises, and retirees—primarily from California—seeking greener pastures. This invasion has more than compensated for the timber jobs loss (which, incidentally, was not the result of spotted owl protections).

Clearly, there are winners and losers in the transition to an environmentally sustainable economy, but the latter are not relegated to a permanent bottom-rung status. Job retraining programs, which teach marketable skills for a rapidly changing labor arena, can speedily transform losers in the workforce into winners.

Still not convinced that environmental regulations contribute to prosperity? The 1994 *Gold and Green Report* by the Durham, North Carolina-based Institute for Southern Studies should put any doubts to rest. ISS researchers discovered that the states with the most stringent environmental protection regulations and enforcement invariably had the healthiest economies; examples include Vermont, Hawaii, and Minnesota.

Still, a strong economy by itself is no guarantee that environmental protection will be diligently implemented. Resolve and understanding must accompany affluence.[22]

Then there are the situations where costs are secondary because the benefits are priceless—preservation of a national park, for example. The financial obligation in those circumstances translates into doing whatever it takes within the realm of possibility and without thought to a traditional monetary return.

One final observation regarding environmental debunkers' treatment of economics: Although the cost of environmental protection often seems to fit the bashers' description of "hefty," don't allow that to legitimize their assertion that we have been shortchanged. Compliance costs are small potatoes compared to what the nations of the world spend on weapons of war: in excess of $750 billion a year, or more graphically, an average of $80 million every hour. It's a classic case of overkill, with an abundance of stark statistical comparisons to instill in all but the most bellicose a sense of shock and revulsion.

For instance, if the money spent to build two B-1 bombers (nearly $500 million) were allocated instead to battle malaria— which kills a million children around the world each year—the disease would be contained.[23] The cost of two nuclear-powered aircraft carriers (nearly $6 billion) would be more than enough to finance a program to reverse desertification of grasslands throughout the Third World over the next 20 years.[24]

Approximately four days of global military spending, the equivalent of $8 billion, is enough money to finance the international community's five-year plan to save the world's tropical forests.

Private Property Righteousness

One of the bashers' pet themes is that the environmental move-ment is an avowed foe of private property rights.[25] This is ridicu-lous on its face. The last time I looked, a large percentage of environmental activists were property owners who—just like everybody else—displayed little inclination to cede their rights to any governmental entity. They simply advocate the environmen-tally sound and sustainable use of property. Why? Because they believe that we are custodians rather than absolute rulers of our personal domains.

The law bears them out. It is well-established legal doctrine that property rights are not absolute. Therefore, one cannot always do as one pleases with his or her acreage. What galls the bashers is that this doctrine has been invoked to protect wetlands and endangered species situated on private property without the fed-eral government providing compensation to the landowners.[26] They view the practice as a violation of the Fifth Amendment, which mandates that regulating private property for a public good constitutes a governmental "taking" of that property for which just compensation is due.

But there is an important caveat to the Fifth Amendment. Any governmental regulation of private property issued to prevent harm to other property owners is not compensable. From this principle evolves the doctrine of public trust. The federal govern-ment is not liable for denying a private landowner the use of a portion of his property when the natural resources that such use would disrupt are vital to the national interest.

Not everybody, however, perceives endangered species and wet-lands as essential enough to qualify as components of the public trust. Jonathan Adler of the Competitive Enterprise Institute, a free-market think tank, maintains that "if the public wants to pro-tect endangered species or preserve scenic vistas, the public should be willing to pay for it, just as it pays for highways, parks, and other public goods."[27] In defining what constitutes the national interest, Adler makes no distinction between preserving endangered species and constructing any old highway, regardless of its necessity, location, and viable alternatives.

Highways (especially local ones) and parks rarely can be deemed essential to long-term national interests and survival. That being the case, these projects are usually classified as sufficient intrusion upon private property to qualify the owner for compensation.

Just so they don't seem completely off the wall, bashers emphasize that the nation's "nuisance laws" would deny compensation to landowners whose use of property was restricted by a regulation aimed at curbing a direct threat or nuisance. But what of a threat whose realization is inevitable, though not immediate? Suppose the adverse impact is a cumulative process, thereby skirting the definition of "direct" until the threshold of harm may well be irreversibly crossed?

Furthermore, many forms of industrial and residential pollution perpetrated by landowners are regulated activities; that is, permits are issued granting pollutant discharge up to a certain level. Pollution that is regulated isn't recognized as a nuisance by the courts, depriving victims of an important means of legal redress. Indeed, nuisance law has such narrow application that legal experts maintain it offers "little, if any, meaningful protection against neighboring environmental abuse."[28] As the National Wildlife Federation points out, "nuisance law is highly unpredictable—varying as it does from state to state—and is reactive, not preventive. Moreover, it cannot address property uses that cause widespread harm to many neighbors or the general public. In fact, the inadequacy of nuisance law to remedy harm to the environment or public health and safety is often the basis for passing anti-pollution and other statutes."[29]

Swamp Dollars

With their nondescript marsh grass and stagnant waters, wetlands don't appear to possess much value to the untrained eye. Fortunately, hydrologists are not fooled by appearances. Their educated estimates of the enormous monetary value of wetlands indicate that the cost of compensating private property owners for preserving such resources would be prohibitive on a national scale.

Dr. Eugene Odum, internationally renowned director of the University of Georgia's Institute of Ecology, concluded in a 1974 analysis that an average acre of wetlands provides society with a $50,000 a year value in seafood, flood control, waste assimilation, and water purification benefits. Eighteen years later, a team of researchers from the University of California/Berkeley's School of Public Policy used a different formula to evaluate wetlands in their state and came up with an appraisal of $22,000 annually per acre in the form of groundwater storage, water purification, critical habitat, recreation, and fishery amenities.[30]

Hence, even though the monetary worth of wetlands is usually calculated in the aggregate and on the basis of fair market real estate values, arriving at an estimated utilitarian worth of a single acre in dollars could be useful in persuading landowners to reconsider the wisdom of paving over the marshes on their property.

Empty Space, Worthless Space

Environmental contrarians have a fit at the thought of foregoing development to preserve open space. They view any push for such constraints as a conspiracy by anti-growth purists to undermine our industrial economy and return us to an "idyllic" pastoral state unencumbered by modern technology. In knee-jerk fashion, they adopt the thesis that's part and parcel of every real estate developer's sales pitch: land devoid of development is an economic liability, open space as a rule is wasted space, and the only way to expand the tax base and jumpstart the economy is to fill up vacant land.

The idea of restricting development conjures up one of the bashers' major bugbears. It is land use planning, which they consider an unwarranted governmental encroachment on civil liberties. Thus, we have the prescription for the suburban sprawl that has desecrated so much of our countryside. Apart from its substantial aesthetic drawbacks, this sort of growth is rarely the economic bonanza it is made out to be.

Studies by the American Farmland Trust (AFT) have found that residential development, spreading out helter-skelter into the countryside from a community's core, creates a fiscal burden that exceeds the tax revenue it generates. The need to provide additional schools, roads, police, fire protection, water and sewer lines, and other public services to accommodate newcomers translates into costs that extra tax revenue can't begin to offset.[31] In an examination of three Massachusetts towns, the AFT discovered that, on average, for every dollar of tax revenue new residential development contributed to municipal coffers, local government had to pay out $1.12 to cover the cost of extra public services.[32]

Commercial developmental sprawl is likely to have a similar negative economic effect on communities because, even though it doesn't require new schools, it tends to attract construction of adjacent residential housing. By contrast, AFT researchers discovered that for every dollar of tax revenue derived from owners of farms, forests, and other undeveloped tracts, only 33 cents in public services was required, giving local government a net gain of 67 cents on every dollar received.[33] Lo and behold, open space is a better deal for tax collectors than are subdivisions.

Does that mean communities should no longer expand? Of course not! Does it mean that prime undeveloped acreage such as fertile farmland, wetlands and old-growth, biologically diverse forests should be preserved? Absolutely!

How do we reconcile these two objectives? With carefully planned development in the form of high-density clusters that minimize the occupancy of open space and are encircled by greenways.

Private Versus Public

The term "planned development," however, is repugnant to the bashers. It conjures up images of a socialist state, "Big Brother's" centralized government control, and the quashing of individual rights. These impressions lead in turn to antipathy toward virtually any form of land management or ownership that is public in character.

Typical is the attitude of former Senator Malcolm Wallop, Republican of Wyoming: "Private property encourages human beings to consider the welfare of what they own; when you own it, if you destroy it, you're the one who loses. Common or public ownership provides far fewer and much weaker inducements to good stewardship; destroy an unowned property, and someone else bears the cost."

That's odd. Most people I know are every bit as proprietary about their stake in national parks and wildlife refuges as they are about their vested interest in their own backyards. If private lands are better taken care of, how come the most popular retreats for the vacation of a lifetime are our great national parks and other public scenic sanctuaries? You seldom hear people talk about a private resort with the same degree of reverence they reserve for the Grand Canyon, the Florida Everglades, Yellowstone National Park, or the California redwoods.

Another thing: I don't know what sort of experiences Senator Wallop has had, but the career civil service employees I've encountered during visits to national parks, refuges, and forests have been extremely dedicated (and motivated) public servants. And I'm not alone. The general public has long held national park and forest rangers in high esteem as a professional group, a marked contrast to the man in the street's perception of real estate moguls and timber barons.

True, private ownership of land would seem to provide a strong incentive for environmentally responsible management. But it's hardly automatic! Suppose the landowner is a speculator who acquired the property merely to resell it and make a fast buck. It's unlikely that conservation of biological resources would be a top priority in management or disposal of this property.

Maybe the land had been bought to extract all the natural resources within its borders for a return far in excess of the purchase price. Then the plan might be for the speculator to dump the tract for whatever sum he could get, knowing full well he would end up ahead regardless of the amount of the sale. Perhaps the landowner isn't out to unload his acreage, but what he considers to be the best use of his property turns out not to be in the best interests of conservation.

Regarding Wallop's contention that we as individuals don't care about abusing public property because "someone else bears the cost," he talks as if he doesn't pay federal income taxes.

Richard Stroup of the Political Energy Research Center (PERC) in Bozeman, Montana, echoes Wallop: "Aristotle had it right. That which is owned in common is taken less well care of than that which is owned privately." Evidently, neither Stroup, Wallop, nor Aristotle ever visited Cape Cod to compare the spectacular national seashore and surrounding locales, with the dispiriting commercial clutter erected by the private sector on the densely populated Upper Cape.

I can speak from intimate personal experience about the Chincoteague National Wildlife Refuge (NWR), where I've frequently vacationed over the years. This forested barrier island with a 10-mile-long pristine beach is the second most-visited wildlife refuge in the entire system. More than a million tourists gravitate annually to the 10,000-acre sanctuary located on the Virginia coast along migratory birds' Atlantic flyway. The refuge has largely remained unspoiled (in contrast to surrounding privately owned environs), thanks to the U.S. Fish and Wildlife Service and the general public, both of which have been very protective of the resource.

No individual landowner has shown more custodial pride than the thousands of volunteers who over the years have cleaned up refuge beaches, cultivated nature gardens, and manned tourist information booths. Then there is Citizens to Preserve Assateague, a lobbying group in the Mid-Atlantic region and beyond, bound together solely by their love of the place. This extraordinary organization has been remarkably effective in its campaign to stave off developers' attempts to undermine Chincoteague's natural beauty.

Contrast the wildlife refuge with some of the privately owned, shoddy development in Ocean City, Maryland, a barrier island beach resort some 40 miles to the north, and you'll feel the urge to enlighten Stroup and resurrect Aristotle.

These revealing comparisons demonstrate an essential fact: There is no guarantee that private land will be managed in a more environmentally conscientious manner than its public counterparts. Nonetheless, the bashers don't hesitate to assert flat out that the free market fosters better environmental stewardship than the federal government. Wallop even goes so far as to say "environmental degradation is caused substantially by government interference."

One has to question Wallop and Company's grasp of American history. Are they unaware of the nineteenth century industrial revolution and its destructive laissez-faire legacy, a legacy that was the object of mounting public condemnation which culminated nearly a hundred years later in the passage of national environmental cleanup laws? Another dramatic contrast between the public and private land sectors can be found in south Florida. Rapacious developers were well on their way to subdividing the region's natural beauty into extinction until federal and state authorities intervened to preserve the Everglades and other open space for posterity.

Wallop nevertheless refuses to back down on his allegation that the feds have been a leading cause of environmental problems. He cites government policies that have resulted in clear cutting, dam construction, loss of wetlands, and excessive pesticide application on public lands. PERC chimes in about surplus elk overgrazing the wild grassland habitat in Yellowstone National Park.

There is no doubt that federal agencies' management of public lands sometimes leaves much to be desired. But in most of these cases, who pressured the government to operate in such fashion? The private sector that the bashers insist can do a better job of land management and should assume such responsibility forthwith. Often out of sheer self-preservation, our political leaders become hostage to the demands of powerful special interest lobbies.

For example, if you are looking to blame someone for the glut of elk in Yellowstone, try the hunters, trappers, and ranchers who leaned on the federal government less than a century ago to eradicate the timber wolf, the chief predator of these ungulates, from the northern Rockies. With no natural check on population, the only way to curb the numbers of elk has been to allow sportsmen to thin them out.

If a huge timber company uses every resource at its command in an unsuccessful bid to persuade the United States Forest Service (USFS) to permit widespread clearcutting on public lands, why should we expect the company to forego clearcutting if it gained managerial control? Surely it would operate differently, you might argue, if it owned rather than just managed the land. Not necessarily. As was previously noted, if the goals were quick profit and quick exit, environmentally unsustainable commodity yield might carry greater weight with the owner than watershed protection and habitat conservation. Even if the private owner were to retain the land, the emphasis might be on perpetuating a monocultural crop or concentrating on a single use, to the detriment of biological diversity.

Some bashers actually concede that private interests are the driving force behind public land mismanagement—yet they continue to urge a formal takeover by these miscreants.[34]

You're Wrong, Comrade

Another basher ploy is to cite the environmental plight of Eastern Europe as proof that a centralized regulatory approach is inferior to a free market system in cleaning up pollution. Without disputing that capitalist countries are quite capable of containing environmental abuse and a number have been relatively successful at doing so, let's set the record straight regarding the former Soviet bloc. The horrendous state of their environment is not due to the laws that were on the books when the Communists were in charge. At least on paper, those laws were stringent enough to have made an appreciable positive difference had they been observed, political ideology notwithstanding.

Unfortunately, the laws were largely ignored by government functionaries who were interested solely in filling production quotas set with no thought to environmental consequences. The functionaries weren't worried about the air and water, only about meeting factory orders at a rate that would ingratiate them with the Kremlin. Further incentive stemmed from the fact that failure to meet the quotas often resulted in demotion.

To reiterate, a large government role in the ownership and regulation of goods and services does not automatically translate into failure from either an economic or environmental standpoint. The Scandinavian nations are much more socialist-oriented than we are, yet they rank among the world's environmental leaders, and their per capita income exceeds ours.

And let's not forget—although American bashers routinely do—that, these days, every government needs some centralized apparatus to deal with pollution that doesn't respect arbitrary borders drawn by human beings.

A Private Affair

Bashers are not content with denouncing federal bureaucrats for managing land less well than their private counterparts. Government employees are accused of purposely engaging in mismanagement to further their own careers. "Federal bureaucrats may have an incentive to mismanage public lands if the resulting environmental policies create pretexts for increasing agency budgets and enacting new regulations," Malcolm Wallop declares. Public land managers have enough problems occurring on their watch without trying to create more trouble for themselves. To suggest that they would concoct crises in order to increase their budget and regulatory power is absurd.

Consider that Congress has always displayed a reflex action when federal bureaucrats have complained of additional burdens: It has told them to do more with less. And if any subversive activity is detected on the part of land management agencies, the remedy is at the ready: Dismissal and demotions for misconduct occur in the civil service as well as in the private sector. Moreover, environmental detractors add insult to inaccuracy by discounting the professional pride of federal employees.

States' Rights Forever

The federal bureaucracy is so deeply entombed in the bashers' doghouse that when free-market economics and the private sector are perceived as unable to provide the total solution, environmental denigrators will invariably turn to the states, not

Washington, for assistance. Indeed, bashers treat states' rights as an offshoot of individual rights.

Certainly, there are instances where states do a better job than Washington in regard to protecting the environment. Conversely, if for no other reason than proximity, state governments are often more beholden than the federal bureaucracy to private business interests with narrow, non-altruistic objectives.

The ability to distance itself from localized special interests plus access to the big picture that no individual state can match have put the federal government in a better position to regulate the bulk of modern-day pollution, which migrates across many different jurisdictions. Our founding fathers recognized the political necessity of this centralized, cohesive approach. Witness the supremacy clause of the U.S. Constitution, which mandates that federal laws supersede state statutes when the two are in conflict.

Those who maintain that the states are inherently more proficient than the federal government in managing public lands are in a *state* of denial.

Most Western states are required by their legislatures to administer public lands (which the federal government conveyed to them as part of statehood compacts) for the maximum possible revenue. That obligation is not conducive to camping, fishing, and hunting when such moneymakers as timber, mineral deposits, or rich pasture are in abundance. Hence, the contrast with the management of neighboring federal lands is often highly unflattering from a conservation standpoint.[35]

The Federal Bureau of Land Management and USFS tracts are mandated by law for multiple use, with substantial allowance for non-extractive pursuits such as recreation and wildlife preservation. Furthermore, a significant amount of the federal acreage has been set aside as wilderness. By comparison, state trust lands—except in rare instances—cannot be protected as wilderness, because the designation would be in direct conflict with their statutory mission.

The bottom line: The states are first and foremost out to derive maximum material gain from their lands, whereas the law directs the feds to place more emphasis on perpetuating their territories' ecological health.

It's not only in land management that states often pale in comparison to the federal government. The Tax Foundation, a non-partisan private research group, has found that state taxes have increased an average of 3.9 percent annually between 1983 and 1993, as opposed to federal levies' 2.9 percent rise for that same period.[36]

If you're looking for state government to run a tighter fiscal ship, look again. Spending by states jumped 272 percent between 1980 and 1994, compared to Washington's 250 percent.[37]

We are also frequently told that states are better equipped than Washington to handle pollution within their borders because of their greater familiarity with the terrain and the source of the problem. Not necessarily. States acting unilaterally are not capable of coping with transboundary pollution, an increasingly pervasive phenomenon due to technological advances.

A recent computer analysis by the U.S. Geological Survey disclosed that much of the water pollution problem in 18 states originated outside their borders. In essence, some states are sweeping their dirt under other states' rugs in a classic exercise of "out of sight, out of mind."[38]

If this situation doesn't warrant the federal government's entry to set matters straight, what does?

There are states complaining about mandatory programs that have been instituted in accordance with the federal Clean Air Act. They argue that they are better qualified than Washington to determine what enforcement strategy works best for them. That may be true up to a point. But all too often, when the going gets tough, the tough get going—in the direction of Washington. During the summer of 1995, Maine and New Hampshire officials, who had previously objected to some of the Clean Air Act's sanctions, became incensed at the air pollution drifting over their jurisdictions from neighboring states. They wasted no time in seeking assistance from the same federal government that was the source of their dissatisfaction only a few weeks earlier.

Another dose of reality for the states' rights contingent: In December 1996, the EPA disclosed that approximately a dozen states were drastically underreporting pollution violations that they were supposed to police as a result of a delegation of authority from Washington.

Home Free

Bashers display an unshakable belief in the healing powers of laissez-faire and volunteerism, making little or no allowance for the mayhem of anarchy and the ubiquity of greed. While environmental regulation is deemed an anathema that "imposes billions of dollars in cost for nominal benefits," the free market "encourages a more effective use of resources, greater stewardship and responsibility, and technological innovation."[39]

Many bashers make a token gesture to cover their flanks. They acknowledge the past achievements brought about by regulation that they claim has run its course. And they keep the door slightly ajar for command and control in the future, so as to maintain an air of "reasonableness." Typical is the Competitive Enterprise Institute's caveat that "there certainly may be environmental risks that call for increased regulation."[40]

But we never hear about these risks. Instead, we are subjected to unremitting condemnation of regulation (whether on the books or under consideration), which is portrayed as a major impediment to the economy. Conversely, the bashers insist that the free workings of the marketplace will sort out what is best for society.

University of Montana economics professor Thomas Michael Power uses a hypothetical situation to demonstrate how flawed the bashers' thinking really is.[41]

Suppose a piece of land is under consideration to become a regional park but is also coveted by a developer who wants to build a subdivision. "Hopefully," Power writes, "the public will pay more for Sunday hikes than the local developer will for the privilege of erecting his structures, because if not, farewell forest." And farewell it's likely to be if the game is played under free marketeers' rules. Assuming the purchase involves high up-front costs, a determined, well-financed developer can almost always outbid public authorities for a parcel of land. In the early stages of the offering, developers usually can concentrate their dollars more quickly, because they have far fewer competing demands on the assets used for acquisition.

The free market approach is all askew under these circumstances. In the long term, the value of retaining the land as a park is incalculable. You can't put a price tag on intangibles such as spiritual inspiration, psychic tranquility, and aesthetic gratification generated by a green oasis. Yet all three can easily lose out to a nondescript subdivision.

This is not to say market incentives don't have their place in the environmental protection universe. As Power points out, "economic instruments are tools, but using them does not require us to embrace a new ideology or jettison all government regulation."

Market incentives must thus take a backseat to specific pollution control goals. They must never—and I mean never—become an end in themselves, or we'll be well on our way to legitimizing the right to pollute. Regulation's raison d'etre is ultimately to keep the captains of industry from shirking responsibility for the environmental consequences of their actions.

While regulation and market incentives can complement each other, it should be emphasized that when they do clash, soundly crafted regulation ought to prevail. Our legal system certainly embodies this philosophy. For example, it dictates that the right to a clean and healthy environment takes precedence over a right to use one's property as one sees fit. From prioritization such as this has evolved the body of common law that mandates command and control regulation as a curb on free-market activity.

Professor Power points out a major irony. While libertarian-minded free marketeers have aligned themselves with conservatives against central government control, environmentalists are far more conservative than free marketeers on ecological issues.

"Environmentalists act collectively to preserve certain qualities associated with the natural and, often, social environments," Power notes. "In this sense, they are fundamentally conservative: they wish things to remain the same, or even to return to a previous, preferred condition."[42]

In another astonishing contradiction, free marketeers display the characteristics they delight in excoriating. By endorsing the "end justifies the means" credo so prevalent in the marketplace, they exhibit a Marxist mentality. And their view that we should be subservient to the bottom line in the face of ethical objections, because the bottom line is the purest form of ethics, has an authoritarian, plutocratic ring to it.

To keep the reward potential of laissez-faire in proper perspective, notes the *Population Reference Bureau Bulletin*, we should remember that "while market signals may prevent depletion of some resources ... no markets exist for many commonly held resources such as rain forests, oceans, and the global atmosphere."[43]

Protecting the Innocent

Bashers are fond of reiterating University of California professor Bruce Ames' contention that it's "counter productive" for government to focus on minor health risks, such as pollution, rather than major risks, such as driving, smoking, alcohol, poor nutrition, and AIDS.[44]

But what regulatory role should the government play in relation to these "major" risks, which revolve around lifestyle choices that we are all free to make?

Bashers and environmentalists alike adamantly oppose any attempt by officialdom to regiment our daily lives (provided we are not clearly endangering the well-being of other people in the course of our activity). That leaves the government with the obligation to do no more than inform the public of the negative odds they face if they wish to continue engaging in voluntary high-risk behavior.

What of the so-called "minor" risks to which Ames refers—the toxic pollutants released into the environment by industry?

There is a significant dispute on just how "minor" they are. But, for the sake of argument, let's accept Ames' assessment. Minor though the risks may be, they are still health risks and certainly not trivial to those unlucky souls who fail to beat the favorable odds.

Moreover, these risks are for the most part imposed upon people without their knowledge, and as such demand the attention of government regulators, because no one else can—or will—protect the unsuspecting public.

Professor Ames and his constituency have a difficult time distinguishing between voluntary and involuntary risk. That explains the non sequiturs that cascade from their mouths, such as "hazardous waste sites, pesticides, air pollution, and other trendy environmental problems get the headlines. But cars are far more dangerous. ..."[45]

The implication is that regulation of automobile use is being neglected because of official efforts to curb industrial pollution. Surely the bashers can't be serious, since they constantly remind us that any heavy-handed government intervention into personal lifestyles is their own worst nightmare.

The bashers' world is one where the government can't protect against major risks because they are questions of personal choice, and shouldn't police minor risks because of disproportionate costs. It's a scenario in which daily existence would amount to one massive free-for-all, much to the liking of anarchists, plutocrats, and scoundrels, but hardly anyone else.

Dose Makes the Poison

The bashers' disregard for involuntary risk is a byproduct of their dismissal of chronic low-level exposure to environmental pollutants as a serious health threat.

It's easy for them to make a prima facie case that prolonged contact with trace elements of highly toxic substances is inconsequential, since the incubation period for a disease such as cancer can be as long as 30 years. In fact, they use this hiatus to justify their mantra: "dose makes the poison."

According to the "dose" theory, there is a linear relationship between how ill you get and how much toxic exposure you experience. It's the basis for bashers disputing the relevance of laboratory tests in which rodents are stricken with cancer after being fed toxic chemicals in much higher concentrations than human beings ever encounter. What these skeptics neglect to mention is that over 90 percent of the chemicals that cause cancer in laboratory animals at high doses do so at low doses as well.

Some of the more ignorant environmental detractors even grouse that if you load up a laboratory mouse with enough of *any* substance, cancer will develop.[46]

This is outright nonsense. If you overdose a specimen with any concoction, it's bound to get sick, but only about 20 percent of substances tested in the lab have been found to be carcinogenic.

Bashers also dismiss animal experimentation with the disdainful aside that "mice are not little men." Of course they aren't, but enough genetic similarities exist to make the lab work meaningful.[47]

Indeed, while most scientists believe that animal tests are far from foolproof, such tests remain the best indicators we presently have of a chemical compound posing a potential danger to human health.

It would thus seem sensible whenever possible to minimize—or better yet, eliminate—low-level exposure to toxic pollutants. This especially holds true if you believe, as most scientists and environmental activists do, that there is no safe threshold for human exposure to a proven carcinogen.

Ames and his entourage are of course skeptical of this reasoning, and that is their prerogative. But under the circumstances, to whom would you extend the benefit of the doubt? The general public, unaware of all the toxic substances to which it is being exposed? Or those who willfully discharge lethal contaminants into the environment?

If you embrace the former school of thought, you are obligated to work for reduction, and preferably eradication, of harmful synthetic compounds in the environment. If you choose the latter, a toxic chemical in commercial use will be deemed harmless to human beings unless proven otherwise. That means no collective corrective action will be taken against a hazardous chemical in the environment until people start dropping in the streets.

Pesticides Forever

Anti-environmentalists' attachment to toxics technology is manifested in their defense of pesticides. They warn that, without those chemical sprays, crops will be decimated by destructive insects, and the yield of the fruits and vegetables that are major inhibitors of cancer will be drastically reduced. In short, badmouthing bug-killing chemicals is downright unpatriotic.

These detractors contend that if pesticide use were eliminated, crop harvests would decline by an estimated 30 percent, farm prices would jump by 70 percent, and U.S. agricultural exports would fall to zero.[48]

Of course, no mainstream environmentalist is suggesting a total ban on pesticides (unless, of course, a full array of effective, non-toxic substitutes ever were to become available).

What is being advocated is an approach known as Integrated Pest Management (IPM), which is designed to minimize and phase out synthetic pesticides as much as possible without disrupting harvests. IPM involves expanded use of biological controls, crop rotation, introduction of genetically pest-resistant crops, and better timing of pesticide application. It has already been shown that these techniques are capable of reducing pesticide use on major crops anywhere from 25 to 80 percent without adversely affecting crop yields.

The agricultural methodology that comes closest to eliminating pesticides is organic farming. It is an alternative often vilified by environmental denigrators for being a prohibitively costly, primitive, low-yield solution to meeting the nutritional needs of a growing human population. Yet recent studies indicate that organic farming is not as utopian as its critics would have us believe.[49]

A research project completed by American and New Zealand scientists in 1992 found that "natural farming not only left the soil in better condition but often was more cost-efficient than an operation dependent on conventional industrial agri-business techniques."[50]

Three years earlier, the National Academy of Sciences concluded that well-managed organic farming nearly always used fewer synthetic chemicals than conventional competitors, thereby reducing production costs and the risk of environmental and health damage without necessarily decreasing per acre crop yields. In some cases, it actually increased them.

As for prices soaring when chemical pesticides are removed from the market, this hasn't happened. Since 1985, the EPA has banned various uses of 12 pesticides on more than 200 crops without any effect on the price or availability of food.[51]

Indeed, well-known Cornell professor David Pimentel has long produced agricultural data indicating that total elimination of pesticides would not result in any serious food shortages. Reason: most staple foods, such as wheat, are not dependent on pesticides and thus wouldn't be greatly affected by the chemicals' disappearance.[52]

Ah, Au Natural

Why are environmentalists so adamant about getting rid of synthetic pesticides? Apart from the risks that their toxicity poses to the health of human beings and many other living organisms, pesticides deplete soil fertility over time. Since most are fossil fuel derivatives, they also cut into our energy resources.

None of these reasons have impressed the bashers, who assert that the menace of pesticides is grossly exaggerated. Here are some of their principal justifications for championing continued widespread use of pesticides:

Charge: *There's no evidence that chronic exposure to low levels of pesticides cause cancer.*

Rebuttal: Circumstantial evidence abounds. For example, it has been found that farmer exposed to herbicides run a six times greater risk of contracting certain cancers than does the average person.[53]

Charge: *There is nothing in the composition of synthetic pesticides to create a health hazard. The synthetics are comprised of the same elements as pesticides occurring naturally in many of the "healthy" plant foods we consume.*[54]

Rebuttal: The configuration of the synthetics differs from that of the naturally occurring toxins. The human immune system has adopted to the latter over thousands of years of exposure. The former quite likely has a long way to go to gain similar acceptance.

Furthermore, edible plants have been found to possess powerful antioxidant properties that appear to offset any natural toxins. Synthetics are not normally graced with such redeeming counterbalance, and there is no evidence to suggest we could change those circumstances in the foreseeable future.

Of Mice and Men

Rather than exaggerate human risk, animal testing actually underestimates it, because laboratory rodents are typically subjected to toxic chemicals for only part of their lives. Humans, on the other hand, are often exposed to pesticides from conception to death.[55]

Nor is there any truth to industry's accusation that the government overreacts to these lab tests by banning every chemical that causes a tumor. In fact, the vast majority of chemicals found to possess some carcinogenic properties are still being used on crops, albeit under far tighter official scrutiny.

If bashers can't convince us that pesticides are harmless, their fallback position is to urge us to chill out because farmers are spreading far fewer chemicals on our cropland. How is it, then, that National Cancer Institute researchers have found farmers to be experiencing elevated rates of several types of malignancies associated with exposure to synthetic chemicals?

Perhaps the explanation lies in farmers using twice as many different chemicals as they did in the 1960s, primarily due to the large increase in herbicide applications.[56] The fact that pesticide use in general is on the rise—by roughly 100 million pounds in both 1994 and 1995 over 1993, according to the EPA—could also have something to do with the farmers' medical problems.[57]

What's all the fuss? asks *Investors Business Daily*. Herbicides almost are never absorbed by food crops but instead remain in the soil.[58] Unfortunately, the newspaper fails to mention that herbicides also tend to migrate into underground aquifers from which many a community's drinking water supply originates.

It should also be noted that toxic sprays to protect crops and combat insects have created a global problem. Scientists have discovered that lethal insecticides used in India and China have been transported by wind currents to such distant locations as the Arctic and Antarctic, where they have descended to the earth's surface and polluted the terrestrial environment.

In addition, the bashers have ignored the special vulnerability of children to those chemicals, a vulnerability resulting from youngsters' higher metabolism and much greater rate of ingestion in proportion to body weight. Studies indicate that kids in homes where pesticide is used are seven times more likely to develop leukemia than their peers in pesticide-free residences.[59] If you are a parent who has been using chemical insect sprays, you will undoubtedly want to reevaluate the frequency of the practice, especially since childhood cancers have jumped 21.5 percent since 1950, a period corresponding with the increased use of pesticides.

The More, the Merrier

There is no issue that sends detractors of environmentalism into more paroxysms of hyperbole than population. Family planning is condemned as a manifestation of totalitarian ambition that places restraints on individual freedom. All that talk about it being an essential element of environmental protection is just jive. Bashers bask in Third World paranoids' denunciation of contraception programs as thinly veiled attempts by wealthy nations to reduce the population in developing countries and thereby consolidate political power.[60]

It thus comes as no surprise that bashers dismiss environmentalists' concerns about demographic pressures as the ultimate red herring, insisting that "there is no real evidence population is a problem anywhere, or ever has been."[61]

Let us examine some of the most egregious misrepresentations that these skeptics disseminate in their campaign to discredit the notion that human population growth is cause for concern.

A persistent theme is that no correlation exists between population density and poverty.[62] Demographic doubters actually contend that high population densities contribute to economic prosperity, and they cite as cases in point the city-states of Hong Kong and Singapore.[63]

One irony is that Hong Kong and Singapore didn't really begin to flourish as modern commercial hubs until their populations stabilized. More importantly, these jurisdictions have thrived because they were able, in their capacity as middle men, to convert other countries' natural resources into domestic investment capital. If they had to rely on their own virtually non-existent natural resource base to support their massive populations, they would not have survived.

In more typical situations of dense urban population, especially in the Third World, entrepreneurial skill is incapable of generating enough wealth to meet the needs of any but a relatively small percentage of the populace. If you have any doubts, visit just about any town in India.

Even in relatively affluent urban centers, the more congested the neighborhood is, the lower it's likely to be on the economic totem pole. Don't bother, however, trying to convince the cornucopian-minded bashers. They insist that "the rate of population growth has little or no impact on the rate of growth of real per capita income in developing countries."[64]

Sometimes I wonder whether we are all inhabiting the same planet.

UN statisticians report that in the 41 countries with slower population growth in the 1980s, incomes grew on average by 1.23 percent annually, whereas in the 41 countries with faster population growth, incomes fell by 1.25 percent a year![65] And a 1990 survey conducted by Population Action International (PAI) found that the five largest cities with the worst living conditions were also among the world's fastest-proliferating population centers, with an average annual growth rate of 3.4 percent during the 1980s. The five in question were Lagos, Nigeria; Kinshasha, Zaire; Kampur, India; Dhaka, Bangladesh; and Recife, Brazil.

Should you be thinking of chalking this all up to coincidence, the five most livable metropolitan areas (Melbourne, Australia; Montreal, Canada; Seattle, Washington; Atlanta, Georgia; and Essen, Germany) averaged 0.98 percent in annual growth during that same period. And keep in mind that livability in this study was determined by economic status as well as environmental quality, public safety, and caliber of city services.

Still not convinced? PAI has another card to play. In 1992, it undertook a statistical analysis of living conditions in 141 countries. The survey was entitled "The International Human Suffering Index," and guess what? The nations with the worst human suffering scores had some of the highest population growth rates. Conversely, the countries with the most agreeable overall quality of life had very low growth rates. Among the indicators used in compiling the rankings were accessibility to clean drinking water, daily caloric intake, life expectancy, and yes, the per-capita financial condition of the citizenry. Mozambique, Somalia, Afghanistan, Haiti, and the Sudan registered the lowest grades. Denmark, the Netherlands, Belgium, Switzerland, and Canada scored highest. (The United States might have finished in the top five if its annual population increase weren't one of the highest in the industrialized world.)

None of these statistics have penetrated the bashers' psychic barriers of denial and self-delusion. Don't be so uptight, they say; there is plenty of room on earth for the human race and then some. If you could fit the world's current 5.6 billion human population into the state of Texas, every individual would have 1400 square feet of space. (Sometimes Alaska or the United States are substituted for Texas, so as to give each individual even more breathing room.)

One would be hard pressed to encounter a more specious analogy. It has as much relevance as the observation that the universe is large enough to provide a galaxy for every individual on earth. True, our world seems uncrowded when you take all the vacant land into account, but much of that consists of desert, mountains, ice fields, and other uninhabitable terrain. By contrast, the much smaller share of the earth's land mass that is hospitable to human existence has been filling up rapidly. In some regions, the number of people has actually exceeded the carrying capacity of the natural resource base.

Providence in Numbers

Many critics of environmentalism are not only unperturbed about runaway population growth, they revel in it. A leading exponent of this school of thought is economist Julian Simon, who argues that the more people there are, the more minds are available to solve the problems besetting the human race.

Taking a cue from this viewpoint, other bashers argue that lower birth rates could quite conceivably deprive civilization of future Einsteins, Beethovens, and the like. They seem to have missed the elemental linkage between human developmental potential and the condition of the surrounding environment. A prospective Leonardo De Vinci or Mozart born in an overcrowded, disease-ridden slum is unlikely to reach maturity and is almost certain to be far too consumed with daily survival to exploit, much less recognize, his or her unique talents.

It's unconscionable as well as counterproductive for the bashers to advocate that human beings have as many children as possible, especially in the developing world, where natural resources are often under severe stress. How can one urge the abandonment of family planning in lands where one billion individuals struggle to survive on a dollar a day, two billion lack clean water, and three million die each year from malnutrition?[66]

Occasionally, the bashers will concede that some couples do want smaller families (although they won't admit this has any utilitarian purpose other than to satisfy parents' personal preferences). But they regard birth control assistance extended by the government as an authoritarian intrusion, even when it's at the couple's request. Indeed, official dissemination of artificial contraceptives is considered an exercise in mind control. Besides, couples don't need contraception to limit family size. They can do it with traditional methods based on abstinence.[67]

This is the Vatican's song and dance. The Catholic hierarchy considers voluntary forbearance, the rhythm method, and prayer a winning combination to ward off pregnancy. Only it doesn't fly. Demographic experts estimate that among couples who rely solely on natural methods, 40 percent experience unintended pregnancy within the first year of practicing these techniques.[68]

So much for Rome's understanding of human sexuality. Celibacy is obviously not the best vantage point from which to gain insight into the vagaries of the libido.

Contrary to bashers' rosy pronouncements that food production is outpacing population growth throughout the world,[69] UN data reveal that, in the past nine years, global increases in grain output, fish harvesting, and beef yields have been unable to keep pace with the rate of expansion of the human race. Indeed, global per-capita agricultural production ceased growing back in 1984.[70]

Africa is a dramatic illustration of this disturbing trend. Population there has been growing at three percent annually since 1970, whereas cereal production has increased by only two percent. Africans are eating 10 percent less than they were 20 years ago, and in 15 nations on their continent, the average caloric intake is below the minimum nutritional requisite set by the UN's Food and Agriculture Organization.

That Was Then, This Is Now

Occasionally, a critic of the environmental movement will admit that a population problem was once in the making, but he or she will quickly add that everything is now under control and we should turn our attention to other matters. To bolster such a view, the critic will point to the declining fertility rate throughout the world.

Omitted from such calculations is the reality that the death rate has dramatically fallen at the same time, offsetting to some extent the lower birth rate. Moreover, so many people are in their reproductive years (due to the population explosion in the latter part of this century) that even if every couple on the planet were to limit themselves to two children or less (which hardly seems imminent), 90 million persons would be added to the human race each year for the next two decades. And make no mistake—if global family planning programs were to falter, the annual increase in total human population would rise accordingly.

In fact, that is in danger of happening. A December 1996 analysis by Population Action International found that the number of women in the developing world aged 15 to 49 was increasing by 2.3 percent, or some 24 million annually. Just to keep the percentage of these potential Third World mothers receiving family planning assistance at current levels (54 percent) will require a similar increase. Yet Congress cut funding for international family planning assistance in 1996 by 35 percent, oblivious to the insidious threat that runaway population growth poses to our future quality of life.

Another reason why a declining birth rate is not yet a cause for unabashed rejoicing is the specter of unemployment. There are already more than 500 million people in the developing world who are underemployed or out of work. Even if the reduction of birth rates proceeds at its current pace, 30 million new jobs will have to be created annually for the next few decades just to keep the unemployment situation from deteriorating further. Obviously, if the lower birth-rate trend should reverse, the task of keeping a lid on an immense political powder keg would become just that much harder. (The latest United Nations report finds one billion unemployed or underemployed throughout the world in 1995, up from 820 million in 1993 and 1994.)

Finally, myopic economists such as Simon argue that the supply of most resources has become more plentiful despite population growth, so there really isn't any demographic problem. Those economists chose to ignore the status of the most crucial resource of them all—*fresh water*. Global per-capita water availability is one-third lower than in 1970 due to the 1.8 billion additional people inhabiting the planet. The good-timers also must not be seafood aficionados. Otherwise, they would be aware that, even when inflation is taken into account, fish prices are 40 percent higher than in 1950, a reflection of reduced abundance due to the demands of an expanding human population.

The Fix Is In

Even if you somehow manage to wheedle critics of the environmental movement into conceding that population growth has the potential to deplete natural resources, you won't get them to recant their conviction that "the more, the merrier." Salvation from resource depletion is always at hand for the cornucopians, in the form of the technological fix. As they see it, human ingenuity can overcome any limitation imposed by nature—creating a rationale for unrestrained entrepreneurial initiatives.

"Unlike most other species, we modify the world to suit our needs; we don't have to adopt to its given constraints," declares environmental-trashing ideologue Ron Baily.[71]

Tell that to inhabitants of barrier islands or the Sahara Desert, Ron. On a more universal scale, farmers around the world are limited by seasonal weather patterns and soil types as to what they can grow, modern technology notwithstanding.

"Human intelligence usually breaks the bonds that 'carrying capacity' imposes on other species," Baily continues. "This is why the science of economics is more relevant to the study of human beings than is ecology."[72]

On the contrary, Baily unwittingly dramatizes the increasing irrelevancy of modern-day economics by highlighting the "dismal science's" failure to take account of the elemental linkage between human activity and natural resource depletion. There is little or no technology, however brilliantly conceived, that does not rely to some extent on the natural resource base. A technique has yet to be developed that enables products to be manufactured from dust.

As author Lindsey Grant points out, the bashers' belief in infinite substitutability "is not based on any systematic rationale nor buttressed by any evidence other than the fact that the industrial world has been doing pretty well, so far ... It's an assumption required by economists to run their models ... but it's a terribly dangerous assumption in a finite world on which human economic activity is pressing ever more heavily. *There are no practical human substitutes for clean air and water or a functional ecological system.*"[73]

Further undermining their case, the bashers display extraordinary inconsistency in their adulation of technology. This equivocation shows they are motivated more by ideology than supreme confidence in the human mind's capacity to overcome the planet's finite limitations. While subscribing to such assertions as "we literally have the technology to make nearly any land arable," they summarily dismiss any chance of people being clever enough to produce technological breakthroughs that would enhance the environmental movement's cause.[74]

Hence, they express conviction that agronomists will find a way to make crops multiply in virtually any terrain, no matter how inhospitable. Yet they ridicule the suggestion that engineers could ever design an automobile that would meet stricter requirements for fuel economy and still retain its current degree of safety (the assumption being that the vehicles would have to be lighter and flimsier to achieve the improved fuel mileage goal). Why bashers' faith in auto-design engineers' capabilities should be any less than in those of agronomists has no rational explanation, only a political one.

A further inconsistency involves bashers condemning big government for creating a dependency that relieves persons of individual responsibility, while eulogizing the technological fix for fostering that same sort of dependency. The promise of the fix springs other traps for the unsuspecting. Even when technology appears to master the natural elements, it may cause unforeseen secondary effects that transform triumph into a Faustian bargain. For example, the initial success of some potent pesticides has backfired as the targeted destructive insects have acquired immunity while non-target beneficial ones have not.

Those who trash environmentalists' opposition to heavy reliance on pesticides should note the cautionary tale of the boll weevil in south Texas. Cotton farmers there have sued to halt the state's repeated application of the pesticide malathian, which was aimed at eradicating the boll weevil. The weevils, it turns out, are already pretty much under control, and all that malathian did was kill wasps and other beneficial insects that ordinarily keep the beet army worm and other pests in check. Free of predators, the worm was at liberty to ravage the region's cotton crop, and so it did, to the great distress of the plaintiff farmers.

Another agricultural-related example: the Green revolution in the Third World. It has been responsible for a dramatic increase in food production, but the vast amounts of fossil fuel-based fertilizers and pesticides used injudiciously in the process have had deleterious effects on the long-term health of the soil.

Environmental detractors are fond of asserting that if the eleven percent of vehicles that are old, highly polluting models were removed from circulation, air quality would be improved far more dramatically than by tightening the regulatory screws on newer vehicles that already have sophisticated pollution abatement devices. Alas, the increase in the number of cars on the road and the total amount of vehicle miles traveled have more than offset the tailpipe emission reductions resulting from improved technology. Despite all the fanfare, we are experiencing a net increase in air pollution from mobile sources.[75]

Many who champion the technological fix as a panacea bestow the ultimate tribute to human ingenuity by reaching the eyepopping conclusion that "while world population is increasing in absolute terms, the planet is actually becoming relatively less populated in relation to such key variables as food and resources."[76]

Bona Fide Positivism

While the bashers portray themselves as eternal optimists due to their belief in the infinite potential of the human intellect, they demonize environmentalists as doomsdayers who predict that humanity will eventually strip the earth clean of its natural wealth. These denigrators of the environmental movement have things in reverse. It is they who are a depressing lot.

Their cavalier stance—if, heaven forbid, it were ever universally embraced—would surely increase the risk of humanity squandering the vast natural riches of our planet.

The true optimists are the environmentalists. Although stressing the finite nature of earth, they are quick to note that the most essential resources are renewable as long as mankind manages them with care.

Net Energy

When it comes to mineral wealth, the false optimism of the environmental skeptics again springs from their failure to make the connection between human activity and resource depletion.

The chief executives of extractive industries who boast that there are a thousand years of coal buried in the ground, 100 years of oil deposits under the sea or whatever, are giving us a gross rather than net figure. Few environmental denigrators admit to the existence of net energy, much less incorporate it into their calculations. Yet it is elemental in defining the relationship between human beings and the world around them.

In essence, net energy refers to the difference between the energy needed to produce an energy supply or product and the actual quantity (measured in energy values) that is produced. For example, extracting, transporting, and producing fuel demand a great deal of energy use in their own right. Thus, if a petroleum deposit contains the equivalent of 10 years of oil but takes eight years worth to bring the lode above ground and into the marketplace, we are looking at only a two-year supply.

Given their proclivity for gilding the lily, politicians are unlikely to own up to the reality that as the richest and more easily recoverable mineral deposits are depleted and industry turns to less accessible caches, much more energy will be needed to produce the same amount of the end product, thereby drastically reducing the yield.

What Wetland Loss?

The feel-good crowd has trouble with net statistics in another realm as well: wetland preservation. Eager to discredit wetland protection regulation that they consider to be overly stringent and in violation of private property rights, they reject environmentalists' claim that the nation is losing nearly 300,000 acres of wetlands annually to development. In fact, they assert that more wetlands are being created each year than are being destroyed, an improvement upon President Bush's "no net wetland loss" goal, which they claim was actually achieved several years ago.[77]

One must view these declarations with great skepticism, given the primitive state of wetland restoration technology. The vast majority of projects throughout the nation have been unable to replicate the complex, biologically diverse character of the original sites.[78]

Skepticism turns to repudiation when one examines the feelgooders' data. The net gain of which they boast is based on statistics compiled by the U.S. Agriculture Department's National Resource Inventory (NRI).

There's a problem here. The NRI is not meant to ascertain national wetland loss rates. The inventory doesn't even monitor 30 percent of the nation's land area, including wetlands in urban, suburban, and coastal locations. Instead, it focuses narrowly on rural, non-federal wetlands used as waterfowl habitat. By contrast, the U.S. Fish and Wildlife Service oversees the much more comprehensive National Wetland Inventory (NWI), which with the help of extensive aerial photos indicates 117,000 wetland acres have been lost each year to civilization during the latest decade on record--1985-1995.[79]

The charge is also made that wetland regulation is not even mentioned in the Clean Water Act (CWA). Overzealous environmental regulators, so the allegation goes, simply invented the authority to impose big government's will over private property owners.[80]

Wrong again. The intent of Congress is unmistakable. When federal lawmakers reauthorized the CWA in 1977, the term "wetland" was expressly included in Sec. 404 (g), which described the scope of the waters to be regulated. Further affirmation of federal officials' authority to regulate wetlands can be found in the CWA's legislative history as well as in court rulings throughout the land.[81]

4

CAUSES CELEBRES

Bashers seek to build a following by disputing the authenticity of the most widely acknowledged environmental threats and most publicized environmental claims. In the course of this campaign, they rely on a standard set of melodramatic accusations and horror stories which they dutifully recycle for shock effect. To the unsuspecting, such presentations may sound quite convincing, for they always contain a dollop of truth. Fortunately, a minimal amount of investigation usually suffices to expose these allegations for what they are—a melange of cant, prejudicial omissions, syllogisms, and outright lies.

The irony of their crusade is that they are done in by their own propaganda. Bashers normally consider technological expertise a panacea for whatever ails the universe. Yet their confidence in mankind's resourcefulness vanishes whenever innovative breakthroughs are part of environmentalists' master plan. For example, detractors refuse to acknowledge that automobile engineers might be capable of designing models that could achieve far better gasoline mileage without a downsizing that compromises the safety of passengers. There are other notable examples in which bashers exhibit a lack of confidence in human ingenuity, at whose altar they otherwise devoutly worship: electric cars, recycling, and renewable sources of energy.

High Voltage Cars

The planned introduction of electric vehicles (EVs) into the transportation mix is a losing proposition in the free market crowd's opinion. These characters consider this technological innovation to be a Machiavellian ploy to tighten the regulatory vise on industry. Conversely, environmental activists are counting on EVs to help ease the substantial air pollution and energy drain caused by motor vehicle use.

While such a theory stokes the paranoia of critics of the environmental movement, they manage to contain their emotions and hide behind a measured public response that assails the Greens' science rather than their politics. Critics assert that EV technology is extremely primitive, resulting in a prohibitively expensive, limited mileage, sluggish automobile of flimsy construction that places occupants at great risk in the event of a collision.[1]

Rush Limbaugh has even weighed in, asserting that no one wants EVs, so the only way they will ever penetrate the marketplace is if the government forces them down our collective throat. "Why," he exults, "they don't even have enough juice to support air conditioning in this day and age. How many people are going to want a car without AC?"[2]

Washington Times Transportation Editor Eric Peters leapfrogs from this criticism to fashion an additional strained argument. He warns that as a result of government compelling industry to build a number of costly EVs for public use (under a provision in the Clean Air Act and California code), automobile manufacturers will have to offset this expenditure by raising prices on conventional models. That in turn, Peters predicts, will persuade people to retain their old "dirty" cars longer, thereby causing more rather than less air pollution.

Recently, much to the delight of EV detractors, a report by researchers at Pittsburgh-based Carnegie Mellon University concluded that a 1998 model EV would release an estimated 60 times more lead per kilometer of use than a car burning leaded gasoline.[3]

What an ideological bonanza! The environmentalists' cure is worse than the disease! Journalists hostile to the environmental movement scrambled to outdo each other in playing up the Carnegie-Mellon study for all it was worth.[4]

Bursting the Bubble

Now for a reality check. None of the critics seem to have touched base with the engineers intimately involved in the development of the EV. If the ideologically driven skeptics had bothered to do so, they would have discovered the following:

- New batteries developed from nickel cadmium and a nickel-metal hybrid are unaffected by cold weather and can propel an EV at speeds in excess of 85 mph, using energy at the equivalent of 126 miles per gallon.[5]

- A converted Honda Civic EV has been clocked accelerating from 0 to 60 mph in 7.8 seconds, a takeoff not all that dissimilar from that of high-performance super cars.

- Engineers have constructed an EV that can be driven 214 miles without a recharge, a distance comparable to the range provided by a full gas tank in some pricey conventional internal combustion engine models with poor fuel economy.[6]

- What about the nightmarish allegations that recharging the EV's battery is a protracted ordeal? A new device can recharge a spent EV battery in less than 20 minutes, not much longer than it takes to fill up a tank at a gas station.

- Some small EV manufacturers are already selling limited numbers of models in the $15,000 to $45,000 range. If EVs were ever mass produced, the economies of scale would lower prices to a level competitive with that of today's conventional automobiles of similar size.

- For those worried about survivability in a highway accident, factory tests of EV durability and toughness have been reassuring.[7]

- Oh yes, the pollution scare. According to a well-documented analysis by the International Center for Technology Assessment (CTA), a public interest group, "much of the data and information used in the Carnegie-Mellon study is flawed and outdated; in addition, it does not take into account significant advances in environmental protection covering lead processing and in improved battery recycling technology and efficiency."

Indeed, CTA declares, EVs produce 97 percent less toxic emissions than gasoline vehicles, even when taking into account the lead pollution discharged by battery manufacturing and recycling facilities.

Noting that the Carnegie-Mellon researchers rely heavily on donations from corporate contributors, the CTA expresses concern that the study's findings may have been influenced by vested oil and automobile interests opposed to integrating EVs into our transportation system.[8]

- Finally, let's tend to Limbaugh's penchant for inaccuracy in environmental matters. His contention that EV engines are unable to support air conditioning is totally untrue. A/C has been an optional feature in EVs since the early 1980s, and most high-performance highway models are equipped with it. The A/C apparatus can also be installed after manufacture in a rather simple procedure.[9]

Recycled Slander

Bashers usually take a dim view of recycling, and not just because of the high esteem in which it is held by the environmental movement. To the Greens' denigrators, the process amounts to an ideologically imposed ascetism in a land of plenty. They tend to regard recycling as an un-American, even dangerously subversive, attack upon a consumption-oriented value system in the world's wealthiest capitalist nation.[10] Free marketeers consider the practice a constraint on entrepreneurs' efforts to convert nature's raw materials into products and hard currency.

But rather than denounce resource recovery as a Communist plot, an allegation they realize is likely to evoke ridicule outside their own circle, most of these critics have substituted more temperate expressions of dissatisfaction. One of their most frequent criticisms is that recycling routinely consumes more energy and natural resources than manufacturing processes that rely directly on raw materials. They then follow up by condemning recycling for failing—contrary to its backers' claims—to conserve iron ore, petroleum, or forests.[11]

This calumny inspires environmentally unsophisticated columnists—who share the bashers' ideological bent—to seize upon the outlandish analogies designed to diminish recycling's stature. Case in point: Mona Charen quotes a Gonzaga University economics professor's observation that "1000 years of U.S. trash would fit in a 30-square-mile area piled 300 feet deep." Even if this statement were accurate, does Charen really think it makes recycling superfluous?

Most homeowners would object to even a *day's* worth of their own community's trash, much less the nation's, being buried anywhere near their domicile. Hence, a 30-square-mile national landfill would have to be located in the middle of nowhere, a decision that would render transportation costs prohibitively expensive for most of the country. Still, critics insist that we are not running out of landfill capacity and then follow up by impugning recycling for its alleged cost inefficiencies.[12]

As with most bashers' claims, truth and falsehood are insidiously intermingled to lure the unsuspecting. A number of locales are indeed approaching the limits of viable landfill capacity. And as Worldwatch Institute researcher John Young points out, "while some cities still have cheap municipal landfills with years of remaining capacity, others do not and are operating well-run programs that collect and market materials at costs well below those of landfilling or burning waste."[13]

Contrary to the propaganda spread by their detractors, environmental activists have never portrayed recycling as a panacea to the waste disposal problem. Indeed, the mainstream environmental movement has made clear that recycling is no more than a partial solution, and in some instances may not even be that. If a market is created, it will succeed; if not, it's likely to fail. Landfills on a modified scale remain a part of the recommended strategy. Most important of all, industry and individuals are urged to find new ways to reduce the amount of waste they generate in order for environmentally sound disposal capacity to keep pace with the trash load produced by an expanding population.

Its limitations notwithstanding, recycling is starting to make a difference. The United States alone is now saving about one percent of its total annual energy use by recycling municipal solid waste.

Since early 1994, prices for nearly all commonly collected recyclables (paper, plastics, and metals, for example) have skyrocketed. Paper diverted from our municipal waste stream into recycling doubled from 13 million tons in 1985 to 26 million tons in 1993. New York City, which two years ago was paying $6 million annually to dispose of its newsprint, expects to earn between $20 million and $25 million over 72 months from selling that material.[14]

Higher prices for raw materials around the world have encouraged manufacturers to look elsewhere. Subsequent decisions by companies and some governments (including our own) to give recycled materials preference have helped considerably. So has increasing consumer confidence in the quality of recycled products. All these factors, in turn, have encouraged greater capital investment in the infrastructure responsible for recycling capacity.

Even when the numbers don't favor recycling in a particular community, environmental, aesthetic, and possibly ethical concerns may lead residents to adopt the practice and operate at a deficit. Recycling, for example, saves trees by easing pressures to turn virgin forests into de facto timber farms. And keep in mind that an unfavorable economic picture for recycling can be misleading. While a recycling program can cost more up front to operate than a landfill, it has the potential to generate revenue and make a profit when the economy is in high gear.

Recycling is undervalued by many economists who neither assign credit for the tonnage saved from going into the landfill nor acknowledge any benefit when the need to build a waste dump is obviated altogether. The reduction in the costs stemming from diminishing air and water pollution damage, as well as from landfill operations, are usually not incorporated into an assessment of a recycling program's value. Neither are the considerable energy savings. It should come as no surprise, then, that a recent study by the Tellus Institute of Boston found that when these external reductions in costs were considered, recycled boxboard, aluminum, and glass were far cheaper for society to buy than their virgin equivalents.

The nation is certainly catching on, even if the bashers aren't. In 1986, we recycled eight percent of the nation's municipal waste stream. Four years later, it was 17 percent, and by 1994, the figure had risen to 23 percent.[15]

Dubious Futurism

Those who forge a career out of disparaging the environmental movement dismiss renewable energy technology as too far-fetched to make any significant contribution to the national and global fuel mix for the foreseeable future. They mockingly label as a work of science fiction the idea that solar, wind, biomass, hydro, and other relatively non-polluting renewable sources of power might serve as the energy cornerstone of our economy.

Aside from the bashers' sudden, startling loss of confidence in the human technological genius they usually sanctify, there is another major irony about this aversion to renewables. These skeptics are for the most part champions of free markets and open competition, yet they turn a deaf ear to pleas that renewables be allowed to compete on a level playing field with conventional fuels. While the nuclear power and fossil fuel companies receive huge subsidies from Washington in the form of tax writeoffs and other fiscal perks, conservative members of Congress are seeking to strip the renewable energy industry of even its modest amount of federal financial aid as well as to virtually eliminate ancillary research by government scientists. The rationale: The private sector can do a better job on its own of developing renewable energy. The flaw: Renewable technologies often require a large initial research expenditure that doesn't pay off in the short term. This discourages many companies from experimenting because of heavy pressure from stockholders to register immediate, substantial gains.

If renewables were permitted to vie on an equal footing with nuclear, oil, gas, and coal in the open marketplace, it would not be such an uneven contest vis-a-vis cost per unit of energy. Economy of scale could come into play, and the difference in prices of the various energy alternatives would narrow.

Why this closed mind among bashers towards priming the pump for renewables? Well, who wants to rely on solutions promoted by long-haired, pot-smoking leftist radicals? Indeed, support of renewables as a remedy could be construed as acceptance of ecologists' contention that some severe environmental problems exist because of—horror of horrors—disruptive human activity involving traditional energy use.

For the skeptics, renewables evoke images of austerity and sacrifice that would consign a capitalist country to a dreary fate. Some even perceive the push for renewables as part of a conspiratorial scheme to halt economic growth and transform the United States into a classless society through a massive redistribution of wealth. Another supposed knock on renewables is that they could divert us from maintaining the fossil fuel base responsible for making us the most powerful industrial complex the world has ever known.

Finally, renewables are considered more of a creature of big government than of private enterprise, inspiring free marketeers to associate the technology with bureaucratic inefficiency and a socialist state. Yet most members of Congress who argue that renewables should be developed by private industry or not at all have consistently sought to curtail the federal financial assistance that businesses desperately need to get off the ground so they can operate on their own.

Clearing the Air

Dismissing renewables as exotic phenomena with little mass application just doesn't square with the facts. While market saturation is not yet imminent for some renewable technologies, it's important to note that renewables collectively supply approximately eight percent of the total energy demand in the United States and have surpassed nuclear power as a source of fuel.

In addition, renewable energy producers furnish about 11 percent of our electricity and, at the present rate of expansion, could serve more than 40 million homes in 15 years.

The U.S. Energy Department's National Renewable Energy Laboratory (NREL) predicts that by the year 2005, solar-powered photovoltaic cells and modules will generate as much as 10 percent of the electricity provided by our utility companies. Another optimistic projection comes from the American Solar Energy Society. It maintains that renewables could meet half of the United States' energy needs by the year 2030 *with presently available technologies* (provided government seed money to the private sector is forthcoming).[16]

The NREL estimates that by 2030, wind turbines could produce 10 percent of our nation's total electric power. Already, 1.5 percent of all electricity consumed in California is derived from wind.

Hydrogen, which is essentially non-polluting, possesses the greatest potential of all. It can be burned as fuel in engines and be used for direct production of electricity through chemical reactions in fuel cells. The main obstacle up to this point has been the high costs associated with its extraction from water.

It's patently absurd to claim that reliance on solar power and other renewables is a component of a duplicitous scheme to foist a monastic existence upon the American people. Anyone who has ever visited a structure either partially or completely dependent upon solar energy will, I venture to say, encounter little in the way of deprivation. Whatever cutbacks you will find are manifested not in creature comforts but in electricity bills.

Red Flags

No incident incites environmental charlatans more than the Alar scare. It is alleged that the outlawed Alar, a chemical that was applied primarily to apples as a growth regulator and color enhancer, was falsely branded as a health hazard by eco-purist groups seeking to further their crusade against free enterprise and attract new members with publicity born of a contrived crisis.[17] The defenders of Alar were infuriated by a 1989 EPA ban on the chemical's use. They felt that the government decision was made on the basis of highly unreliable laboratory experiments in which some mice developed malignant tumors after exposure to Alar. From the results of these tests, authorities concluded that the chemical possessed carcinogenic properties that posed a particularly grave risk to apple juice-drinking infants.

Bashers charged that the tests were rigged by massively overdosing the mice with Alar to elicit adverse reactions.[18] A favorite analogy was to characterize the animal tests as the equivalent of giving a human being 50,000 pounds of Alar-treated apples or 19,000 quarts of apple juice to consume every day for a lifetime.[19]

They added that Alar had never been conclusively proven to cause cancer in humans, and noted that the chemical had been used for 21 years with no observable negative effects. Finally, they criticized the discrepancy between the estimates of the EPA and environmental activist groups regarding how many pre-school children would eventually develop cancer from Alar exposure (nine out of a million versus 240 out of a million, respectively).

"The basic problem," wrote the authors of the environment-trashing Apocalypse Not, "is that there is simply no way to assign a potency factor that states the number of cancers induced by a given dose of Alar or any other perceived carcinogen."[20]

Conceding the difficulty of assigning a precise risk factor to exposure, are these authors suggesting we do nothing? Who should get the benefit of the doubt, the pre-schoolers or chemical manufacturers and apple growers?

What about the contention that Alar should be exonerated because lab tests proved positive only after the ingestion of massive doses? The overwhelming majority of the scientific community regards animal laboratory tests (even when conducted with the maximum tolerated doses) as the best—albeit admittedly imperfect—indicator currently at our disposal for assessing cancer risks to humans.

In addition, children are considered much more prone than adults to damage from toxic exposures. Even at trace levels, youngsters may be inordinately vulnerable to Alar because of not fully developed immune systems, high metabolic rates, exposure to a multitude of trace pollutants, and intake of more toxic substances per unit of body weight. It follows that in the bashers' ideal world of relaxed regulation, children would bear the brunt of the pain. Many of the existing anti-pollution regulations that the bashers would roll back, after all, have proven inadequate to protect the young. For example, the Center for Disease Control warns that some 1.7 million youngsters each year are still contracting lead poisoning from paint in buildings. More than 100,000 children accidentally ingest pesticides each year. And studies have shown that youngsters suffer decreased lung function at levels *below* the current ambient air quality standard for particulate matter.[21]

Bashers remain impervious to expressed concerns over the younger set's vulnerability to Alar. They argue that this color enhancer may not be a carcinogen because many, if not most, lab animals subjected to the chemical did not develop tumors.[22]

When listening to such claptrap, it's important to remember that non-carcinogenic chemicals don't cause malignant tumors, even when administered in maximum doses. The claim that no discernible ill effects from Alar have been recorded in the past 21 years is specious. Cancer's incubation period is often lengthy (except in fast-growing infants, whose rapid metabolic changes can accelerate the process), obscuring the cause. To compound the difficulty, awareness of Alar's threat has been relatively recent, and so has monitoring for any correlation between exposure and disease.

Despite trashers' dire prediction that the banning of Alar would bring apple growers to their proverbial knees, the industry is doing right well, thank you. Prosperity certainly undermined the industry's legal attempt to overturn the Alar ban. But an even more potent factor was the U.S. Supreme Court's April 1996 decision upholding a trial judge's dismissal of the growers' complaint of unfair treatment.

The Rio Earth Summit and Heidelberg Appeal

While the 1992 Rio de Janeiro Earth Summit is considered a watershed event in the evolution of the international environmental movement, the bashers have quite a different take on this historic gathering. They characterize it as a convocation of elitists more worried about saving trees than people.

I concede that holding the summit in grandiose surroundings at an isolated site more than 30 miles from the Brazilian city identified with the gathering did smack of elitism. But the truth is that the summit—which attracted all but a handful of nations—focused more on human beings than vegetation (with the latter being assessed primarily in the context of its importance to the former). To verify that, all one has to do is examine the conference's final declaration, which links poverty to environmental degradation and warns that addressing one without the other will cure neither.

Another denigrating tack depicted the conference as a platform for environmental purists driven by Rousseauistic ideology rather than science. To support this allegation, bashers repeatedly cited the so-called Heidelberg Appeal, a proclamation signed by more than 500 scientists (including 62 Nobel Prize winners) of different nationalities several months before the summit. This document was often disingenuously portrayed as a repudiation of the Rio Summit and its philosophical underpinnings.

Even the venerable *New York Times* was duped into publishing a distorted characterization of the declaration, having been deceived by a reporter who aspired to notoriety as an environmental iconoclast. *Times* reporter Keith Schneider described the Heidelberg Appeal as a denunciation of the environmental movement for articulating an irrational, anti-scientific ideology that exaggerated ecological problems and sought to obstruct technological progress. In fact, nothing in the Heidelberg Appeal's text alleged that the environmental problems highlighted at the Earth Summit were being exaggerated. The Heidelberg signatories actually concluded by identifying over-population, starvation, and worldwide disease as major concerns, an assessment with which no participant at the Earth Summit would have quarreled.

The Heidelberg Appeal did not attack the environmental movement per se, but it did single out for criticism those who would "idealize a natural state." That was all the eco-bashers needed to hear. They immediately pounced on the declaration as an endorsement of their portrayal of the environmental movement as a bunch of back-to-nature, anti-science extremists.

Again, nonsense. There are environmentalists who reject most of the amenities of modern civilization and yearn for a simpler life, but they are relatively few in number and outside the environmental mainstream. To call them representative of the environmental movement is no different from typecasting any relative of a convicted felon as a hardened criminal, purely by virtue of family lineage.

Die-Die-Dioxin

Environmentalists' labeling of dioxin as one of the most toxic chemical compounds in the world immediately exonerates the substance in the bashers' eyes. Here is just a sampling of their responses to what they call the phony "dioxin scare."

- Dioxin is harmless.[23]

- "Dioxin is a natural occurring substance that has a safe threshold."[24]

- "There is no evidence of low-level exposure to dioxin being harmful."[25]

- "Little basis exists for believing dioxin
  has subtle effects on human endocrine
  and reproductive systems."[26]

- Given that animal testing is at the core of the
  deductive process implicating dioxin as a carcinogen, the credibility of such experiments is
  constantly under attack. "One cannot extrapo-
  late from rodents to humans, or even rodents
  (guinea pigs) to rodents (hamsters)," intones
  Fumento.[27]

- The mother of all sound bites, from the environmental detractors' perspective: "Exposure to
  dioxin is now considered by some experts to be
  no more risky than spending a week sun
  bathing."[28]

The Notorious Spinoffs

Dioxin is a chemical byproduct of high temperature incinera-
tion, chlorine-based paper bleaching, and many other industrial
processes. Its capacity to pervade a localized area and its
suspected toxicity have triggered governmental responses that
environmental detractors have sought to portray as ludicrous
overreactions. I'm talking about the federally mandated evacuations that occurred at Love Canal in upstate New York and Times
Beach, Missouri. Also roundly criticized is the indictment of the
defoliant Agent Orange as a cause of serious disease among
Vietnam veterans.

The bashers have characterized all three of these cases as surrender to alarmist propaganda.[29] They point to the Italian town of
Seveso, where a chemical factory explosion in 1976 sent dioxin
dust swirling through the community. After 20 years of Seveso
residents being closely monitored, the bashers declare triumphantly that the only noticeable pathologic effect that has
been detected is a skin rash (chloracne).[30] Fumento does mention
a 1989 study that found above average incidence of certain types

of cancers in Seveso males, but he dismisses the sampling as too small to be statistically significant.[31]

How convenient! From his comfortable Washington perch, Fumento can shrug off as an anomaly a few extra cancer cases in a village across the Atlantic. To those living in Seveso, however, it's hard to be so dispassionate. They derive scant consolation from there not being sufficient evidence to prove that their toxic past is slowly but inexorably catching up with them.

Anyway, the picture is not as murky as the bashers suggest. Fumento and other debunkers of Seveso fail to acknowledge a 1991 international conference in which scientists made a convincing case that there were an abnormally high number of liver cancer and soft tissue sarcoma victims in the Seveso population.[32] Also omitted: mention of a peer-reviewed study published in the October 1993 issue of *Epidemiology* in which a significant increase in cancer among Seveso survivors was reported.[33] Finally, Doctor Pier Alberto Bertazzi of the University of Milan recently conducted epidemiological studies and found an abnormally high incidence of Hodgkin's disease, non-Hodgkin's lymphoma, and leukemia in Seveso residents who were exposed to the blast.

Reality Check

In September 1994, the EPA completed an exhaustive review and reassessment of research on dioxin and related chemicals. The report's conclusion: Dioxin and most of its chemical byproducts at low levels cause a range of adverse health effects, including reproductive and immune system disorders, alteration of fetal development, and cancer.[34] Furthermore, contrary to the claims of those parroting the chemical industry's line, the EPA's Science Advisory Board (SAB), a collection of independent scientists recruited to peer review the EPA study, in general confirmed the report's conclusion.[35] Criticism that emanated from some SAB members centered around a request for EPA to provide more documentation, not retract its conclusion.

EPA's grim assessment of dioxin evolved from 17 long-term animal studies suggesting that dioxin is a direct cause of malignant tumors. This presumption is challenged by the few scientists who contend that dioxin is a promoter rather than initiator of cancer, i.e., that it enhances the capacity of other poisons to cause malignancies.[36] Even if this were so, it strikes me as little more than a semantic splitting of hairs. A distinct negative effect may be delivered in a roundabout way, but it is still sufficient to qualify dioxin as a carcinogen for all practical purposes.

As to the credibility of animal tests and the questions raised by the different responses that various species have to dioxin exposure, Assistant EPA Administrator Lynn Goldman's spirited defense of the methodology reflects the sentiment of the overwhelming majority of the scientific community. "Though a wide variety in health effects can be observed from dioxin exposure," she says, "the chemical compound affects organs in all species in roughly the same way."[37] That means the cellular and genetic reaction of humans to dioxin exposure resembles in kind, if not degree, the reaction of laboratory animals.

False Alarms

When bashers can't sell the exoneration of dioxin in general terms, they turn to specific controversies involving Love Canal, Times Beach, and the use of Agent Orange. The bashers maintain that no cause-and-effect relationships between dioxin exposure and disease have been conclusively established in those widely publicized instances. Typical are the authors of *Apocalypse Not*, who declare that "we know not of a single accepted scientific study that has shown widespread harm to residents of Love Canal."[38]

Let's set aside for the moment what dioxin doubters routinely choose to ignore—the time lag of 20 or even 30 years that often occurs between exposure to a carcinogen and the actual incidence of cancer. And let's not dwell on the disparagers' unconscionable prerequisite that dioxin cannot be considered a credible threat until it can be conclusively demonstrated that human life was lost as a result of exposure. Even though the doubters have been proclaiming that the evacuation of Love Canal was unnecessary and the company that discharged industrial chemical waste was unfairly maligned, the manufacturer is paying hefty damages.

Occidental Chemical Company, whose corporate parent and predecessor buried 22,000 tons of hazardous waste under the site where the community of Love Canal was built, agreed in 1994 to compensate New York state in the amount of $120 million to settle a 14-year-old lawsuit. And on December 21, 1995, the EPA announced that the company had consented to fork over $129 million to cover the federal government's cleanup costs at the contaminated site. Environmental denigrators, take note. Would Occidental Chemical, or any company, part with that kind of money if it and its product were not at fault?

Still, the aforementioned fines relate to hazardous waste cleanup, not adverse health effects per se. Is there no evidence of the latter? Because of cancer's lengthy incubation period, definitive answers are hard to come by. A comprehensive New York State Department of Health study of the fate of Love Canal residents is still in progress; with an infusion of money from the Occidental settlement, the agency hopes to complete work on the survey within the next four years. Meanwhile, earlier contradictory studies on Love Canal's health effects were so flawed in their methodology (and probably premature in their findings) that no conclusions can be reliably drawn either way.[39]

That hasn't deterred bashers from flatly asserting that the concerns raised by environmentalists are blatant false alarms.[40]

False alarms? Not quite. We do know that some eye and skin burns were detected at Love Canal. Even Occidental doesn't dispute that.[41] Furthermore, results of laboratory tests on animal subjects since these government-ordered evacuations took place suggest that authorities acted prudently at Love Canal and Times Beach.

Bitter Fruit

What of the defoliant Agent Orange?

In 1993, the National Academy of Sciences (NAS) conducted an exhaustive review of all available data. Based on statistics derived from industrial operations, it concluded that there was a link between Agent Orange exposure and cancer. The NAS added, however, that a definitive decision on the merits of ill Vietnam vets' demands for compensation would have to wait for better documentation regarding the extent of exposure to the toxin. Still, enough "statistical association" was established between Agent Orange and three types of cancer as well as two skin diseases (chloracne and PCT) to bring about this telling result: In 1984, 40,000 soldiers won a $184 million class action settlement from manufacturers.[42]

In 1990, President Bush overruled an industry-weighted scientific advisory committee and made three diseases compensable: chloracne, non-Hodgkins lymphoma, and soft tissue sarcoma. Troops who were exposed to Agent Orange in Vietnam and came down with any of those illnesses were to receive their full active-duty pay in civilian life, and when they died, their widows were entitled to their full military pension.

Then came the 1993 NAS report. It served as the basis for declaring seven more diseases compensable, but dissatisfaction still festered. Retired Admiral Elmo Zumwalt, who commanded U.S. naval forces in Vietnam from 1968 to 1970 and is leading the fight for veterans' compensation, has maintained that military victims of numerous other diseases related to service in Southeast Asia should be indemnified (e.g., neurological defects, heart defects, diabetes, birth defects in vets' children). He adds that only about one-third of the troops who deserve financial aid are receiving it.[43]

On March 14, 1996, a panel of 16 independent scientists completed their review of Agent Orange for the National Academy of Sciences. In particular, they scrutinized the health of the Vietnam veterans (and their families) who oversaw "Operation Ranch Hand," which entailed the manufacture and aerial spraying of Agent Orange on enemy jungle encampments. The "ranch hands" were the American military personnel most exposed to the toxic defoliant. And what did these scientists find? They confirmed earlier reports of sufficient evidence to link ranch hands' Agent Orange exposure to soft tissue sarcoma, non-Hodgkin's lymphoma, and Hodgkin's disease. In addition, the latest data suggest that ranch hands' children are at greater risk of being born with spinal bifida, a deformity of the spine that can cause neurological problems.[44] In 1996, the federal government designated as "compensable" this malady as well as prostate cancer in Vietnam veterans.

Zumwalt pledges that if the list of compensable illnesses is not broadened further, American environmental groups and veterans' organizations will press the federal government to arrange epidemiological studies of the Vietnamese population for further documentation that will assure justice to the veterans.

Meanwhile, a higher-than-average incidence of cancer cases has been discovered among workers at Agent Orange production facilities. Furthermore, dioxin has been detected in mothers' breast milk, an especially unsettling development given that babies' untested immune systems don't provide much protection.

Recently Dr. William Farland, research director at EPA, warned Congress that "lack of a clear indication of disease in the general population should not be considered strong evidence for no effect of exposure to dioxin-like compounds. Rather it is an indication of the inability of our current scientific tools to directly detect effects at low levels of human exposure."[45]

One postscript to the supposed debunking of dioxin's toxicity: Despite its attribution to "some experts" by New York Times reporter Keith Schneider, the catchy analogy of exposure to dioxin being no more dangerous "than spending a week sunbathing at the beach" was not a quotation from a scientist.[46] It turns out that Schneider, who at the time seemed to be striving to become a journalistic icon by challenging the conventional thinking of the American national environmental movement, invented the quote for dramatic effect.[47]

Three Mile Island

Three Mile Island (TMI) is another occurrence that has prematurely received a clean bill of health from those eager to diminish the national environmental movement's stature. Again, the lag time between toxic exposure and the outbreak of cancer has not been taken into account.

The March 28, 1979, malfunction at the TMI nuclear plant in Lancaster County, Pennsylvania, became a cause celebre for environmentalists, symbolizing the darker side of atomic power. As such, it has attracted the attention of debunkers of the environmental movement, a large percentage of whom are diehard champions of nuclear energy. Their message is reassuring: "No one hurt, no one killed, no harm done at TMI."

No small wonder that the debunkers admire University of Pittsburgh epidemiology professor George K. Tokuhata for declaring that "at such low doses of radiation, no major health effects would be expected."[48] Yet even over the short term, the aftermath of TMI was not benign. Tokuhata himself concedes the existence of documentation that women in the vicinity of the mishap on average have given birth to underweight babies. He blames this and other health anomalies on psychological stress, not radiation poisoning—and he's certainly entitled to his opinion.[49] But not every scientist thinks TMI's radioactive release was that benign. Radiology professor Ernest Sternglass, who teaches at the same university as Tokuhata, believes the accident's pollution caused an increase in infant mortality—though, again, the statistics are inconclusive.[50]

Another source of uncertainty: The monitors for the type of radiation that TMI emitted were not widely in place back in 1979, so evaluation of the accident's scope remains speculative at best.

Thus, part of the TMI story has yet to unfold, a condition that even Tokuhata admits in a closing paragraph, thereby undercutting his inferential thesis that the low-level radioactive releases were essentially harmless. "Insufficient time may have elapsed to allow experts to detect cancer," he declares. Further studies are desirable."[51]

Prince William Sound

The bigger the environmental cause celebre, the more motivated the bashers are to demolish its credibility. That explains why they have eagerly sought to portray Alaska's Prince William Sound as fully recovered from the massive, 11 million gallon Exxon oil tanker spill that occurred on March 24, 1989. In celebrating nature's restorative powers, they are in effect thumbing their noses at environmentalists' grave concern for the ecology of the Sound. This recovery, say the disparagers, proves their contention that environmentalists are shoot-from-the-hip alarmists.

Of course, no one was declaring at the time of the spill that it was the end of the world. Yes, environmentalists were apprehensive about Prince William Sound's ecological future, but so was virtually everyone else. In fact, representatives of national environmental groups were rarely quoted in the national media.[52] That role was reserved largely for government and independent scientists, who shared the fears expressed by environmentalists.[53]

It's easy to sail the waters of Prince William Sound these days and be dazzled by scenic grandeur that displays no visible sign of the Exxon spill. As you might expect, the detractors of the environmental movement have sought to deceive the uninformed with this calm after the storm. "Overall," writes self-anointed environmental sage Gregg Easterbrook in his wildly schizophrenic literary assault on the environmental movement, "nature shrugged off the Valdez disaster as if shooing away a mosquito."[54]

It was not a catastrophe, he declared, and after three years, Prince William Sound was "almost like new."

Easterbrook takes extremely generous literary license with the adverb "almost" since, by his own admission, the population of murres (a type of sea bird) has fallen off, fewer killer whales have been spotted in the sound, and the Pacific herrings' spawning has significantly declined.[55] Retaining Easterbrook's figure of speech, nature may have swatted away one mosquito, but others are still hovering in a most annoying and menacing fashion.

Many other detractors join Easterbrook in ridiculing the idea that the Exxon spill was a major disaster and could have long-term adverse ecological effects.[56] Dr. Jo Kwong in *Freeman* points out triumphantly that after the spill, the fish catch topped 40 million, far exceeding the previous record of 29 million set in 1987.[57] What she failed to mention was that most of those fish were out to sea when the Exxon spill occurred and thus were not affected by the accident.

How about the increase in the salmon catch in the two years subsequent to the spill? Those numbers were based largely on hatchery fish raised in the sound. The population of wild salmon has yet to recover, and scientists say it will take several more years to determine whether the fish make it all the way back.[58]

Bashers maintain the Exxon spill was not a true catastrophe. But massive wildlife mortality at the time (including the largest human-induced bird kill in history) and the subsequent one billion dollars in reparations paid by Exxon suggest that the incident was very much a major ecological disaster.

As for the long-term ecological fate of Prince William Sound, there is no dispute that the region will eventually recover. The unresolved questions are how long, how fully, and at what cost in human suffering? Contrary to Easterbrook's sanguine appraisal of the spill's long-term effects on wildlife, the latest data—released more than six years after the fact—indicate that populations of harlequin ducks, pigeons, and sea otters have been slow to rebound. Six years after the spill, oil residues continue to cause contamination of some mussel beds. And on the basis of data collected so far, scientists have been unable to ascertain how much of a recovery such species as clams, rockfish, and river otter have made.[59] Circumstantial evidence thus points to at least some lingering effects from the malfeasance of the Exxon Valdez.

The exact overall degree of nature's resiliency also remains a mystery. Ecosystems, of course, recover from human-induced oil spills; but how many times can they snap back completely from pollution insults? At what point, if any, does wholesale degradation acquire some permanence? Uncertainty about the ability of our life support system to absorb repeated punishment dictates that we use every means at our disposal to eliminate gross insults to the environment. Our survival might just depend on it.

ANWR From Afar

Environmentalists consider the preservation of the coastal plain of the Arctic National Wildlife Refuge (ANWR) a top priority. They argue that the ANWR's plain is the closest thing to a completely intact ecosystem that our nation has left and, as such, must remain off limits to industrial development.

Entrepreneurial-minded foes respond that the fossil fuel potential of the region is crucial to national security and technology has advanced to the point where oil can be extracted without damaging the environment. They cite the oil development at nearby Prudhoe Bay as evidence that a portion of ANWR can be industrialized without disruption of the surrounding ecology. Why, even the caribou herd in the vicinity of the complex has flourished, or so it is maintained.

Yet an average of 500 oil spills occur annually at Prudhoe, and air pollution from the facility exceeds the total emissions of at least six states.[60] Though the petroleum industry contends that its "footprint" on the tundra at Prudhoe Bay is only about the size of a commercial airport, one will find a network of roads, pipelines, and production facilities that extends over an 800-square-mile area. The birth rate of the local caribou herd has dramatically declined in the past 10 years, and numerous bird and fish populations in the vicinity have suffered grievously.

Plans for ANWR offer little in the way of improvement. Although the actual drilling site in the 1.5-million-acre coastal plain would be only about 12,000 acres, the entire industrial complex would include 280 miles of roads, hundreds of miles of pipeline, 11 production facilities, and two ports. Indications are that the project's environmental impacts would be felt in an area as large as 235 square miles.

If the "localized effect" argument doesn't work, many of the environmental movement's adversaries shift gears and challenge the need for preservation of any of the coastal plain in a pristine state. Typical is the argument that the area is little more than a frozen, treeless desert, so why all the angst? In fact, the coastal plain is the nation's last, best concentration of wildlife, serving as the calving ground for the 152,000-strong porcupine caribou herd and home to 200 species of animals, 350 species of plants, and, in season, countless numbers of migratory birds.[61]

If denigrating the ecological worth of the coastal plain falls flat and the "limited impact" pitch makes few converts, proponents of oil development resort to reassuring us that any scars inflicted upon the landscape will disappear either naturally or as a result of remedial action. Government officials charged with evaluating the credibility of such claims do not share this optimistic view. According to the Interior Department's latest analysis, the mitigation measures touted by industry "are speculative and unproven ... and the odds are that the coastal plain would be irreparably altered by development."

When all else fails, proponents of opening up ANWR play what they regard as their trump card—namely, that national security necessitates that we search for whatever recoverable oil lies beneath the coastal plain's surface. Remember, avers the conservative think tank Heritage Foundation, that we had a $51 billion oil trade deficit last year.

The grim warning that failure to exploit ANWR is putting the nation at the mercy of the potentates in Middle Eastern oil-producing states has a hollow ring to it. Why the sense of urgency when the very same champions of ANWR development are either ardent advocates or tacit supporters of legislation to export Alaskan oil to Japan? Furthermore, Interior Department geologists recently disclosed that forecasts of the potential oil find in the ANWR have been inflated, and what at best could be hoped for is a petroleum equivalent to what the nation uses in a 90-day period.

Rather than sacrifice its wildlife heritage for a stop-gap energy fix, the United States ought to wean itself from dependency on oil imports by relying more heavily on renewable energy. Mass application of "clean" renewables is no longer a science fiction pipe dream, with many experts predicting that such energy sources will fill more than half of our fuel requirements by early in the next century.

Let's examine some other causes celebres whose well-publicized threats to public health are peremptorily dismissed as hoaxes by environmental detractors.

Raging Over Radon

Radon is a colorless, odorless, radioactive gas that occurs naturally and can seep into poorly ventilated basements of structures situated above rock formations with high radioactive content. Extrapolating from studies done on uranium miners, government scientists estimate that approximately 7,000 individuals a year contract lung cancer from radon exposure. The EPA regulates radon by requiring that houses for sale be tested prior to transfer to determine if they meet the federal guidelines of four picocuries per liter of air or less.

All this is a fiasco to the bashers. "Radon regulation is a huge, costly, government-bred hoax," whines conservative columnist Tony Snow, a graduate of the school that believes manipulation of the facts is acceptable if that's what it takes to reach an ideologically correct conclusion. Hence, Snow declares that low levels of radon may actually help fend off various cancers.[62] Would you believe that a gas the EPA is seeking to have purged from our homes as a preventive measure against cancer is actually an inhibitor of the disease? Those EPA officials must be either dolts or sadists!

Where are the bashers getting this nonsense from? They are twisting out of proportion the theory behind medical radiology, in which small radiation doses are considered beneficial just as large ones are deemed harmful. Radiologists operate on the premise that full-body exposure to low-level radioactivity stimulates the immune system and thereby builds resistance to disease. But radon molecules leaking into basements can attach themselves to dust particles that are inhaled by humans. The particles then lodge in the lungs, which lack adequate defenses to repel these carcinogenic attackers.

Undeterred, bashers attempt to consummate their argument by citing the most definitive study to date, an analysis using human rather than laboratory animal subjects and conducted by scientists at the National Cancer Institute (NCI).[63] According to critics of the EPA policy, NCI scientists concluded that household radon was not a major threat.[64]

To put it charitably, the critics are engaging in wish fulfillment. While it is true that uncertainty surrounds radon's lethal nature at the low concentrations that sometimes seep into the ground floors of residential structures, NCI researchers in no way suggested that the absence of answers justified dismissing the radioactive gas as a cancer threat.

"Studies of indoor radon have not yet provided a clear picture of the level of risk associated with lifetime low-level exposure," they declared.[65] "Incompleteness of the data thus suggests a cautious approach to interpreting the results." The term "cautious" may be too conservative from a precautionary perspective. NCI scientists did find a suggestive correlation between home radon exposure and the incidence of adenocarcinoma, a lung-based malignant tumor that can originate in non-smokers and is every bit as lethal as the more common forms of lung cancer. Researchers who interviewed patients also uncovered a discernible association between lung cancer and radon, although no correlation was detected in data obtained from the next of kin of deceased lung cancer victims.

Rutgers epidemiology professor Leonard Cole has written a book in which he expresses skepticism at the degree of danger that authorities are associating with radon. He argues that there is no firm epidemiological evidence that low-level radon is a menace. "EPA's politics are way ahead of the science."[66]

EPA's politics are not "way" ahead of the science, but they are ahead—and that's the way it should be. Politicians have a responsibility to protect public health, and they must make their decisions based on the best information available. To do otherwise would be to abdicate the mandate to govern. Authorities can't afford to wait for conclusive scientific proof because that would delay remedial action until after the fact. Instead, they must gear their response to the weight of the evidence in a potentially hazardous situation. It's a process that incorporates social, economic, and moral considerations, as well as scientific ones. Bashers miscalculate badly when they treat scientific findings and policy decisions as interchangeable.

Asbestos

Asbestos vaulted to the forefront of the bashers' "Rogues Gallery" of issues with the publication of a June 1989 *New England Journal of Medicine* article. The authors energized critics of the environmental movement with the declaration that asbestos wasn't the health menace EPA was making it out to be. Drs. Brooke Mossman of the University of Vermont and Bernard Gee of Yale argued in their paper that EPA's program to remove the substance from schools was essentially a waste of time and money.

Prior to the article, the main criticism leveled against federal regulators was that they made things worse instead of better by requiring the removal of safely encapsulated friable asbestos.[67] The end result of such a procedure was to release toxic asbestos fibers into the air where little or none had existed before.

In some instances, criticism was justified. A number of unwarranted asbestos removal operations were undertaken in the nation's schools. But these mistakes were the products of misunderstanding the law, not adherence to it. EPA guidelines were misconstrued from the start, although they always directed that securely sealed asbestos should be left untouched. The only caveat was that conditions should be inspected periodically to make sure no flaking had begun to occur. Four years after passage of the 1985 Asbestos School Management Abatement Act, the EPA finally dispelled the confusion by restating officially that tightly sealed asbestos should be left alone.

The fact that the major controversy revolved around the appropriate methods of asbestos control would seem to constitute a tacit admission that the substance is a serious health hazard. But many bashers' ideological machismo won't allow them to make even that concession. They close ranks behind the Mossman-Gee contention that 95 percent of the asbestos utilized in the United States is of the kind—chrysotile—that is relatively harmless compared to the less commonly employed types of the silicate mineral.

Unfortunately, Mossman and Gee took excessive liberties with the term "relatively." While chrysotile's association with a form of chest tumor has been weaker than that of its fibrous cousins, no such divergence has been detected with other diseases, including lung cancer and asbestosis. A 1990 study done for the U.S Public Health Service disclosed that "statistically significant increases in lung cancer mortality have been reported in workers exposed primarily to chrysotile."[68]

No less prestigious an institution than the National Academy of Sciences concurred with the EPA that enough doubt existed about chrysotile's health effect potential to justify regulating it.

And in response to the Mossman-Gee article, a number of doctors wrote to the *New England Journal of Medicine* in protest. They asserted that the abandonment of asbestos inspection and abatement was unjustified, given that numerous epidemiological studies had established a relationship between asbestos exposure and lung cancer.

Environmental detractors were undaunted. They took heart from a 1988 Harvard University symposium in which participants from the worlds of academia and industry dubbed EPA's asbestos policy "fiber phobia." Conservative columnists such as George Will and Tony Snow gleefully trumpeted the symposium's conclusion that a person stood a 300 percent better chance of getting hit by lightning than dying from asbestos exposure.

There's a lot more (or less, depending upon your perspective) to the Harvard symposium than meets the eye. It was an informal series of discussions dominated by industry representatives and sympathizers whose conclusions were not subjected to peer review and were subsequently embraced by only a small minority of the scientific community.[69] The sponsors of the gathering were the National Association of Realtors, the Safe Buildings Alliance (an association of former asbestos products manufacturers), the Institute of Real Estate Management, and the Urban Land Institute—a coalition stridently skeptical of the need for asbestos remediation, whose cost, coincidentally, they would largely bear.[70]

Chlorine

The bashers' crusade against a chlorine phaseout makes repeated use of distortion, particularly in regard to the chemical's role as a drinking water decontaminator. Environmentalists are accused of a purist mentality that compels them to risk the outbreak of cholera and other waterborne diseases in order to terminate the commercial usage of chlorine. The following allegation is typical: "Environmental groups are actually calling for a zero discharge, despite the fact that chlorine is used in 85 percent of all pharmaceuticals, 96 percent of all pesticides, and purifies 98 percent of all drinking water."[71]

Another frequently invoked argument is that chlorine is a natural occurring substance, so why all the anguish? That observation is usually punctuated with the refrain that there have never been any known fatalities from chlorine exposure.[72]

Let's set the record straight without further ado. Neither the environmentalists nor Clinton administration officials (whom are depicted in cahoots with the Greens on this matter) have been advocating a total chlorine ban—at least not right away. If a less toxic, economically viable substitute is found for purifying drinking water, perhaps at some later date, all the better.

For the moment, however, the environmental mainstream's approach coincides with the one articulated by EPA Chief Carol Browner. "The Clinton administration will develop a national strategy for substituting, reducing, or prohibiting the use of chlorine and chlorine compounds." While it may not be practical to remove chlorine totally from the marketplace, the chemical has been found to be expendable in most of its uses, including its role in the manufacture of medicine. Only 20 percent of the drugs in which chlorine is utilized contain the chemical in the end product. For the vast majority of these drugs, chlorine is employed in processing and can be readily replaced by a more benign substitute.

Yes, chlorine is part of nature in such stable forms as sodium chloride (salt). But manmade, highly toxic chlorinated organic compounds are not present naturally in the environment. And they have been found to infiltrate the food chain and ultimately accumulate in human body tissue, adversely affecting health in the process.[73]

While there is no conclusive proof that chlorinated compounds cause malignancies, several studies have demonstrated that women exposed to high levels of organochlorines suffer from significantly elevated rates of breast cancer.[74] Empirical evidence has also circumstantially linked organochlorines to reproductive problems and immune suppression in people and wildlife.

Second Hand Smoke, Third Rate Jibes

Bashers' ideological enmity towards big government and centralized regulation is so fanatical that official efforts to protect public health are usually characterized as mere pretexts for the federal bureaucracy to extend its control over Americans' private lives. That's the category into which environmentalists' adversaries place regulatory initiatives to protect nonsmokers against cigarette smoke. Research has implicated environmental tobacco smoke (ETS)—also known as secondhand smoke—as a carcinogen and provided the basis for the government's campaign to ban cigarette smoking inside public buildings and other non-residential structures. Already greatly alarmed at increasing constraints on the use of their product, tobacco companies are alleging that the action proposed against ETS is merely the first step in a draconian plot to prohibit cigarette smoking altogether.

There's not a grain of truth in the suggestion that an outright smoking ban is in the works. But in their single-minded campaign to disparage what they deem to be an autocratic federal government, the bashers have sought to transform ETS into a symbol of regulatory excess. They have eagerly made the tobacco industry's arguments their own, no matter how contrived and convoluted the claims might be.

Hence, the ultra-conservative *Washington Times*, a newspaper that's virtually a house organ for environmental denigrators, published an editorial impugning the motives of those who would curb ETS. The crackdown on ETS was dismissed as an exercise in "regulatory empire building."[75] Two months later, in the same newspaper, William Rusher of the Claremont Institute wrote an op-ed column in which he called those who wanted to restrict ETS "health fascists."[76]

Skeptics argue that the EPA has failed to establish any conclusive link between ETS and fatal disease.[77] If by that, the critics mean there is no open-and-shut case against ETS, they are absolutely right.

But as EPA Administrator Carol Browner testified before Congress in May 1994, "ETS contains more than 4,000 substances, of which more than 40 are known or suspected human carcinogens. Based on the total weight of available scientific evidence, the EPA concluded that the widespread exposure to secondhand smoke in the United States presents a serious and substantial public health risk ... We are able to see a consistent cancer risk at typical environmental levels."

The operative words here are "total weight of available scientific evidence." That must guide our leaders in potentially hazardous situations. Let it be emphasized again that, with a statutory and moral obligation to protect public health and safety, authorities cannot afford to wait for ironclad proof that either may never come or arrive too late. A proactive policy is designed to avert catastrophes; a reactive policy concedes them.

As you might expect, the Phillip Morris Tobacco Company didn't buy into the "weight of evidence" approach. It noted that "in rigorous science, close doesn't count."[78] Perhaps not, but in responsible administration of public health policy, it does.

Scientists are information providers, not decision-makers. The latter task is reserved for elected officials who must take into account other considerations besides scientific data in issuing their directives. Obviously, the weight of evidence counts heavily when lives may be at stake. It's one reason why the tobacco industry's disputation of ETS's lethal effects has drawn little support.

An EPA four-year study, completed in 1993 and peer-reviewed by an independent scientific panel who unanimously endorsed the findings, concluded that ETS was a Class A carcinogen that caused an estimated 3,000 lung cancer deaths annually. While the EPA conceded there was no irrefutable case, it added that the preponderance of available evidence pointed to an increased risk of lung cancer for nonsmokers and thus warranted a regulatory response.

That conclusion was supported previously by such eminent institutions as the U.S. Surgeon General's Office, the National Academy of Sciences, the National Institute for Occupational Safety and Health, and the National Cancer Institute.

Other research has reinforced the EPA's finding. Ross Brownson, division director of the Missouri Department of Health, oversaw a recent study of 1,906 nonsmoking women living in households with smokers. The data indicated that these women had up to a 30 percent greater chance of developing lung cancer than nonsmokers living in a smoke-free environment. Another study undertaken at Louisiana State University over a five-year span examined the case histories of 653 nonsmoking female lung cancer victims and found a correlation with dose exposure to ETS.[79]

Scientists also discovered a linear correlation between ETS exposure and Sudden Infant Death Syndrome. The risk of this disease doubled, sometimes tripled, in homes permeated with ETS.[80] ETS triggers and exacerbates asthma attacks in an estimated 200,000 to one million kids and causes 150,000 to 300,000 bronchitis and pneumonia cases annually.[81] Youngsters under five years old with mothers who smoke have nicotine and carcinogens in their blood.[82] A recent Center for Disease Control survey determined that children exposed to ETS in their homes had substantially more acute respiratory infections and absences from school than kids living in smoke-free residences.[83] And children who undergo surgery have been found to need post-operative oxygen therapy far more frequently if they are exposed to secondhand smoke in their homes.[84] Also, based on a review of 80 studies, scientists have concluded that nonsmokers are more sensitive to heart damage from ETS than smokers are.[85]

Researchers at North Carolina's Bowman Grey School of Medicine in Winston-Salem, N.C., discovered that exposure to secondhand smoke made individuals more predisposed to stroke because their arteries thickened at a faster rate than those not in contact with the fumes.[86]

What of the study published in the August 1996 edition of the American Heart Association journal, *Circulation*? Medical investigators found that individuals who never smoked but lived with partners who did had approximately a 20 percent higher risk of dying of heart disease than when both parties abstained from tobacco. Perhaps as telling as anything, five out of seven of the tobacco industry's own special panel of medical advisors agreed that ETS was a human lung carcinogen, and six out of seven concurred that ETS poses a serious and substantial health threat to children.[87]

Nevertheless, the industry and its sympathizers have persisted in some rather pathetic attempts to discredit this impressive body of evidence. Take the tobacco industry's chief mouthpiece in Congress, Rep. Tom Bliley (R-Va.), who also happens to be chairman of the powerful House Commerce Committee.

In testimony before his own committee, Bliley asserted that the Brownson study, which he labeled "one of the largest and best designed studies ever conducted," "reported no significant association between ETS and lung cancer among nonsmokers."[88] The American people deserve better than this semantic chicanery, especially when their health is at issue. To put it charitably, Bliley misrepresented the conclusion of the Missouri research.

"Our study and others conducted during the past decade," Brownson states, "suggest a small but consistent elevation in the risk of lung cancer in nonsmokers due to ETS. The proliferation of federal, state and local regulations that restrict smoking in public places and work sites is well-founded."[89]

Industry has tried to argue that ETS and tobacco smoke directly inhaled from a cigarette are two distinct phenomenas. Yes, ETS and primary tobacco smoke have differences. But both possess toxic components suspected of being detrimental to human health, and they do display some common elements. Moreover, ETS burns at a lower temperature with less oxygen, thereby making it capable of producing a more toxic byproduct.

Dead Meat

Bliley and his sympathizers seek to foist their "don't stop 'til you drop" philosophy on the American people. "Epidemological studies can show only a statistical association, they cannot prove causality," the congressman proclaims, with the clear implication that this is reason enough to award ETS a clean bill of health. The tobacco industry invokes the same rationale in an ad, noting that while approximately 30 epidemiological studies found a positive association between ETS and pulmonary disease in nonsmoking women living with smokers, only six studies were "statistically significant."

These nicotine apologists don't seem to realize they are under-cutting their own position by conceding a statistical association between ETS and illness. Who cares if the linkage is statistically insignificant if you have a chance to end up as one of the statistics? Besides, is it so terrible for smokers on their cigarette break to be segregated from nonsmokers? If even a few cases of lung cancer are prevented by such separation, how many people are really going to care that smokers must puff away in specially ventilated rooms or the great outdoors?

Finally, there are defenders of ETS who out of desperation actually claim that smoking is beneficial to one's health.[90] You'd be flabbergasted to learn that smoking appears to offer some protection against such serious illnesses as Parkinson's Disease, osteoarthritis, endometrial cancer, colon cancer, and Alzheimer's.[91] The basis for these startling claims is an article in—wouldn't you know it—*The American Smoker's Journal. Forbes* magazine editor Peter Brimelow cites a number of studies which he says indicate the frequency of the aforementioned diseases is less in smokers than non-smokers.

I wonder if it ever occurred to Brimelow or anyone using his article as a frame of reference that the diseases in question take quite a while to develop and thus are largely confined to one's senior years—a period of life most tobacco users never reach because of terminal smoking-related illnesses.

But let's not just limit our rejoinder to anecdotal evidence. If you still need to be convinced that cigarette smoking has no place in cancer avoidance strategy, review the 1989 and 1990 U.S. Surgeon General's reports. They identify tobacco use as a direct cause of cancer of the lung, larynx, mouth, esophagus, and blad-der, as well as a contributing factor to cancer of the pancreas, kidney, cervix, and stomach.[92] That linkage with cervical cancer would certainly distress those who previously took heart from Brimelow's contention that there is "extensive long-standing evi-dence" that "women who smoke are up to 50 percent less likely than nonsmokers to develop cancer of the womb."

Climate Hotheads

No environmental issue riles the bashers more than global warming. Much of their frustration stems from what the threat of accelerated climate change does to the credibility of their cornucopian vision. The potential for massive environmental disruption is so formidable that after most people are informed of the existing evidence, skepticism is considered irresponsible.

Exasperation in the climate-change doubters is often manifested by paranoia. Typical is their refrain that global warning is not just a hoax but also part of the environmental community's grand design to replace our democracy with a socialist state—or worse.

Wrote the late Aron Wildavsky, political science professor at the University of California/Berkeley: "Warming through its primary antidote of withdrawing carbon from production and consumption is capable of realizing the environmentalist's dream of an egalitarian society based on the rejection of economic growth."[93] Adds S. Fred Singer, another critic lukewarm on global warming: "A 10 percent reduction in greenhouse emissions would cost the average household about $1500 a year ... raising the price of gasoline to about $4 a gallon."

These are scare tactics practiced by bashers who conveniently ignore the capacity of renewable energy sources to fill at reasonable cost the void that would be created by the gradual phaseout of fossil fuels.

In railing against reductions in fossil fuel use, Wildavsky was clearly taking enormous and unjustified liberties with his characterization of environmentalists' ultimate objective. Their intent is not to engage in social engineering. Their concern stems from the combustion of fossil fuels being the primary manmade source of carbon dioxide (CO_2) buildup in the atmosphere. CO_2, in turn, is one of the principal greenhouse gases, that is, a gas that allows solar radiation to penetrate to the earth's surface but then traps the heat in the lower reaches of the atmosphere. Environmentalists link this greenhouse effect to global warming, which they maintain has the potential to cause disastrous ecological consequences.

This stark assessment galvanizes the bashers to insist it's the opening gambit in constricting corporate America's freedom to conduct business. Indeed, they challenge the validity of just about every facet of the global warming theory.

To buttress their thesis that warmer temperatures are quite likely part of a natural cycle rather than the byproduct of human activity, they assert that most of the temperature rise in the last century occurred before 1940, while most of the increase in man-made CO_2 emissions took place after that date.[94]

No linear relationship, right? Well, not exactly. It should be pointed out that major industrial revolutions accompanied by extensive coal burning did take place before 1940. In addition, it was an era without pollution controls; indeed, pollution was welcomed as a sign of prosperity.[95]

Nor is the temperature data as conclusive as the bashers would have us believe. The nine warmest years of the twentieth century have all occurred since 1980. Moreover, after slipping briefly (due, scientists believe, to the floating debris from Mount Pinatubo's eruption acting as a temporary shield and cooling influence), the average temperature of Earth's surface in 1994 rose to the high levels of the 1980s.[96]

The telltale statistics regarding increasing temperature don't stop there. Siberia is warmer than at any time since the Middle Ages. A chunk of Antarctic glacier as large as the state of Rhode Island recently broke off and collapsed into the south Atlantic.[97]

The link between increasing concentrations of greenhouse gases and global warming is inconclusive but highly suspect. Chris Flavin of Worldwatch points out that "by 1995, concentrations of CO_2 had reached 360 parts per million (ppm), higher than at any time in the past 150,000 years and far above the 280 ppm that existed when fossil fuel burning began."[98]

Bashers make a habit of rearranging facts so that their theories appear in a more favorable light. A leading practitioner of this "art" is Ron Baily, whose book *Ecoscam* spews out global warming inaccuracies eagerly snapped up by his cohorts in environmental bashing. Among Baily's claims:

- *Most of the recent warming occurred between 1976-80, with little change since then.*[99]

As I've previously noted, Baily is way off on temperature readings in the 1980s and mid-1990s.

- *There has been a significant increase in snow and ice in the Antarctic and Greenland ice caps.*[100]

Au contraire. Records show the average Antarctic temperature has increased over the past 45 years. It should thus come as no surprise that the 350-square-mile Prince Gustav Shelf has disappeared and Wordie Iceshelf, which covered 800 square miles in the 1940s, has lost two-thirds of its mass.[101]

Skeptics are also fond of noting that temperature readings recorded by satellite sensors are unchanged over the past 17 years. What they don't tell you is that surface readings have risen and are, at present, considered more reliable. Ground monitors are calibrated to discount the heat retention of big cities, while satellite accuracy is questionable. The reasons for the latter: atmospheric disturbances, including stratospheric ozone depletion, which has a cooling effect that masks the warming taking place at lower altitudes, and satellite readings that haven't been recorded over a sufficient period of time.

To bolster the theory that any climate change is due to natural fluctuations, skeptics quote the United Nations Intergovernmental Panel on Climate Change in 1990: "It is not possible to attribute all, or even a large part, of the observed global-mean warming to the enhanced greenhouse effect on the basis of observational data currently available."[102] In effect, the IPPC was saying that while global warming was occurring, it could conceivably be the result of natural variability.

Alas for the bashers, five years of additional research led the IPPC to alter its views. On November 29, 1995, it concluded a landmark international global climate conference in Madrid, Spain, by producing a consensus document that stated "the balance of evidence now suggests a discernible human influence on global climate."

But skeptics have their own version of scientific consensus. From Dixy Lee Ray to George Will, from Ronald Bailey to Rush Limbaugh, they have seized on an infamous 1991 Gallup Poll which they contend shows that a majority of scientists actively involved in global climate research do not believe that global warming has even begun.[103] Some doubters of global warming don't go quite as far in their interpretation of the poll's results. They merely assert that the survey demonstrated that a majority of scientists don't think the climate change is attributable to human influence.

Either way, they have misrepresented the results of the poll in their zeal to discredit Vice President Al Gore and other foes they have sought to demonize for putting the global warming theory on the map. In fact, the overwhelming majority of scientists questioned in the poll concurred that global warming was taking place. There was less agreement on whether this climate change was human-induced, perhaps because the question was phrased in an ambiguous manner. Nonetheless, two-thirds of the respondents answered that greenhouse warming resulting from human activity was in progress.

Still not satisfied that this poll has been distorted by the global warming skeptics? A majority of the respondents thought the odds were better than 50-50 that human-induced global warming would raise the global average temperature two degrees Celsius or more during the next 50 to 100 years!

That the bashers could portray this Gallup Poll as a rousing affirmation of scientific skepticism towards global warming, or towards the human contribution to the phenomenon, illustrates just how desperate they are.

And the mendacity continues to mount. Greenhouse skeptics brand environmentalists as "doomsday" alarmists because of the latter's dire warnings about the potential harm of global warming. But look who's accusing others of being alarmists!

Crocodile Tears

"Stringent limits on carbon dioxide emissions would lead to reduced standards of living and wrenching social changes," warns Ron Baily.[104] Come on, what are we talking about here? Is it "wrenching social change" to be more energy efficient, plant trees, rely more on renewable energy sources, place greater emphasis on recycling and mass transit, and buy food and manufactured products of local origin to minimize transportation-related fuel consumption?

These are "no regrets" strategies; that is, they possess merit no matter how great a threat global warming turns out to be. By no means an exhaustive list, they are practical steps that benefit society in their own right. So is substituting natural gas for coal and oil. That promises to decrease pollution with minimal disturbances to human activity. Telecommuting and telemarketing offer tremendous opportunities for reducing emissions, particularly in the transportation field.

The bashers routinely disparage renewable energy sources—solar, wind, hydro, and biomass—and would have us believe the state of knowledge is too primitive to produce viable substitutes for the fossil fuels we use today. But the available technology can already more than hold its own, while innovative advances are coming on line at a rapid clip.

Still, bashers can't resist engaging in sophistry. They ask us why, if energy conservation is so sound economically, must it be mandated by law?[105]

The answers are straightforward enough. A need for conservation isn't always obvious, even though it might be very much a necessity. Markets are often artificially manipulated, especially when a quick buck is in the offing. Future supplies can be overdrawn to meet popular demand without the public recognizing the burden being placed on succeeding generations. Furthermore, where abundance prevails, frugality usually does not. It's simply human nature to be cavalier about waste when surrounded by surplus.

Through the exercise of government, collective responsibility is supposed to offset individual fallibility. Unfortunately, political leaders all too often balk at interfering with constituents seduced by immediate gain and, in the process, abdicate their custodial obligation to future generations. The Clinton administration is certainly not immune to this shortcoming. As of mid-1997, the president's first-term pledge to reduce the nation's greenhouse emissions to 1990 levels by 2000 seemed laughable. Carbon emissions had actually risen eight percent *above* 1990 levels on his watch, and were continuing to climb. Fuel prices were being kept artificially depressed by subsidies emanating from Washington, which encouraged energy waste that could very well make life significantly more difficult for Americans who come of age in the years ahead.

Adding to the obstacles that conservation must surmount is the acquisitive orientation of our culture. The materialistic cast of the American value system prompts many of us to view conservation in the same way we regard cod liver oil. We know it's good for us but, unless forced to do so, we would just as soon not partake. That's another reason why mandatory requirements have a role.

Slippery Slope

The bashers have a fallback position in the event their denial of global warming becomes too ludicrous even for them to expound. If somehow forced to concede that a long-term warming trend is taking place, they simply shrug their shoulders and exclaim: "So what! Human beings can easily adjust to the projected climate changes."[106] Indeed, they continue, global warming could well be a boon to mankind—by creating improved growing conditions for plants that thrive on carbon dioxide and normally prefer warmer weather.

Let's just say that, at the very least, this scenario is fraught with variables and unknowns. For example, some scientists raise the question of what greenhouse-induced drought would do to the composition and compaction of soil.[107]

What of plants' need to experience cold weather to germinate? Suppose increased carbon dioxide causes them to sprout so fast that they outgrow their nutrient supply in the soil, making them far less wholesome for human beings?[108]

Fighting Fire With Fire

Spinning the global warming roulette wheel could be playing with fire—perhaps literally in a drought-stricken area. Yet we have University of Virginia professor Pat Michaels, an outspoken critic of conventional global warming theory, imperiously dismissing any justification for immediate concern.

That should come as no surprise. For the better part of a decade, the self-absorbed Michaels has fancied himself a leading gadfly of conventional global warming thinking (and he has been generously financed by an energy industry eager to harness his egomania for propagandistic advantage). The problem is that Michaels' professional identity has become so wrapped up in his contrarian role vis-a-vis the greenhouse effect that he appears inherently incapable of ever admitting he has taken a wrong turn. The loss of face would be unbearable. And so it is with most prominent bashers on most environmental issues. They withdraw into an ideologically rooted insularity that no dissenting view can penetrate.

Hence we have Michaels declaring: "That the greenhouse effect might warm the planet is not the point. The point is how much it warms it and how it warms it."[109] But the mere warming of the planet is *precisely* the point—certainly for officials responsible for protecting public health and safety.

When faced with the possibility that a process is being set in motion that could severely disrupt the planet's climate and might not be readily reversible, officials don't have a pedant's luxury of waiting until all the evidence is collected. Their obligation is to take every precaution within reason until it is convincingly demonstrated there is no cause for alarm. The benefit of the doubt must be given to assuring the preservation of our life support system, *not* to the hope that protracted scientific examination and discourse might some day expunge our concerns.

The latter strategy is favored by Michaels and like-minded critics, who argue that we don't know enough to take remedial action against the greenhouse effect. That's troubling enough to anyone who believes it is better to be safe than sorry. But Michaels and company make an even more indefensible leap of faith by insisting we know enough to justify *not* taking immediate action.

One wonders how, in good conscience, they can be so cocksure when the latest annual temperature readings have been among the warmest of the century. What of the 80 percent decline of zooplankton off the southern California coast over the past

40 years, as a result of an air temperature increase that reduced upwelling of nutrient-rich deep water?[110] How about the disease-carrying *Aeles aegypti* mosquito in parts of Latin America suddenly being able to frequent higher altitudes which were previously too cold for it to inhabit?[111]

The breaking off of an iceberg the size of Rhode Island and the disintegration of a smaller ice shelf due to a 2.5-degree Centigrade warming in the Antarctic can hardly give aid and comfort to Michaels' fan club.[112] Then there is a 1995 EPA economic analysis of climate change's impact on freshwater recreational fishing. Computer models project the disappearance of cold- and cool-water habitat range, resulting in an annual estimated loss of between $85 million and $320 million to the recreational fresh-water fishing industry.

Can we afford to mark time when researchers are reporting that spring is arriving a week earlier than it did 20 years ago, with global warming a prime suspect?[113] Should we be blase when scientists have found that a type of butterfly highly sensitive to subtle shifts in temperature has moved northward up the California coast from its traditional range, evidently in search of a cooler climate?[114] Is nonchalance the right response when warmer temperatures are likely to expand the range of virulent disease-carrying vectors and increase the frequency of heat-related illnesses?

Computer simulations, which are becoming more sophisticated and consistent with on-site observations, also project a potentially disruptive three degrees Fahrenheit global warming by the middle of the next century if business proceeds as usual. How can Michaels and Company be so complacent when most climatologists believe there is a better than 50-50 chance that the earth's climate will warm by at least 3.5 degrees over the next century? Who would counsel inaction when carbon dioxide's atmospheric life extends anywhere from 50 to 200 years, precluding any quick turnaround should the greenhouse buildup continue unabated?

Certainly, none of the detractors could continue in this vein if they subscribed to the following words in the UN Climate Convention drafted at the 1992 Rio Summit: "Where there are threats of serious or irreversible damage, lack of full scientific certainty shall not be used as a reason for postponing cost-effective measures to prevent environmental degradation." This prudent strategy is called the "precautionary principle," a conceptual mainstay of an effective environmental protection policy.

Ozone Sham

Human-induced depletion of the stratospheric ozone layer that shields the earth from lethal solar rays is another environmental threat that bashers dismiss as nothing more than a sham. The motivations driving them to portray ozone depletion as merely a natural fluctuation are the same that inspired the campaign to debunk global warming. Environmentalists are resented for the credibility they have gained among the general public as a result of publicizing the possible disruption of the earth's atmosphere. Bashers also harbor an ideologically engendered anxiety that any response to "alleged" human-induced stratospheric ozone depletion will come in the form of tightened regulatory restraints on industry and individual freedom. Finally, their contrarian challenge would not be complete without casting aspersions on environmentalists' reasons for sounding the alarm.

We're fed the same tired old wives' tale of treachery: environmentalists are conjuring up fears of ozone depletion to advance their diabolical plot for undermining capitalism. This line of thought leads to some wild accusations. One of the most outspoken environmental detractors, Dr. S. Fred Singer, president of the Science and Environmental Policy Project, charges that the environmentalists are "ideologically opposed" to the use of chlorofluorocarbons (CFCs) in air conditioners.[115] Singer got it half right. Environmentalists are opposed, but for scientific, not ideological, reasons. They advocate a phaseout of ozone-destroying CFC chemical compounds, a phaseout that because of the long life of the pollutants unfortunately cannot occur overnight.

Actually, environmentalists don't rule out CFCs in air conditioners. They support the use of recycled CFCs. And they remind those who complain about the cost of a phaseout that existing equipment will not have to be abandoned. That's because it is adaptable to recycled CFCs or more benign alternatives.[116] Furthermore, the EPA estimates, the public health benefits of the existing CFC ban and ultimate phaseout will exceed industry's and individuals' replacement costs by 700 to one, not exactly a death blow to the American economy.[117] Most of the skeptics try to nip the ozone depletion hypothesis in the bud, but in the process are tripped up by bad science and their refusal to accept the "precautionary principle."

Shooting from the Hip

Skeptics challenge the government-mandated CFC ban by asserting it is unnecessary. They frequently characterize the fluctuations of the stratospheric ozone layer as a natural reaction to sunspot cycles.[118]

In reality, monitoring of solar cycles (which run for 11 years) discloses changes in global ozone levels of one to two percent. Downward trends in ozone concentrations since the early 1980s have been far greater than that, suggesting much more is at work than sun spots.[119]

Okay, then, on to the next argument. Maybe sun spots don't cause the changes. Maybe the culprit is chlorine periodically eroding the ozone layer. The chlorine, after all, comes from natural origins. Oceans and volcanoes emit far more of it into the atmosphere than manmade CFCs. Hence, we are still looking at a natural phenomenon.

Again, the bashers' rendition doesn't square with the science. Researchers have never found significant amounts of naturally generated chlorine in the atmosphere. Why? Oceans emit chlorine in salt particles that are quickly washed out of the atmosphere by precipitation and water vapor. That's the reason no sodium has been detected in the lower atmosphere.[120]

A similar explanation applies to volcanoes. They release chlorine in the form of soluble hydrogen chloride acid, which is dissolved by rainfall and the steamy water vapor that is also part of the eruption. (One caveat to all this: The massive eruption of the Philippines' Mount Pinatubo did release sulphur dioxide, which rose to the stratosphere and briefly interacted with CFCs to accelerate ozone depletion. But the operative word here is "briefly," since sulfur dioxide fortunately has a short life span.)

Undeterred, the bashers maintain that CFC molecules are too heavy to rise to the stratosphere.[121] California professor Sherwood Rowland, who received the 1995 Nobel Prize for his work on ozone depletion, quickly disposes of their hypothesis. He explains that powerful wind currents propel CFCs into the stratosphere, where inert chlorine molecules are freed by radiation and proceed to break down the ozone shield over long stretches of time. Nor is the CFCs' presence in the stratosphere a recent revelation. Dr. Rowland notes that as early as 1975, air samples taken by high-altitude balloons and aircraft contained CFCs.[122]

Critics try to undermine this body of evidence by raising the issue of why the notorious ozone hole over the South Pole was detected long before CFCs were widely used as refrigerants.[123] The authoritative Geneva-based World Meteorological Organization explains that the detection of a South Pole ozone hole in 1958 was based on a single report of extremely low ozone from one location by unproven techniques. More importantly, this report has been superseded by readings from the instruments of four different monitoring stations throughout the Antarctic. In the early 1980s, a sharp, progressive decline in ozone concentration over the South Pole first began to appear and was dutifully recorded by scientists at the four facilities.[124]

So what? exclaim many of the skeptics. There is no upward trend of chlorine in the atmosphere, and the ozone layer has not eroded over North America.[125] Come again? Both ground stations and satellites have registered ozone readings 10 to 20 percent lower over the middle latitudes in North America in 1995 than in the early 1980s.[126] Ozone losses have also been detected over the Arctic.[127] Satellite measurements have recorded chlorine and CFC levels rising in tandem in the stratosphere the past few years.[128] It's a correlation that persuasively refutes the contention that humans are not at the root of ozone depletion.

When all this data starts to crowd even them, the bashers play their ultraviolet-B (UVB) card. If the ozone shield is really being depleted, they ask, why isn't there evidence that more of the sun's

potentially lethal ultraviolet rays are reaching the earth's surface?[129] Actually, there is. Instruments have detected increases in
surface UVB radiation at Antarctic sites as well as in parts of
South America when the ozone hole has formed over the South
Pole.[130]

No Pain, No Gain

If bashers are compelled to admit more ultraviolet radiation is
striking the earth, what arguments remain to disparage the CFC
threat? You guessed it. "Don't worry about more UV-B. Contrary to
the environmentalists' claims, there is no proof it is a serious
health threat. Indeed, no substantial reports exist of adverse
health effects from ozone depletion."[131]

Wrong again. Scientists have established through numerous
clinical studies a cause-and-effect relationship between exposure
to high levels of UV-B and non-melanoma skin cancers, cataracts,
and incidents of immune system suppression.[132]

When forced to give ground on this score, some critics retort
that non-melanoma skin cancer isn't all that big a deal.[133] It's not
a killer like melanoma, which they hasten to add is in no way con-
nected to UV-B exposure. This rationalization of UVB is a combination of bluff, inaccuracy, and cold-blooded insensitivity.

First, the inaccuracy. Though non-melanoma skin cancers are
highly curable if detected and treated early, some can become life-
threatening if ignored.[134] Even if most non-melanoma skin cancers rarely metastasize, they are big deals, both emotionally and
financially, to their victims. At the very least, these tumors can
become disfiguring if not attended to in a timely fashion. To
imply they are relatively innocuous because they usually do not
signal imminent death is a crass, ideologically driven exercise in
sophistry. Cataracts and suppression of the immune system are
also no walk in the park, particularly for those who cannot afford
routine medical care to combat these maladies.

As for melanoma, ruling out high UV-B exposure as a cause is,
to put it mildly, premature. In testimony before a House Science
Subcommittee in September 1995, Dr. Margret Krippe of the

University of Texas' Department of Immunology declared that "recent molecular studies implicate UV-B as a causal factor in melanoma." At the same hearing, EPA Assistant Administrator Mary Nichols told lawmakers that "the preponderance of evidence suggests that UVB does in fact play a significant role in triggering melanoma, although the exact dose-response relationship appears complex."

Our old friend Singer tries to discredit this testimony by citing the work of Brookhaven National Laboratory scientist Richard Setlow, who concluded that melanoma seemed more related to exposure to UV-A, which cannot be filtered by the ozone shield. But Setlow also admitted he was unclear whether UV-B had any relationship to melanoma—hardly the disclaimer of UV-B's complicity that Singer and like-minded critics attribute to him.[135]

Here Yesterday, Gone Today

As a matter of fact, the evidence for ozone depletion is so compelling that some bashers actually make an exception to their unrelenting dismissal of environmental concerns. They concede that the phenomenon is genuine, though they regard the environmentalists' characterization of the problem as grossly exaggerated.[136]

This deviation from their deprecating norm produces quite an uneven response. They acknowledge the ozone depletion problem by cheering the reduction in CFC manufacture. Yet they can't bring themselves to credit the international treaty responsible for the cutback. Evidently, praising a regulatory regime that is revered by environmentalists would be losing too much face.

To justify their feel-good stance, they argue that whatever ozone depletion problem has existed is no more. But declaring victory at this juncture would invite defeat. CFC molecules have a 40-year life span in the stratosphere, so the ozone layer will not recover expeditiously. Indeed, as a result of the pollutants already in the stratosphere and what is continuing to rise to those heights, ozone depletion over the next 10 to 15 years will get worse before it gets better, regardless of what we do. Should the CFC phaseout falter under false assurances that the threat has been extinguished, whatever progress has been made would soon be nullified and we would be back to an ominous square one. Just as with global warming, the "precautionary principle" applies to ozone depletion. The weight of evidence clearly dictates that doing nothing creates a far greater societal risk than implementing the preventive strategies that are at our disposal.

Specious Species

Detractors of the national environmental community regard the Endangered Species Act (ESA) as another thinly veiled contrivance to transform capitalist society into a socialist state. The way they see it, protection of animals and plants classified as on the brink of extinction is really a reordering of land use patterns and priorities to promote pastoral conditions at the expense of industrial expansion and private property owners' developmental rights.

But objections to the ESA are not just enunciated in political terms. "There is no evidence that the ESA has led to reclaiming a single endangered species," proclaim Robert Gordon and James Streeter of the National Wilderness Institute, in what has become a familiar refrain for the bashers.[137] This allegation is flat-out wrong. You can even discern that directly from the complaints of some bashers. They lament that out of more than 800 animals and plants currently designated endangered or threatened, only 21 have been removed from the list. Although seven of those were deleted because they were found to have become extinct, that still leaves 14 ESA success stories—though, of course, you'd have a hard time getting critics to concede the recoveries had anything to do with the statute.

The achievements of the ESA don't end there. Mollie Beatie, the late U.S. Fish and Wildlife Service director, noted that extinction rates had slowed dramatically since inception of the law.[138] Ken Smith of the FWS adds that populations of 38 percent of all listed species have stabilized or are improving.[139]

ESA Science

A key reason why the ESA is a major disappointment, the detractors say, is because it is not based on sound science. They gripe that there is no peer review of FWS decisions on petitions to list species. The implication is that protection is extended regardless of the societal merits of doing so.

Not true. Contrary to the bashers' claims, extensive peer review of FWS decisions does occur. In a congressionally commissioned study completed in the autumn of 1995, the National Academy of Sciences found that ESA regulators were using sound science in their decision-making and were quite successful under trying circumstances. In view of the accelerating loss of habitat, regulators were actually urged to redouble their efforts. To those who contend that approval of every request for protection is automatic, Beatie had this response: "Over the last five years, on the basis of scientific information, the FWS has turned down 75 percent of the petitions asking it to list species."[140]

Inconsistency characterizes those in Congress who have been the most strident in criticizing the science behind the FWS's decisions. They turn out to be the same ones who have voted to downsize drastically the federal government's capacity to provide the technical basis for determinations whether protection is warranted.

Another line of attack is to assert that regulators are violating the statute's intent. "The ESA was primarily intended to protect threatened bears, eagles and wolves," proclaimed a *Wall Street Journal* editorial writer.[141] Only later, he complained, was the law expanded by courts and bureaucrats to encompass everything from beetles to rats. There's something wrong, critics incessantly fret, when the ESA affords the same protection to a bug as it does to a bear.[142]

This is an argument born of inaccuracy and ignorance. There is no indication in either the law's language or legislative history that Congress intended the ESA to safeguard only the better-known species. Beyond that is the appalling intellectual parochialism of those who think that the ESA should protect only mammals and birds. Anyone with even a rudimentary grasp of ecology knows that invertebrates are more integral to our survival than large mammals. Indeed, invertebrates are an essential part of the biological foundation for our life support system, performing such indispensable tasks as pollinating our crops and breaking down waste products that would otherwise transform the world into one giant garbage dump.[143]

We also ought to keep in mind that every species has a niche in the biosphere. When some element of our planet's complex food chain is eradicated, its absence creates a ripple effect. Certain competing species may actually benefit. Others whose survival is highly dependent on the extinct life form in some way will surely begin their own slide towards oblivion.

We don't understand all the interrelationships between species. But as the years pass, it is becoming increasingly evident that the health of organisms in the wild is an important index of the condition of the environment on which we rely for our survival.

Flaws in the Statute

ESA detractors maintain that the statute fails to take economics into account, resulting in animals and plants being protected at the expense of human beings. Consequently, the charge goes, the law has thwarted economic development, cost thousands of jobs, and infringed on private property rights because of the demands of habitat preservation.[144]

Again, the facts don't jibe with the allegations. Implementation of the ESA does require consideration of economics, except in the biological determination of whether the species should be listed in the first place. Economics come very much into play in shaping the actual steps to be taken to rescue a listed species from extinction.

Between 1987 and 1992, for example, the FWS conducted 97,000 consultations under the ESA regarding proposed development projects. Only 54 failed to receive the green light. Another series of data reveal that during the 1988 to 1993 period, there were just four cases in which a private landowner was enjoined from proceeding with development of his or her lands because of the ESA.

As for direct economic impacts, states with high numbers of listings have not suffered. In fact, compared to other states, they boast superior statistics in agricultural production and employment.[145] Indeed, the argument can be made that in many instances the ESA has been essential to a robust economy. Look at the Pacific Northwest, where the law's protection of endangered salmon runs has been crucial to preserving a commercial and recreational fishing industry providing 60,000 jobs and $1 billion annually in personal income to the region's economy.[146]

A Spree on Species

If other smear tactics fail, some ESA denigrators will argue that the implementation of the statute is prohibitively expensive. For example, the National Wilderness Institute (a euphemistic mouthpiece in spirit, if not body, for property rights extremists and other ESA foes) asserts that recovery plans for 388 species will cost taxpayers approximately $884 million. Furthermore, it maintains, an additional 400 listed species still without recovery plans will drain the U.S. Treasury of $1 billion.

These numbers are grossly inflated. Well over half the species awaiting recovery plans are plants, whose extremely limited range and distribution make their restoration far less expensive than that of endangered animals. Even if the NWI's estimates were accurate, the sum would be a pittance in the context of the total federal budget. For example, more than $100 billion is conferred annually upon farmers alone, in the form of federal subsidies. And what of waste? Researchers for national environmental organizations didn't have to look hard to find 47 federally-funded, ecologically destructive programs that are sheer boondoggles and could save the U.S. Treasury $39 billion if terminated. Nor have we begun to address the potential economic benefits of species preservation. More than 40 percent of all modern medicines are derived from wild species, mainly plants and often endangered ones at that. Furthermore, only about two percent of the world's plants have been tested for their medicinal value.[147] It is therefore mind-boggling that humanity has allowed this irreplaceable treasure trove to vanish at an estimated rate of three species per day.

Some of the more euphoric bashers won't even concede the need for an ESA at this point in time. They dispute the existence of an extinction problem, or at least one that is as serious as the environmentalists claim.[148] An oracle of this school of thought is University of Maryland economics professor Julian Simon. "There is no evidence whatsoever that extinction is faster now than it was in the past," he declared during a St. Louis symposium.

Simon is a master of sophistry in buttressing his case. He bases his argument largely on the historic rate of documented extinctions of birds and mammals: an average of one of each bird and mammal species has vanished from the earth every year since 1600. But his statistical presentation is severely flawed. He conveniently leaves out any references to losses of insects, amphibians, reptiles, fish, and plants—a rather glaring omission considering that insects alone comprise approximately 90 percent of our planet's life forms (excluding bacteria).

Simon is guilty of sins of commission too. The Union for the Conservation of Nature (IUCN), which is the main source for Simon's mammal and bird data, also tracks insects as best it can. IUCN scientists estimate conservatively that there is an annual global loss of 2,300 insect species, "with the probability that the number is much higher," especially due to humanity's massive leveling of biodiverse tropical rain forest.[149] When confronted with this disclosure, Simon's response is to shrug and declare that "we don't know what is happening with invertebrates" and thus cannot speculate about their rate of extinction.

There it is. In Simon's idiosyncratic world, species cannot be classified as extinct unless one can count the carcasses. After all, he reasons, if a species' habitat is destroyed, perhaps the creature can flee to other surroundings. That certainly would be a difficult maneuver for endangered plants. But what makes this thinking truly perverse is that it creates an impossible standard for intervention to rescue a stressed species.

As you then might expect, most ecologists have no use for Simon. Loss of habitat is powerful circumstantial evidence that species are on the wane, declares Dr. Peter Raven, director of the Missouri Botanical Gardens and one of the nation's leading biologists. And noted Harvard biology professor Edward O. Wilson retorts that "all biologists know that as habitat is reduced, species go extinct. Hundreds of independent studies demonstrate this."[150]

Raven, who shared the platform with Simon at the now infamous St. Louis gathering, notes that the Maryland economist and his cohorts have conveniently ignored the 800 to 1,000 *documented* extinctions of plants, the loss of two-thirds of the freshwater fishes of Indonesia, and many other instances where species' disappearance has been scientifically corroborated. "With the enormous surge in human population growth and destruction of natural habitat, it would take wishful thinking combined with an incomplete understanding of the facts and massive denial to conclude species were not being adversely affected," Raven asserts.

Many ESA skeptics respond that they can't understand why there is so much anxiety when extinction is a natural phenomenon. That answer misses the point completely. Yes, extinction is an elemental facet of evolution, but not at the pace it has been occurring since the human race grew large enough to adversely effect much of the earth's surface. Raven points out that scientists have calculated that since 1930, known extinctions of living organisms have taken place at a rate *100 times faster* than during the earliest years of civilization. How much more affirmation does anyone need to incriminate human activity as a major factor in ecological disruption?

Simple Simon

Simon and his cornucopian groupies dispute the validity of the extrapolation techniques that scientists use to identify accelerated extinction. But the way Simon et al. arrive at their conclusions is hardly reassuring. They simply argue that, without precise physical evidence that the last animal or plant of a species has drawn its final breath, there is no proof of extinction—hence, no extinction.

This is the height of speciousness. How can one arrive at an exact tabulation, considering the millions of species, their scattered and often remote locations, and the relatively limited resources available to monitor their comings and goings?

The skeptics do not even acknowledge the de facto extinction of plants and animals whose populations have been decimated and survive only as scattered individuals, too isolated to engage in any kind of sustainable propagation. Being a literalist in these instances is either a myopic exercise in self-denial or a calculated cold-blooded deception, especially in the face of an extrapolation process grounded in sound science.

The ESA is not perfect. Sometimes its implementation has been too little, too late. And on occasion, it has been imposed heavy-handedly on private property owners. All sensible environmentalists acknowledge these failings. Unencumbered by doctrinaire rigidity, they have no compunctions about urging that regulatory controls be refined and blended with the market-based incentives the bashers so ardently advocate.

For example, during 1994-95, the Washington-based environmental group Defenders of Wildlife held a series of roundtable discussions with farmers, ranchers, developers, and business people. The objective: to produce recommendations for giving private land owners fiscal incentives for protecting endangered species on their property. Among the proposals agreed upon were granting estate tax deferrals as well as income tax deductions and credits to property owners who extended hospitality to resident endangered species.

By contrast, most detractors of the environmental movement are inflexible about solutions. Disputes can only be resolved in accordance with ideological correctness. Thus, the most dogmatic bashers would like to see the ESA abolished altogether and endangered species protection on private land maintained purely on a voluntary basis, with monetary incentives as inducements.

The problem is that the monetary incentives might not be enough to compete with the sum the private landowners could realize from developing the acreage. Well, you might say, money isn't everything. What about that noble streak that supposedly runs through even the vilest of human beings? Wouldn't that be enough to tilt the scales in favor of preservation? It's true that most of us possess some altruistic instincts, but they are incessantly at war with cupidity, and they don't always win.

We therefore need regulation as a backup to assure the preservation of our common heritage, which by definition does not belong to any one individual, regardless of physical location or possession of title. Enter the ESA, which overall has had a positive effect despite a human population explosion, intense developmental pressure on habitats, and other trying circumstances.

A final point: Please don't agonize over private property rights. They are sacrosanct unless they clash with public use. When conflict occurs, the merits of the private and public sector are weighed to determine which side should prevail. The courts have been engaging in this balancing act for centuries and, in general, they have performed admirably.

Anecdotal Warfare

The so-called reformers of the ESA have sought to make the case for dismantling the statute through a series of attention-riveting anecdotes in which private landowners are persecuted in horrendous fashion by federal authorities. These sagas throb with melodrama. But in the vast majority of cases, poetic license has been shamelessly exploited on behalf of ideological correctness. The result is gross distortion in which perpetrators are portrayed as victims, while the law of the land and those assigned to enforce it are depicted as the embodiment of evil.

That the most persuasive argument the ESA critics believe they can make consists of doctored anecdotes is a measure of their desperation and lack of substance. Several of the tales are so inflammatory that they have been emotionally recounted on numerous occasions in congressional debate by lawmakers with a thespian bent.

At the top of this list is the saga of the endangered Stevens Kangaroo Rat. What could turn the public more virulently against the ESA than to demonstrate that the law places the survival of a rodent ahead of human life, limb, and property?

Be serious. What official in his right mind would make such a socially repugnant decision? After all, bureaucrats are human beings too, and on that basis alone would be most reluctant to establish any precedent in which the interests of their own kind would be subordinated to any other life form—much less a rat. Moreover, since the regulators are public employees, they would hardly want to institute policies that shortchanged their taxpayer employers and thereby jeopardized job security.

But the critics of the ESA are not engaging in logic here. They are counting on the passion of the moment speaking louder than hard facts. Hence, when wildfires destroyed 29 houses in southern California's Riverside County in 1993, ESA detractors branded the U.S. Fish and Wildlife Service the culprit. To protect the endangered Stevens Kangaroo Rat's habitat, the allegation went, the FWS banned the removal of weedy brush, thereby preventing homeowners from creating firebreaks. In reality, landowners were permitted to establish firebreaks, provided they did so by mowing with light equipment rather than disking, a high-powered, mechanized process that loosens and turns over soil and vegetation, destroying most wildlife habitats. The absence or presence of firebreaks was a moot issue anyway, because the intense wildfires leapfrogged every obstacle in their path.[151]

The EPA detractors have also manufactured a whale of a tale out of a shrimp story. They never get tired of recounting the saga of how a tiny crustacean known as the fairy shrimp—which they claim is not even endangered—is about to devastate the economy of northern California, due to implementation of the ESA. The Interior Department designated the fairy shrimp and two closely related types of shellfish as endangered after finding that 75 percent of their habitat—temporary pools of standing fresh water—in California's Central Valley had disappeared while another two percent was swallowed up annually by agricultural use and urbanization.

ESA critics refuse to acknowledge biologists' conclusion that it's wisest to measure the population of this creature by habitat loss and fragmentation (which hinder recolonization) rather than by actual numbers.

It must also be pointed out that no project has ever been halted as a consequence of the fairy shrimp's listing. Conflict resolution between federal authorities and landowners has been very effective in northern California and elsewhere in the nation. To state or imply otherwise is to distort the issue of species preservation.

Wolf at the Door

Reintroduction of the grey timber wolf to the Rocky Mountain region by the Interior Department under the protective mantle of the ESA is another flash point for detractors of the statute. They argue that the animals are not endangered, since plenty of the beasts inhabit the wilds of Alaska and Canada. Furthermore, they assert that federal authorities have no business returning the wolves to a region where they were eradicated more than a half-century ago by the government (acting at the behest of residents who considered the creatures an economic liability because they preyed on livestock and the wild game prized by hunters).

To critics, the reasons for not reintroducing the wolf remain the same as the ones used to justify eliminating it, only with greater urgency since the region now has a larger human population. But that's not all. Since the wolf is viewed as an egregious symbol of the ESA, the statute's denigrators have pulled out all the stops. Why restore an animal that will menace not only livestock but humans, they ask. Injecting a sinister ulterior motive into the controversy, some critics suggest that wolf reintroduction is merely a federal ploy to solidify control over local officialdom. Environmentalists are accused of wanting to return the Rocky Mountain region to a primeval state at the expense of humans, an absurd allegation if ever there was one.

Canine Clarification

While the wolf is not endangered in the far north, biologists stress the genetic importance of maintaining distinct populations wherever possible. Voila, we have the rationale for reestablishing the Rocky Mountain timber wolf. What about the prospects of mangled human beings and livestock losses? According to Dr. L. David Meck, an expert on wolves, there is not a single docu-mented case of a healthy wild wolf killing or seriously maiming a human in North America. In contrast, more than 20 people are killed and 3 million attacked each year by domesticated dogs.

As for livestock, given a choice, wolves prefer wild prey. Scientists have the benefit of empirical evidence from Minnesota, where approximately 1,500 wolves reside. Only 50 or so of 7,200 livestock operations there report any losses each year due to the predator's activity.[152] Meanwhile, wolves in Alaska have helped reduce a caribou herd from 220,000 in the 1920s to 22,000 today (documenting not only their culinary preferences but their capacity to cull surpluses of grass eaters).[153] Don't worry, however, about wolves gobbling up all the deer and antelope. Nature has escape valves to prevent that from happening. Predator populations fluctuate with the abundance of available prey, thereby maintaining a ratio that assures survival of the hunter and the hunted.

Allegations that the return of the wolf would damage the Rocky Mountain region's economy and constitutes a federal attempt to usurp local control are unfounded. Many western communities have welcomed the predator's return as a boost to a rapidly growing tourist trade. Provisions to compensate ranchers for any wolf-related losses have been arranged through private donations administered by the environmental organization Defenders of Wildlife.

The Interior Department released the wolves into national parks in its legal capacity as administrator of federal lands. If the animals stray onto state territory and attack livestock, state authorities and ranchers are duly authorized to kill the marauders or take other action dictated by local regulations—hardly a nullification of states' rights.

PART 3

PROPAGANDA
TECHNIQUES

5

CHARACTER ASSASSINATION

There are a handful of individuals whom the bashers especially love to hate. No doubt, these individuals evoke such animosity in part because they are the environmental movement's most visible spokespeople and have attained the widespread recognition that has always eluded their detractors.

The list changes as popularity fluctuates and an individual occasionally fades from the limelight. But a hardcore cadre has remained at the forefront on a consistent basis. They include Stanford biology professor Paul Ehrlich; Worldwatch Institute president Lester Brown; ecologist Barry Commoner; Harvard biology professor E.O. Wilson; Dave Foreman, founder of the militant organization Earth First!; Vice President Al Gore, particularly since the publication of his evangelistic opus *Earth in the Balance*; and Bruce Babbitt following his ascendancy to the post of interior secretary in the Clinton administration.

These *bete noires* are denounced as leaders of a movement that derives its energy and direction from a jaded view of human nature and the future of the world.

The Prince of Prophets

No one serves as more of an ideological lightning rod for the bashers than Paul Ehrlich. He is their chief nemesis because his descriptions of potential environmental decline rank among the grimmest, and his flair for the dramatic has brought him national prominence. He is one of that small band of celebrity environmental activists whose voice resonates far beyond the halls of academia and other relatively unnoticed outlets to reach a mass audience through best-selling books and appearances on television talk shows.

The bashers attempt to discredit him by asserting that none of his dire predictions has ever materialized. They are outraged that his allegedly dismal record of accuracy has not cost him his large following and nullified all the prestigious awards he has won. One critic ridicules Ehrlich for prophesizing in the 1960s that humanity would experience atomic wars, killer smogs, massive famine, food riots, contaminated water, and global epidemics.[1] Errors galore? Hardly. Five out of six ain't bad!

Detractors also challenge some very specific and particularly calamitous predictions that Ehrlich allegedly made in his 1960 bestseller *The Population Bomb*. At issue are supposed forecasts that hundreds of millions would starve to death in the 1970s, food shortages would kill 65 million Americans in the 1980s, the oceans would be lifeless by 1979, the U.S. population would be reduced to 22.6 million by 1999, and leukemia would increase by 70 percent.[2]

Ehrlich's critics either didn't read the book or chose to ignore what it said. The aforementioned "predictions" don't appear in *The Population Bomb*, although some potential outcomes of a comparable nature are described by the author. His critics' most glaring omission is that Ehrlich made clear that his dire scenarios were only possibilities, not predictions.[3] Indeed, Ehrlich admits in the book that he is just engaging in speculation and none of the catastrophes he describes are a foregone conclusion.

It is true he isn't a riproaring optimist. Overpopulation in his view poses a terminal threat to modern civilization, at least as we know it, and he doesn't believe human beings' ability to keep their numbers sufficiently in check is preordained. Nonetheless, Ehrlich believes that the human race has a reasonable chance to achieve a stable, environmentally sustainable world. He also thinks we could prevail, even if we don't move as quickly as he would like to curb population growth.

"Perhaps with care, the world could at least temporarily support a population of 10 billion," he declares. "Success would require a degree of cooperation, care for our fellow human beings and respect for the environment that are nowhere evident now. *But society has shown it can change rapidly when the time is ripe.*"[4] No inevitable apocalypse here!

For Ehrlich, the optimum level to stabilize global population over time is two billion people. He adds that the current level of approximately five billion is a workable number, just not as comfortable. Unfortunately, he declares, the population bomb has not been defused, an observation with which any self-respecting demographer would agree. Until couples worldwide average no more than two children each, population cannot stabilize. Despite the declining birth rate, women are still averaging 3.4 children each on a global scale. Were that pace to continue, human population on Earth would rise to 100 billion by the end of the next century!

Keep that in mind when Ehrlich's critics deride his views by citing the decline in birth rates. All that decrease has accomplished is to slow the population explosion somewhat. As one expert notes, "It has not been stopped, and certainly not averted."[5]

Ehrlich's plea for the human race to reduce its numbers prompts his detractors to brand him a misanthrope.[6] But clearly, he is a people-lover, not a people-hater, given that the objective of his work is to help set the stage for humanity to enjoy a better quality of life.

Oh yeah? retort his critics defiantly. What about the professor's assertions that coercive population control may be necessary? How benevolent is that?[7] Again, Ehrlich is misquoted. Although he explored in his books the idea of instituting coercive population control, he concluded that it would not work. The only viable option, he contends, is "to halt human population growth as quickly and humanely as possible ... and then bring about a gradual decline."[8]

And how does one manage that? The solutions Ehrlich espouses are not new, and they have been widely embraced by population policy specialists throughout the world. At the top of the list is expanded education concerning the advantages of and urgency for reduced family size. Women especially need this knowledge, due to their subservient position in many cultures. Other strategies include cultural and economic incentives to have smaller families, greater availability and more effective distribution of artificial contraceptives, and improvement of living conditions in countries with high birth rates, so that couples won't feel compelled to breed prolifically to ensure that at least some offspring will survive and provide support in old age.

A New Kind of Growth

Disparagers of Ehrlich allege that he portrays economic growth as a disease, not a cure.[9] This is balderdash. Ehrlich very much favors growth. It's just different from the largely unrestrained growth that has dominated this country. He is talking about *sustainable* growth (i.e., growth in which one generation uses natural resources only to the extent that it leaves the earth in at least as good condition for succeeding generations). It is economic growth that tends to be qualitative rather than quantitative, placing more value on the durability rather than the number of products in one's possession. It is growth that will lead humanity to tread much more lightly upon the earth.

This unconventional celebration of economic growth doesn't appease the bashers, who continue to snipe at Ehrlich's fiscal philosophy. Insinuating that the Stanford professor is a closet Marxist, they quote him as saying that population stabilization and saving the environment can only be achieved through the creation of a new civilization in which inequitable distribution of wealth is corrected.[10]

Ehrlich is portrayed as a modern-day Robin Hood, with the bashers quite aware that robbing the rich in order to compensate the poor does not possess the panache that it did back in the Middle Ages. A benevolent thief as a positive role model might appeal to Americans in the context of authoritarian medieval England, but it doesn't resonate nearly as well when applied to a twentieth century democracy in which upward mobility is not restricted.

Once again, Ehrlich is being maligned. He is actually advocating a redistribution of wealth within the framework of a capitalist-oriented global community. His scenario does not require well-to-do countries to reduce their living standards to close the gap, as his denigrators suggest, but rather that less affluent nations be assisted in elevating their quality of life.[11]

How can this be accomplished while keeping citizens of both rich and poor nations happy? The strategy that Ehrlich advocates is widely endorsed by environmental activists and some prominent politicians. It entails the industrial world transferring environmentally friendly technology to developing countries, and all nations reallocating portions of their massive military expenditures to peacetime uses. This strategy would involve a buildup of environmental protection infrastructure both at home and abroad, since the ramifications of major ecological transgressions routinely extend beyond sovereign borders. The Worldwatch Institute estimates that for $774 billion, which is just under 10 percent of the world's annual military spending, the international community could reverse negative trends in soil erosion, deforestation, and energy availability around the planet within a decade.[12]

What are the chances of humanity pulling this off? Ehrlich's answer demonstrates that he is anything but a doomsdayer. "There is hope of achieving the change on the massive scale that is required, although the political battles will be brutal."

His grounds for optimism? He believes that it will become apparent to rich and poor alike that future generations, regardless of economic status, will only inherit a highly livable planet if everyone works together to make it so. Such recognition will lead to cooperation that will narrow the material disparity between peoples.[13]

Bodacious Babbitt

Bashers seek to portray Interior Secretary Bruce Babbitt as a theocrat who constantly violates the constitutional requirement of separation of church and state.

His invocation of spiritual inspiration as a rationale for supporting a strong endangered species law is supposedly a manifestation of this sin. "I believe all the plants and animals in the natural world are together a direct reflection of divinity, that creation is a plan of God," he is quoted as saying.

That's enough to infuriate right-wing columnist Cal Thomas, who fulminates: "Babbitt's theology comes close to animism—the attribution of conscious life to nature or natural objects. It is certainly not mainstream Christian doctrine."[14]

Thomas advises Babbitt to consult a Gideon Bible next time the Secretary is in a motel room, in order to gain an understanding that it is appropriate to worship the Creator but not what God created. Another writer accuses Babbitt of formulating conservation policy on the basis of nature worship rather than scientific evidence.[15]

Enough of this semantic prevarication! Since when is it sacrilegious to revere God by scrupulously caring for his works?

In his anti-Babbitt diatribe, Thomas conveniently omits the interior secretary's follow-up statement. Given the sacred status of nature, Babbitt declares, "it is left to us to translate a moral imperative into a way of life and into public policy."[16]

The secretary's advocacy springs from an ethical decision, not ritualistic worship, and is entirely consistent with Christian thought. Evangelical Christians themselves proclaim that "we care for creation because we know and worship God, and He has given us the responsibility to be stewards over His creation until He returns to make all things new."[17]

A supreme irony of these verbal attacks on Babbitt is that they originate from a faction that promotes itself as a defender of fundamental Christian principles in an increasingly amoral secular world. Nonetheless, the bashers are partially right. Environmentalism does have a religious strain coursing through it, but in an ethical rather than ritualistic sense. In that regard, it is no different from political parties, labor unions, and charitable enterprises.

Critics of the environmental movement misconstrue the separation of church and state. Our founding fathers established the distinction in relation to funding and the physical act of governing, not the sharing of spiritual values. The conduct of most inhabitants of the United States is influenced by a code of ethics rooted in religion, and Babbitt is no exception. But to suggest that by taking his cue from religion-oriented values he is in effect substituting religious tenets for the law of the land defies reason. Values provide the prism through which officials weigh the evidence—scientific and otherwise—that helps them make regulatory decisions. Values are not the decisions themselves.

Demonizing the Environmental Movement

Detractors of the environmental movement persist in using the phony nature-worship charge to typecast their foes as misanthropic theocrats who care more about animals and plants than people. In fact, environmental activists are preoccupied with the health of animals and plants *because* of people. Although they believe we are part of nature rather than separate from it, they acknowledge that our superior cognitive ability vests us with a special custodial responsibility. The fate of other life forms is in our hands, just as the Good Book says.

So there you have it. Those trying to label environmentalism a religious movement are muddying the difference between the rituals and the moral values of organized religion. The former have no place in political decision-making; the latter are at its core.

Environmentalists are also branded as a collection of wealthy power brokers wielding disproportionate political influence. If you swallow this line, you'll have no trouble believing the corporate world is being persecuted by anti-pollution crusaders. What a pity the *Fortune* 500 cannot seem to muster the resources to adequately defend themselves!

Such alleged omnipotence is of course absurd. The environmental community is hardly a citadel of opulence, encompassing as it does the full spectrum of economic strata, with substantial representation at the lower rung of the income scale. Over the years, it has become increasingly evident to economically depressed citizenry that their lack of political clout places them—more than anyone else—at risk from pollution. One would have to be blind not to notice how effectively affluent neighborhoods have been able to fend off the siting of contamination-spewing facilities in their midst, while poorer communities are left to languish in the dust—polluted, that is.

The awareness of the economically disadvantaged is reflected in the voting patterns of their congressional representatives, who invariably have some of the best environmental voting records on Capitol Hill.

Not So Deep Pockets

Let us return to the bashers' astonishing claim that corporate America is a pauper in comparison to the environmental movement. Anyone familiar with the struggle to curb pollution and natural resource depletion over the years knows that the movement's expenditures are dwarfed by the sums their corporate adversaries lavish on lobbying and litigation.

Public interest lawyers and lobbyists generally receive a fraction of the salaries earned by those in industry's employ. Further, when a court battle erupts, the legal team handling the corporate side of the controversy usually outnumbers its environmentalist counterparts by at least five to one. Not surprising when the profits of a single *Fortune* 500 company exceed the total annual expenditures of the entire national environmental movement. It's a tribute to the skills of a small cadre of environmental activist lawyers and lobbyists that they have been able to prevail consistently against such odds. The widespread support for their cause, reflected continuously in public opinion polls, obviously helps.

Ludicrous Luddites

Ascribing princely wealth to environmental groups only scratches the surface of the absurd. Dig deeper and you will find many bashers spreading the word that environmental activist organizations are anti-capitalist and anti-technology, with a particular distaste for modern urban life.[18]

On the contrary, mainstream environmentalism has a positive vision for contemporary society, at least when society functions in an environmentally sustainable manner. A cornerstone for reaching this objective is modern technology. No one is preaching the end of capitalism, only a major reduction in the waste that need not be an inevitable byproduct of free enterprise.

Fissure in the Ranks

Media critic Mark Dowie writes that environmental groups have become increasingly bureaucratic, estranged from grassroots supporters, and bereft of ideas.[19] To a degree, this has been true of some national environmental organizations. But the malady has hardly been terminal. In fact, in most cases, a fullblown recovery is underway, galvanized by the 1994 ascendancy of a Republican congressional majority that threatened to unravel the nation's environmental protection laws.

If you need proof of this resurgence, note the successes the movement has scored in thwarting Congress's recent attempt to roll back environmental regulations. The mighty forces arrayed against environmental protection could not have been stymied without the Greens' display of extraordinary perseverance and tremendous grassroots support.

Some try to sully the national environmental movement by misrepresenting the modus operandi of its earliest days.[20]

Keith Schneider, who covered environmental issues for *The New York Times*, wrote a piece in 1993 suggesting that the national movement had built its impressive record of accomplishment by rejecting negotiation and compromise for a tough, unyielding stance. It was an attempt to portray environmental activists as inflexible dogmatists hovering on the fringes of society. In fact, the movement from its inception has been solidly in step with the mainstream of American society, in spirit if not in body. I say "spirit" because the public's affinity for a clean and healthy environment was no less when Rachel Carson wrote *Silent Spring* in the 1960s than it is today. What has changed is the level of citizen awareness, concern, and participation. These have heightened considerably, due in no small part to the environmental movement's educational efforts.

It should also be noted that from the beginning, the national environmental movement used negotiation, conciliation, and alliance building (albeit in varying degrees, depending upon the circumstances). How else does Schneider think our landmark environmental statutes became the law of the land in the ecological "golden age" of the 1970s? We owe a lot to that tiny band of intrepid Washington-based environmental lobbyists whose acumen in weaving powerful factual documentation into their appeals for major reforms turned the tables on a far more affluent, politically well-connected, pollution-prone corporate America. Incidentally, those early leaders of the environmental movement were not wild-eyed radicals, as Schneider implies. Such individuals as Joe Browder, Louise Dunlap, and Brent Blackwelder of the Environmental Policy Center, Gus Speth, Dave Hawkins, Dick Ayers, Jonathan Lash, and Dave Donniger of the Natural Resources Defense Council, Bill Butler and Michael Bean of the Environmental Defense Fund, Brock Evans, Mike McClosky, and Debbie Sease of the Sierra Club, Jay Hair and Barbara Bramble of the National Wildlife Federation, Paul Pritchard and Destry Jarvis of the National Parks and Conservation Association, Cliff Curtis of Greenpeace, Christopher Flavin of the Worldwatch Institute, and Maureen Hinkle of the National Audubon Society were fresh out of the establishment. As such, they projected a reassuring image that came in mighty handy in dealing with the staid, tradition-steeped Congress and court system.

Detractors of the environmental movement tend to identify with populist ideology, railing against big government's intrusive presence. Yet they object strenuously to laws that enable public interest groups to collect legal fees from the federal bureaucracy when successfully challenging its authority. Consistency is expendable in matters of ideological rectitude.

Lester Brown — Feasting on Famine

Another prime target of the bashers is Lester Brown, president of the Washington-based environmental think tank, the Worldwatch Institute. Only Ehrlich eclipses Brown on the enemies list. Brown's notoriety stems from his warning that humanity's burgeoning population is rapidly overtaking the carrying capacity of the earth's natural resource base and poses major threats to our future quality of life. Attempts to tarnish him usually take the form of grossly overstating his assertions and creating the false impression that he is devoid of solutions.

Reluctance to credit Brown with any positive message stems partly from the nature of his remedies. They involve family planning and environmental taxes to slow population growth and rates of consumption respectively, strategies that bashers consider examples of government "encroachment on individual freedoms." Brown thus ends up being portrayed as one who believes the world is hurtling towards global famine, rejects the potential of modern technology, and pines for a return to a primitive, pre-industrial society.

Typical is an ad hominem attack launched by Denis T. Avery, director of global food issues for the free-market-oriented Hudson Institute.[21]

He accuses Brown of opposing the use of pesticides and other modern farming techniques that could combat famine, and charges that the Worldwatch president "for 25 years has discouraged public investments in agricultural research."

Envy and frustration at Brown's fame appear to have driven Avery to misrepresent the Worldwatch president's position. "Overall," Brown has stated, "there is a need for much greater investment in agricultural research, although not because of the likelihood of another breakthrough like the development of hybrid corn ... that will lead to a huge gain in world food output. But in a world of food scarcity, *every technological advance that helps expand production, however small, is important.* Each one buys a little more time with which to stabilize population."[22]

If Avery and others have problems with Brown's ultimate solution of population stabilization, they should explain why instead of putting words in his mouth. That they feel compelled to distort his position time and again strongly suggests that they cannot refute his convictions on their merits.

Dr. Epstein and the Cancer Apocalypse

Dr. Samuel Epstein, a professor of environmental medicine at the University of Illinois School of Public Health, is pilloried as a scaremonger because of his persistent and well-publicized assertions that environmental causes of cancer are being largely ignored. This insistence that a significant amount of cancer results from exposure to manmade environmental toxins infuriates the bashers. If Epstein is correct, an increased governmental regulatory role that restrains free-wheeling capitalism would seem in order. And, of course, such an expansion would run counter to environmental denigrators' ideological bent.

Epstein irritates not only the bashers. Take the medical profession: He accuses it of fixating on diagnosis and treatment of cancer, as well as basic research, while ignoring or trivializing prevention strategies. Why, he asks, isn't more attention paid to avoidable exposures to industrial carcinogens in the air, water, food, consumer products, and the workplace? The professor also chides government regulators for kowtowing to industry and not moving as aggressively as they should against known or suspected carcinogens in the workplace and marketplace.

In short, Epstein has been a thorn in the establishment's side for many years, particularly with his demands that more comprehensive and conspicuous warning labels be affixed to products containing toxic ingredients. As you might expect, those who parrot the industry line and publicly dismiss Epstein as an eccentric pariah never seem to want for money and platforms to express their views.

But Epstein is not easily cowed. Though he doesn't claim to have all the answers, extensive documentation gives him the confidence to spout his theories with dogged persistence, unshakable conviction, and a healthy dose of credibility. If you believe that the potential victim deserves the benefit of the doubt, and the burden of proof to show that a product is *reasonably* safe rests with the manufacturer, Samuel Epstein is your man.

6

SINS OF OMISSION

Bashers routinely commit sins of omission in attempts to discredit their adversaries. The technique is frequently used to build the phony case that the federal government cannot manage land as effectively as the private sector. A typical example: "The National Park Service has allowed elk and bison populations in Yellowstone National Park to greatly exceed the habitat's carrying capacity."[1] Just a minute! Wasn't it the private sector that pressured federal authorities to exterminate the wolves in the region and thereby eliminate the principal natural check on the populations of big game animals?

The law expressly forbids sports hunting in national parks. But hunters take heart, all is not lost! Scientific culling is allowed, and hunters may kill a certain number of elk when the creatures stray outside the park's boundaries.

False Incompatibility

On a broader scale, bashers constantly disseminate half-truths to portray the environment and economy as being irrevocably at odds. They know full well that public support for the environmental movement's mission will ebb if that mission is perceived to be in conflict with people's pocketbooks. The principal way that they promote this alleged conflict is to complain unceasingly that "costs are not considered in decision-making under such landmark environmental statutes as the Clean Air, Clean Water, and Endangered Species Acts."[2]

They got it half right. The anti-pollution standards and endangered species listings are determined solely by health and ecological considerations respectively. What the bashers fail to disclose is that cost factors can and do come into play in formulating the strategy for complying with these laws.

Discarding All Caution

One of the most egregious omissions relates to the precautionary principle, the basic strategy promoted by environmental activists when a suspected ecological hazard is at hand. The principle is that when enough evidence of a potentially hazardous situation exists to outweigh the risk of standing pat, those in charge have a clear-cut obligation to take whatever *reasonable* preventive actions are at their disposal.

State of the Planet misrepresents the principle as meaning that "humanity not interfere with nature until all the ecological consequences of an action can be taken into account."[3] What nonsense! If that definition were taken literally, humanity would be in a state of perpetual paralysis. Who could possibly know in advance all the consequences of any action he or she took?

The Mountebank of Ellipsis

Nearly a quarter of a century ago, environmental writer Jeff Stansbury and I submitted to the now venerable *Washington Monthly* magazine an article analyzing a then rather novel concept known as "net energy." Net energy means simply that it takes energy to produce energy, but it is a principle with far-reaching ramifications.

The magazine decided to publish the piece, which was assigned to a young editor named Gregg Easterbrook. There was some communication between us and Easterbrook during the course of the editing process, and everything seemed to be proceeding smoothly. But when the article finally made it into print, major portions were unrecognizable. Easterbrook had taken unauthorized liberties not just with our words but also with our thoughts. Jeff was so incensed that he hired a lawyer, a move that triggered a settlement in which the magazine's publisher printed a sizable retraction.

Following that episode, I lost track of Easterbrook until he resurfaced years later as a reporter for *Newsweek*.

Needless to say, I approached his material warily, and the accuracy of his recent opus *A Moment on the Earth* strongly suggests that my caution was well taken. I've encountered no one more adept at using ellipsis than Easterbrook, who eventually became an environmental reporter not only for *Newsweek* but for the *Atlantic Monthly* and a number of other well-known publications.

His pretentious, 731-page *A Moment on the Earth* appears to be a vehicle designed to canonize him as an oracle. He is evidently intent on attaining literary immortality by remaking the environmental movement in his own image. This voluminous exercise in self-puffery has plenty of impressive research packed into its pages. Unfortunately, Easterbrook's ambition compels him to manipulate the facts and consequently taint his ultimate global vision, which he labels "eco-realism" (a misnomer if ever there was one).

Eco-realism is the truth according to Easterbrook, a truth he claims runs contrary to a mainstream environmental movement topheavy with fearmongers. Conditions aren't as bad as the movement makes them out to be, insists Easterbrook, and the earth's resiliency in recovering from manmade ecological perturbations is vastly underestimated.

Most of Easterbrook's prose reflects a tug of war between ambition and conscience. Evidently well aware that he is often playing fast and loose with the facts, he scatters throughout his prose numerous caveats to his most outrageous assertions. His journalistic background, if nothing else, appears to have driven him to cover his flanks. This incessant equivocation not only vitiates the credibility and flow of his book, but also draws attention to the disingenuous techniques that he uses in attempting to sell so many flawed premises.

Here are just some of the favorable conditions that Easterbrook maintains the environmentalists are ignoring:

- "The bulk of the world's forests remain, and in them, the dance of the ages continues."[4]

Well, the dance may continue, but the tempo has slowed drastically, due to biodiversity loss resulting from virgin forests being leveled and replaced by secondary growth. These trends are particularly severe in the tropical regions of Southeast Asia and our own Pacific Northwest.

- Easterbrook tries to finesse this reality with some statistical sleight-of-hand. He argues reassuringly that even if some forestland and other natural resources are being decimated by civilization, there's no need to worry when "only about two percent of the United States' surface is built up."[5]

In fact, four percent of the land in the lower 48 states has been paved over. Perhaps that doesn't seem to be much of a difference, but keep in mind that most of that four percent consists of the best land in the nation, valued for its soil fertility, scenic grandeur, proximity to fresh water, and/or favorable climate. Hence, the loss of a portion of our limited supply of prime farmland, wildlife habitat, wetlands, and old-growth forests to bulldozers is double what Easterbrook says it is. That makes the depletion far more numerically significant to our well-being than what appears at first blush.[6] Easterbrook also neglects to describe the other side of the coin, namely that less than five percent of our land and one percent of our rivers remain completely pristine.[7]

Spotting the Owl

Easterbrook writes that, in northern California, there are more wild spotted owls living in "industrial forests than in wholly natural forests."[8] It's his justification for contending that environmental activists are playing down the "threatened" spotted owls' abundance in order to seal off national forests from timber cutting.

There may be some increase in sightings of spotted owls in northern California secondary-growth forests. However, ornithologists warn that the overall spotted owl population in the Pacific Northwest—not healthy to begin with—is in serious decline, largely due to shrinkage of its natural, old-growth forest habitat. That has been made quite clear by data compiled through a universally accepted ecological monitoring system known as the "Leslie Matrix."

Easterbrook interviewed the scientists who were applying the Leslie Matrix in the spotted owl situation, but he chose to omit their findings when they didn't support the conclusion he desired. Indeed, he seems willing to go to any lengths to embellish his rose-colored hypothesis. He exults that "world emissions of chlorofluorocarbons (CFCs) peaked in 1988 and have been declining ever since," implying that mankind has resolved the stratospheric ozone depletion crisis and environmentalists should therefore turn their attention elsewhere.

Before you savor humanity's triumph, however, consider that Easterbrook glossed over an important fact. It's the "rate of emissions that has been declining, not the emissions themselves."[9] That means that even if society exercises all due diligence, the CFC problem will be around for quite a while. Furthermore, if we let down our guard and allow the production of ozone-depleting chemicals to resume, we will soon be right back where we started.

Then there is Easterbrook's euphoric crowing over DDT's disappearance from the American environment: "DDT was banished, and its biocumulative effects are nearly gone from the U.S. biosphere."[10] Easterbrook didn't get it even half right. While DDT is outlawed for general everyday use in the United States, it can be exported as well as deployed here if authorities judge the situation enough of an emergency. The chemical is thus extensively used in other parts of the world, particularly Southeast Asia, where it has come back to haunt us in the form of residues transported by wind currents that have infiltrated our food chain.

Easterbrook also failed to mention that DDE, the toxic, metabolic breakdown product of DDT, remains ubiquitous in the environment because of its capability to biomagnify as it is passed up the food chain. Indeed, DDE residues have been found in the body tissues of individuals eating contaminated fish, an alarming trend that has led to consumption bans or advisories on fish caught in a number of states, primarily those bordering the Great Lakes.[11]

To establish his credentials as the patriarch of eco-realism, Easterbrook must set himself apart from the mainstream crowd. He attempts to do this by painting so detestable an image of environmentalists that, in comparison, he comes across as a savior to readers gullible enough to buy such guff. "A central tenet of environmental doctrine," he writes, "is that things only get worse, never better."[12] This is ellipsis at fever pitch and with defamatory intent. It is also blatantly transparent. We all know that perpetual pessimists are turnoffs, and that if environmentalists truly fit that mold, they would never enjoy the enviable level of popularity that they do.

Easterbrook asserts repeatedly that environmentalists are wedded to an inexorable downward spiral when, in reality, they envision an endless series of fluctuating highs and lows. It's true that victories in environmental battles have no permanence, while defeats often do (at least in generational terms). But constant vigilance is far different from abject despair. An attitude of vulnerable well-being is not the same as resignation to unremitting decline.

Agro-Libel

Easterbrook accuses environmentalists of spurning the benefits of high-yield agriculture. In fact, they duly acknowledge the contribution of the "Green Revolution."[13]

There is concern, however, that population growth is starting to outpace agricultural productivity in some parts of the world. Many high-yield agriculture techniques are also fossil fuel-intensive and a drain on soil fertility. Environmentalists believe that the solution to an adequate, sustainable global food supply rests more with population stabilization than perpetual reliance on an anticipated—but by no means guaranteed—procession of technological breakthroughs.

Easterbrook twits environmentalists for suggesting that damage to nature might be irreversible. Only extinction falls within that category, he sermonizes.[14] Technically, he is correct. But he glosses over the fact that nature's resiliency is not always instantaneous. A significant amount of the damage that humans inflict on the environment is for all practical purposes irreversible, because it will take generations—in some instances, even centuries—for nature to recover completely from the defilement. And that assumes mankind gives it the opportunity to do so.

One of Easterbrook's favorite ploys for undermining environmentalists' concerns is to contrast human environmental abuse with nature's destructive force.[15] Sure, in many respects, humanity's capacity to inflict environmental damage seems puny alongside catastrophic natural events. Left out of the equation, however, is the fact that the biosphere has had eons to adapt to nature's trials and tribulations, but only a relative blink of the eye to adjust to human assaults.

It's also quite possible that, in the course of evolution, the biosphere has developed an equilibrium that has an ecological stress saturation point beyond which the system starts to deteriorate. If this is the case, human perturbations could be dwarfed by natural disruptions in absolute terms, yet be just enough to push some components of the biosphere over the edge.

Finally, let's return to the principle theme of Easterbrook's *A Moment on the Earth*, namely that mainstream environmental activists are congenital doomsdayers.[16]

It cannot be stressed enough that this is a defamatory use of omission in its purest form. Environmentalists may frequently harp on problems and even characterize a few as crises. But what Easterbrook fails to note is that the reason environmentalists raise a commotion is because they believe these problems are solvable.

That hardly constitutes an end-of-the world mentality.

Sleight of Hand Artist

In order to establish himself as an icon of eco-realism and the sage who will lead environmentalism into the twenty-first century, Easterbrook constantly seeks to portray himself as more humane, objective, and upbeat than your everyday, run-of-the-mill mainstream environmentalist. He is particularly fond of embarrassing environmentalists through use of analogies, which under scrutiny turn out to be highly flawed by the omission of crucial information.

Some of the most flagrant examples:

- Easterbrook dismisses the ozone depletion threat as overblown by noting that millions of years ago active volcano emissions rising into the stratosphere probably caused severe ozone shield depletion, yet life managed to survive.[17]

In fact, the situation he is talking about occurred too long ago to be relevant to existing life forms, which have adapted over millennia to today's higher level of ozone shield protection.[18]

- Easterbrook also ignores evolutionary adaptation when questioning the significance of humanity's role in the rise of global temperatures, implying that the greenhouse effect may be simply part of a natural cycle.[19] "Ice-core records are clear on the point that natural carbon-dioxide levels bounced up and down long before the first flint struck steel," he intones.

The Environmental Defense Fund (EDF) points out in its lengthy refutation of *Moment* that, while natural carbon dioxide variations have contributed to large climate shifts for eons, conditions have been different for the last 10,000 years. During this period, civilization has evolved and the earth has enjoyed a fairly stable climate—that is, until now.

Over the past 200 years, human beings have increased carbon dioxide levels more than 25 percent above what they were during the previous 10,000 years, creating a strong circumstantial case for their complicity in global climate change.[20]

Birds of a Feather

If two similar species of wild owls in different parts of the country are genetically different (and receive special protection on that basis), Easterbrook asks, why can't we say the same about two human beings who live thousands of miles apart?

It's his snide way of suggesting that similar rare species within the same family are not so different after all and should be lumped together, making them not quite as unique or deserving of protection. The answer that Easterbrook won't—but should—give to his own question is that humans are a relatively homogeneous species, because they are in an early stage of evolution compared to most other species on earth.[21]

Phony Misanthropy

Easterbrook writes that "the green movement does contain a puzzling antipathy towards its own genus: not so much a hatred of people as a wish they would just go away. Enviros' desire is to be alone with nature."[22]

One can't help but be taken aback at the author's temerity in suggesting that he is privy to the subconscious ruminations of millions of people, much less that he has found an emotion pulsating in unison through their psyches. This is an effort to vest literary license with omniscience, and if there is one thing that Easterbrook is not, it's omniscient.

To attain credibility, his presumptuous stereotyping of the environmental community would need documentation, and it should come as no surprise that his data are non-existent.

"Sore Thumb" Preserves

Omissions play an important role in Easterbrook's specious attempt to depict mainstream environmentalists as elitists placing the concerns of animals ahead of those of people. He uses the creation of nature preserves, particularly in Third World countries, to illustrate the supposed callousness of environmentalists toward their fellow human beings. It is environmentalists, after all, who applaud the establishment of these "elitist" sanctuaries in the midst of poverty and are often instrumental in their formation. The case studies he cites are Amboseli National Park in Kenya and the Royal Chitwan National Park in southern Nepal.[23]

As luck would have it, I have visited these two sanctuaries and find much of his description unrecognizable.

"When Kenya established its justly famed Amboseli Wilderness Preserve, it first drove out the indigenous Maasai," Easterbrook declares. Wrong! The Maasai were not prohibited from using the preserve.[24] When they did vacate much of the park, it was of their own volition, based on the determination that the benefits they would receive from withdrawal (in the form of tourist revenues) would far exceed any drawbacks.[25]

"Today," writes Easterbrook, "the indigenous Maasai, a cattle-grazing tribe that for centuries lived in reasonable harmony with Amboseli wildlife, dwell in poverty on the park's outskirts." Wrong again, unless he is comparing the Maasai with Long Island's Hamptons set. The Maasai's income from tourist concessions in Amboseli has soared over the past decade.[26] With this money, they have built schools and other modern facilities as well as created new tourist concessions that operate under their own management. Indeed, their enthusiasm for this new direction in their life inspired them in March 1996 to open a for-profit game sanctuary on their own lands bordering Amboseli Park, and they are preparing to establish two similar ventures.[27]

The Maasai may not be living in luxury, but they are not mired in the abject poverty that Easterbrook suggests either. His claim that environmental activists' yearning "to be alone with nature blinds them to the condition of the indigenous poor" in such places as Amboseli is a load of bunk designed to enhance by contrast his "kinder, gentler" paradigm that he hopes will immortalize his role in the evolution of the environmental movement.[28]

A U.S. conservation organization, the New York Zoological Society, was actually the prime mover in persuading the Kenyan government and international lenders to support the plan that melded the Maasai's economic interests with wildlife preservation.[29] One of the leading environmentalists in Kenya and currently that country's wildlife service director, native-born David Western, devoted much of his considerable energy and skill to integrating the Maasai into the operation of the park. He even oversaw construction of a pipeline to carry water out of Amboseli to Maasai cattle, thereby eliminating the need to herd the domestic beasts into the actual park, where they would compete with the wildlife.

The facts simply don't square with the accusation that the environmental movement deprives native peoples of access to their own backyards and transforms those lands into exclusive safari playgrounds for rich Westerners.

Regarding Royal Chitwan in Nepal, Easterbrook writes that, as a token gesture, local villagers are permitted to enter the park once a year to collect thatch for their huts. He makes it sound as though they have only a few hours to harvest the park's resources. It's actually two weeks! More importantly, Easterbrook does not tell the full story of the relationship between the villagers and the park. Aside from furnishing home construction materials, the nature preserve also provides year-round flood control benefits to the adjacent communities. But where the author is really derelict is in failing to inform the reader of the progress made in integrating the locals into the park's tourist economy. (It's an effort, by the way, in which the U.S.-based World Wildlife Fund has been active in an advisory capacity.)

One must concede that Easterbrook wrote his book before the Nepalese Parliament's decision to recycle 30 to 50 percent of Chitwan's tourist revenues back into local development. But even prior to that long-overdue decision, indigenous people on the border of the park were benefitting from tourism, albeit not nearly as much as they should have. (Less than 25 percent of the local work force were deriving any income from Royal Chitwan visitation.)

Happily, that situation is changing dramatically, again with the enthusiastic participation of the World Wildlife Fund. Management of park buffer zones that were in existence when Easterbrook was writing his book is being turned over to the locals. Jungle tree houses have been built in these buffer zones to allow tourists to observe the nocturnal meanderings of rhinos, tigers, and other wildlife, and such facilities have proven immensely popular. Villagers have been awarded these franchises, and training programs for nature guides are also underway.[30] (Incidentally, linking the local economy to conservation objectives of adjacent nature preserves is a widely used formula nowadays.)[31]

Compatibility between local villagers' needs and park preservation may not yet have reached an ideal stage in either Chitwan or Amboseli, but the shortcomings can't be attributed to a lack of effort.

Easterbrook downplays these strategies without offering any alternative. He seems to imply that a choice must be made between meeting the basic needs of people and preserving the native flora and fauna. If mankind's survival requires the decimation of our planet's biodiversity on which the quality as well as quantity of life ultimately depends, we face a bleak future, indeed.

A Glaring Omission

In such places as Chitwan and Amboseli, human populations are increasing at a rapid rate, threatening to overrun the nature preserves if growth continues unchecked. On the fertile alluvial plain at the edge of Chitwan, population has exploded due to high birth rates, an influx of Indian migrants, and the arrival of Nepalese fleeing eroded mountainsides. The birth rate in Kenya is one of the highest in the world, putting pressure on parks such as Amboseli and open space in general throughout the country.

Therefore, humanity must at some point stabilize its numbers, not only to preserve nature sanctuaries but also to assure sufficient carrying capacity to support future generations. Easterbrook, of course, does not acknowledge the urgent need to contain population growth surrounding nature preserves if the sanctuaries are to survive. His preconceived notions are so deeply entrenched that he is their prisoner, ordinarily a fatal flaw for a purported writer of non-fiction.

The Chameleon Syndrome

Environmental bashers are so consumed by ideology that inconsistency is of no concern. Their vacillation can also be symptomatic of a subconscious—or even conscious—desire to cover their flanks in the event their inaccuracy is exposed.

When a controversy involves their scientific credibility, they will straddle both sides of an issue to fend off critics. Presentations are fudged to provide escape routes if they find themselves about to be pinned down in an embarrassing position. Here are some typical examples:

- Jonathan Adler, director of environmental studies for the Competitive Enterprise Institute, condemns wilderness legislation for intending "to exclude man from nature." A mere two sentences later, he quotes the law as stating that wilderness is an area "where man himself is a visitor who does not remain."[32] When did we begin defining visitation as exclusion?

- How about the authors of *Eco-sanity* protesting the idea of placing the burden of proof on manufacturers to demonstrate that their products are safe? Demanding absolute proof is a "logically impossible task," complain the authors.[33] The implication: consumers themselves must demonstrate that they're at serious risk.

This is a straw man. Manufacturers must show that their products are "reasonably," not "absolutely," safe.

These same authors assert several pages later that "a suspicion that a chemical may be causing harm is not science" and should not be used as a basis for public policy decisions.[34] If it's impossible to prove conclusively that a chemical is safe, the manufacturer gains the benefit of the doubt. And if a strong suspicion that a chemical is dangerous is insufficient to trigger a thorough evaluation of the substance's properties, the manufacturer once again gets the benefit of the doubt. This sure looks like a formula for freewheeling, unregulated release of toxic substances into the marketplace. What about the fate of the potential victim in the *Eco-sanity* authors' scheme of things? He or she would appear to be out of luck!

Bashers' schizophrenic nature manifests itself in this same work when the authors sing the praises of U.S. environmental protection accomplishments[35] and then later criticize the government's environmental record for being "poor."[36]

- A similar ambivalence surfaces in Michael Fumento's *Science Under Siege*.[37] The writer declares that "in almost all measurable ways, the environment in the United States has improved markedly in the 70s and 80s." Only nine pages later, he writes that "there is little evidence that the country is much, if at all, safer as a result of the environmental crusades of the past decade and a half.[38] If betterment of environmental conditions cannot be attributed in any significant way to our landmark federal laws, to what do we owe the improvement?

- Bruce Ames is a scientist with a bias against conventional environmental thinking. He has a contrarian agenda that revolves around absolution of pesticides and other toxic chemicals as serious health threats. That is fine in the context of political opinion. But to gear his research to fit these fixed notions is not reputable science, no matter how many awards he has won. The guy is on a mission, one that blurs important distinctions and encourages heavily biased selectivity in presentation of data.

"Cancer is a degenerative disease of old age, although external factors can increase cancer rates," Ames declares.[39] Shortly thereafter, he says, "we estimate that roughly three-quarters of human cancers are preventable through a combination of good dietary and lifestyle practices."[40]

Ames' first statement assigns an inevitability to the incidence of cancer, thereby weakening the case against environmental pollutants as a cause of the disease. The second statement suggests that cancer is largely a preventable illness, not an inevitable stage in the evolution of life. Besides contradicting his first point, it enables him to downplay the fear of cancer and thereby further diminish concern about pollutants in the environment.

The increasing incidence of malignancies among our young amply demonstrates that cancer is more than just a degenerative disease of old age. It also builds a prima facie case for implicating environmental pollutants as a causative factor. As you might expect, Ames does not call attention to this trend.

Phantom Risk, Specious Risk

Phantom Risk (MIT Press, 1994) is a compendium of scientific papers by authors who attempt to downplay the risk to humans of low-level chronic exposure to toxic pollutants. If the objective of the book is to convince us that concern about this sort of exposure is hysterical and totally unwarranted, the authors fail miserably.

For the most part, *Phantom Risk's* contributors are engaging, in the name of science, in the unscientific practice of making highly selective use of facts to substantiate preconceived hypotheses. They are not following the trail of evidence wherever it might lead, as would truly professional researchers. Their polemicized tracts creak, groan, and sometimes crack—telltale signs of the authors' insecurity with subordinating their professional discipline to ideological imperatives.

For example, University of Pittsburgh epidemiology professor George K. Tokuhata spends an entire chapter attempting to discredit the idea that serious adverse health effects resulted from the Three Mile Island (TMI) mishap. "In short," Tokuhata writes, "the risk from the TMI radiation to the nearby residents is trivial compared with ordinary risks of everyday life."[41] Thirteen pages later, however, he asserts that "perhaps insufficient time has elapsed since the accident for some effects, such as cancer, to have been detected in our studies. Further studies are desirable." This second observation makes scientific sense—and it neutralizes his earlier conclusion.

State of the Planet is another anthology of mostly pseudo-scientific essays hawking cornucopian refutations of the environmental movement's well-documented concerns.[42] Again, we frequently find equivocation symptomatic of a struggle within the authors between the absolutism of ideology and the careful qualifications that are a trademark of sound scientific work.

Hence, Stephen Edwards of the International Union of Conservation and Nature (IUCN) writes that "though there is an impression we are experiencing a very rapid increase in extinctions, this may not be the case. It is clear that documented extinctions peaked in the 1930s, and the number of extinctions has been declining since then."[43] Yet, in the next sentence, he lets the air out of the balloon by declaring that "the reduction in the number of extinctions over the past 60 years may be because we do not have sufficient data to designate the species as extinct."

Let us close with two of the most flagrant contradictions in the bashers' standard repertoire, contradictions that result not from confusion but from a strong streak of hypocrisy that underlies their sanctimonious public posture. The first comes when the free marketeers condemn the welfare state but support corporate welfare, in the form of federal subsidies to companies extracting natural resources from public lands. The second involves ultra-conservative types who denounce government regulations for infringing on our individual freedoms, but lobby fanatically for the most intrusive invasion of privacy: interference with a woman's reproductive rights through a total ban on abortion.

7

IT'S ALL IN THE TECHNIQUE

Apart from sins of omission, what other basic techniques do the slanderers of environmentalism routinely employ to attract converts? Prominent in their arsenal is the dissemination of outright falsehoods that, if believed, will demonize the environmental movement, its individual members, and its philosophy. The bashers hope that even the most outrageous assertion will win acceptance among the unsuspecting if the pronouncements have a sufficiently authoritative ring.

Environmental issues lend themselves to deception on account of their complexity. Such intricacies often discourage laymen from learning enough about the subject matter to detect when hyperbole is supplanting reality. One wonders how the slanderers can in good conscience circulate deliberate lies. Have they conjured up some rationalization that allows them to sleep soundly at night despite engaging in ethical misconduct? The human psyche is always hard to analyze, but the quest for ideological purity appears to have legitimized a Marxist modus operandi. Put bluntly, there's apparently nothing wrong with doing or saying whatever it takes to get Americans back on the "right track" in their daily lives.

Disparagers frequently cite phony statistics as evidence that environmental alarmists grossly exaggerate ecological threats to attract donors. Typical is the bashers' assertion that "95 percent of the rivers in the United States are fishable and swimmable."[1] A proponent of this rosy picture, author Ronald Baily, also reiterates the bashers' familiar, albeit ludicrous, claim that "there is no evidence pollution has reduced overall life expectancy worldwide."[2]

Those who rhapsodize about the condition of our rivers blithely ignore official government statistics revealing that more than one-third fall short of the fishable, swimmable classification.[3] Government data are derived from national, scientifically conducted surveys. Where do the cockeyed optimists' numbers come from?

As for the contention that pollution hasn't reduced overall life expectancy around the globe, the statement defies the imagination, not to mention the actual situation. According to the World Health Organization's 1996 annual report, "about half the world's population suffers from diseases associated with insufficient or contaminated water ... Typhoid caused over 600,000 deaths and cholera some 120,000 fatalities." Most starkly of all, "diarrheal diseases, mainly spread by contaminated water or food, kill nearly three million young children every year."

Ideology or not, it takes a pretty cold-hearted individual to ignore so much human misery and, by extension, the policies that would lessen it.

Defaming Big Brother

Anti-ecology and anti-big government tirades are often punctuated with total fabrications designed to paint federal bureaucrats and environmental leaders as architects of oppressive regulations that stifle individual freedom and initiative. Here is just a sampling:

- *The federal government totally banned DDT.*[4]

Perhaps it should have, but it did not. EPA provided for emergency use of the insecticide in this country, and for export on request from foreign governments.

- *"Some environmental laws make it impossible to use the 700 million acres of federal land."*[5]

This accusation appears frequently in "Wise Use" treatises, and is particularly brazen in its disregard for accuracy. The truth is that *all* federal lands are open to the public for exploring and hiking and, on more than 80 percent of them, varying degrees of commercial activity are permitted.

- *"Every year, federal environmental regulations cost $450 billion, and force each family to pay out $6000,"* alleges columnist Paul Greenberg.[6]

He is typical of journalists who have only a passing acquaintance with pollution issues but are eager to hop on the contrarian bandwagon and assail the supposed heavy-handedness of environmental regulation. In this instance, Greenberg came across some provocative numbers, no doubt gleaned from fellow environmental bashers, and eagerly seized upon them to make his iconoclastic case. No fact-checking took place, since he was clearly more interested in making a flap than making a case. If he had bothered to investigate, Greenberg would have discovered that he was quoting the cost of all federal regulations, as opposed to the $123 billion annual price tag of solely federal environmental regulations. Don't get me wrong, the latter sum is no small change, but amortized over the breadth of society and given the health benefits it confers, the American people are receiving good value.

- *Fuel efficiency standards are an onerous environmentally inspired regulation.*

The contention is that these standards compel manufacturers to reduce automobile size and weight, making vehicles more damage-prone in collisions and increasing death rates on the highways. It's a viewpoint that collapses under scrutiny. When fuel efficiency doubled between 1974 and 1991 in response to regulatory mandates, traffic fatalities per mile traveled fell 40 percent.[7] One should also note that the vast majority of fuel economy gains during the last two decades have stemmed from technology improvements, not weight reductions.[8]

Additional debunking came from a General Accounting Office report in 1991. It concluded that auto weight reductions since the mid-1970s have had virtually no effect on total highway fatalities. Indeed, newer model cars have been successfully designed to improve fuel efficiency and safety simultaneously, not that startling an achievement when one realizes that just because a material is lighter doesn't mean it isn't stronger.

Finally, to demonize the National Park Service (NPS) and stereotype the environmental movement as a bunch of elitists, columnist Alston Chase creates a parable out of a flap between the NPS and the family of the Reverend Martin Luther King over the management of the African American leader's Atlanta, Georgia, birthplace as a historic site.

Chase uses the squabble as a pretext for ranting that the NPS neglects the needs of the urban poor in favor of an affluent upper middle class with the means to travel to remote wilderness areas.

- *"The NPS' concern for providing solace in inner cities is zero,"* he declares.

If that is the case, how does one explain that the majority of trips to national parks are to those parks close to or actually in urban areas?[9]

Sleights of Mouth

Most of the detractors of the environmental movement are shrewd enough to present their case, if at all possible, in the form of half-truths rather than outright lies. It's obviously harder to disprove allegations that contain some kernel of accuracy. Even a scintilla of truth provides some semblance of a moral sanctuary to which one can beat a hasty retreat if his or her subterfuge begins to unravel.

Among the most common variations of this rhetorical sleight of hand is the portrayal of the pronouncements or actions of a fringe group or individual as representative of the mainstream. A corollary is to take the statements of a minority faction that are mildly provocative and distort them to the extent they would repel any sane human being. "The fringes of a sect always seem to set the tone for moderate believers, and mainstream environmentalists remain strangely quiet as the fringe [Earth First] moves inexorably towards lunacy," write Ben Bloch and Harold Lyons in *Apocalypse Not*.[10]

With more than 80 percent of Americans identifying themselves as mainstream environmentalists, they could hardly be categorized as a sect. And if radical fringes do in fact set the tone for the mainstream, where is the evidence? Don't bother looking. You won't find any. The mainstream environmental movement, as an integral part of America's traditional value system, rejects unequivocally any activity violating existing law.

Meanwhile, bashers stumble over each other to portray Earth First! as the dominant voice of environmental activism, when it's neither that nor the anathema its detractors make it out to be. By its own admission, EF! takes a more aggressive tack than other environmental groups, but it still subscribes to a code that is quite benign in the overall scheme of things. In support of its devotion to wilderness protection, EF! has never advocated violence against fellow human beings, and as of late it has even eschewed civil disobedience as its tactic of last resort. Depending on the circumstances, mainstream environmentalists have both praised and criticized Earth First!'s operations.

Bashers have no interest in an objective depiction of what constitutes consensus within the environmental movement. They jump at the chance to taint all activists through association with any self-styled environmentalist who spouts radically abhorrent bombast guaranteed to alienate the average American. Hence, we have Rush Limbaugh and fellow professional polemicists placing the Unabomber, of mail-order homicide fame, squarely in the environmental camp.[11] The reason: publication of a rambling discourse in which the Unabomber denounces modern technology's impact on the natural world.

Limbaugh informs his radio audience that the Unabomber is a member of Earth First!, which the conservative commentator alleges was created by other environmental groups to bring down capitalism. It's demagogic propaganda lifted straight out of right-wing scandal sheets. The truth is that there is no evidence that the alleged Unabomber, Theodore Kaczynski, attended any EF! meetings, much less became affiliated with the organization.

EF! was not created by other environmental groups and does not call for the overthrow of our democracy. It does urge a reordering of national priorities to give more weight to wilderness preservation. Whether you agree with EF!'s objective or not, its mission hardly seems tantamount to insurrection.

Finally, the anti-technology philosophy spouted by the Unabomber clashes with both the current tenets and future aspirations of mainstream environmental activists.

From the Ridiculous to the Absurd

A common technique used to denigrate environmentalism is highlighting cases in which regulators appear to have overstepped their authority in enforcing such statutes as the Endangered Species and Clean Water acts. In these instances, accused lawbreakers are depicted as victims of injustice rather than perpetrators of nefarious deeds.

No one disputes that there have been occasional instances in which federal regulators have exceeded their bounds in dealing with private citizens. But despite considerable lobbying pressures on our officials to bend the law, our environmental regulatory system has in general persevered quite nicely in providing the protection intended by Congress. Where improvement is warranted, shouldn't the appropriate remedy be to refine the enforcement process and the mechanism for the public to air its grievances, rather than to resort to emasculation of our statutes? Furthermore, in the anecdotes time and again cited by professional anti-environmental polemicists, it turns out that the alleged victims of federal regulators were penalized in accordance with the law.

An example is the saga of one Ben Lacy. A Virginia apple cider producer, Lacy was cited for violation of the Clean Water Act after releasing waste water into a local stream. His malfeasance was detected when discrepancies appeared in his discharge permit application, and he refused to cooperate with state regulators in correcting the situation. His intransigence eventually led to federal charges, and a jury found Lacy guilty on 8 of 12 counts of violating the act, a conviction that carries a maximum sentence of 24 years in jail and a $2 million fine.

Lacy's defenders claim he made some honest mistakes (even though irrefutable evidence of his premeditated tampering was introduced in court) and that the effluent he released into the stream did not harm the environment. Well, the same arguments were made in Lacy's behalf at the trial, and they did not convince a jury of his peers.

If the critics of the environmental regulatory regime think our jury system is defective, they ought to say so. If they are not advocating any drastic reform of our judicial process, their recourse is to appeal the verdict. In addition, when they believe that a democratically enacted law is onerous or that an injustice has been perpetrated, they have the option to lobby for legislative change or repeal. Applauding arbitrary defiance of a statute's strictures amounts to glorification of anarchy, which is not a viable alternative in a democracy.

Another common technique (a "sin of omission" variation) entails taking a prominent environmental activist's remarks out of context and presenting them as the individual's pronouncement in its entirety. Imagine declaring that Hitler's Nazi Party had exceptional organizational skills but was evil incarnate—and then having others repeat the statement, deleting the second half of the sentence.

A frequent manifestation of this technique is depiction of mainstream environmental activists warning that "cars pose a mortal threat to the environment."[12] Omitted is the qualifying phrase—"as currently constituted." Environmentalists do not oppose cars per se, but there is wide agreement that fossil-fuel vehicles powered by internal combustion engines are severely contaminating the air over cities.

The environmental movement's solution is not to ban automobiles. Instead, the movement seeks to concentrate resources on development of pollution-free vehicles, while engineering a reduction in (not elimination of) dependency on cars. Its prime targets are cities, its principal tools expanded mass transit and land-use planning that puts homes, offices, shopping, and recreational facilities within walking distance of each other.

Half A Truth Is No Better Than None

The half-truth syndrome is a dominant trait of would-be debunkers of environmentalism and government regulation. In a state of ideological rigor mortis, they peer at the world through a narrow prism that transforms fragments of truth into a passel of falsehoods.

Thus we are told that countries engaging in free enterprise—meaning us—are more successful than those with "mixed economies," such as the Scandinavian nations, where proportionately more government-controlled entitlement programs and land management regulations are the norm.[13]

Few would dispute that, in the aggregate, we are the wealthiest and most powerful nation. But the bashers won't acknowledge that while the United States' gross domestic product may be the highest, our individual citizens are not the most affluent on a per capita basis. In that regard, residents of the "mixed economy" Scandinavian countries and Japan actually have higher incomes.

Unbalancing Nature

The more pedantic and ideologically contentious of the bashers challenge the environmentalists' basic tenet that there is a balance in nature. They argue that change and turmoil are more the rule than constancy and balance.[14] That muddles (in my view, purposely) the difference between "static" and "stable." Environmentalists would be the first to agree that nature is not static. You would have to have spent your entire life in solitary confinement not to be aware that nature is in perpetual and sometimes tumultuous flux.

Admittedly, stability is often not immediately obvious, especially when localized dramatic change is viewed in isolation from the entire ecosystem. But the alterations, deviations, and outright turmoil are occurring within the context of a cosmic natural process that constantly adjusts to maintain an overall equilibrium.

If environmental changes are precipitated by human activity, they usually occur far more rapidly than those evolving naturally, thereby leaving nature far less time to adjust. In these instances, it may take longer to detect the restoration of equilibrium at the local level. If the human insult is acute enough, equilibrium may not be discernible for generations, if at all. Sadly, human beings appear to possess the capability to cripple natural systems indefinitely.

This is not to say bashers don't embrace the concept of "balance" when they think it works to their advantage. They exploit it for all it's worth in their quest for favorable media coverage, playing on major news organizations' fears of appearing biased in reporting the events of the day. Bashers have thus had some success in persuading the media to construe "balance" as parity where none exists.

Many publications and electronic news sources feel compelled to initially bestow equal stature upon opposing sides in an environmental controversy, regardless of past performance and reputation.

Celebrating an exercise of fairness totally disconnected from reality, my friends, is not a balanced presentation. Balance is providing as complete a picture as possible of all aspects of the dispute, and then letting the facts speak for themselves, however unflattering they might be to one side or the other. In a clash between a public interest group whose expressed mission is pollution clean-up and a company which is known to emit pollutants in the course of doing business, there is no presumptive ethical equivalency. The former starts out with the prima facie image of a Good Samaritan, purely by virtue of its avowed mission; the other is cast as the prospective villain solely on the basis of its past record. Of course, as the story unfolds, their roles may be modified or even reversed.

If false parity is left unchallenged, it can lead to an undistinguished maverick scientist who touts the bashers' widely discredited notions receiving as much legitimacy as the opposing consensus of world-renowned experts in the matter at hand. This is apt to bewilder the general public, which is just the way environmental denigrators want it, for their convoluted propaganda is much more likely to prosper in a climate of confusion.

Zoning Out Ozone

Half-truths have been used in recent attempts to downplay the ozone hole threat that holds such a prominent place in environmentalists' roster of potential ecological disasters. Typical is the assertion that "crop yields wouldn't suffer even if a thinning ozone layer were deemed a problem."[15]

It turns out that a determination of what constitutes a lack of suffering can be quite subjective. Who would want to be sentenced to a regimen of soybeans for the rest of their lives? Experiments have demonstrated that most crops would be adversely affected by increased ultraviolet ray exposure resulting from the depletion of the protective stratospheric ozone layer. Soybeans appear to be one of the few food plants with some built-in resistance to this added solar radiation, though presumably they have a threshold as well. In any event, why would one wish to gamble with the world's food supply, especially when we know how to halt and hopefully reverse the stratospheric ozone diminution caused by synthetic chemicals?

Good Cop, Bad Cop

Among corporate polluters in league with foes of the environmental movement yet eager to project a contrary public image, a common modus operandi is "good cop, bad cop." These companies make highly visible donations to environmental groups and produce flattering annual reports on their own pollution abatement performance. At the same time, they are often behind-the-scenes players in legal actions and lobbying maneuvers to thwart the reforms being pushed by the beneficiaries of their environmental largess. The companies are also unobtrusively funneling money to groups and individuals committed to weakening anti-pollution regulation and discrediting the environmental movement.

Another variation of this split personality is for foes of the environmental movement to remind us that there is no way they could not be environmentalists, given that they and their families live on the same planet and are subject to the same pollution threats as the rest of us. The argument is compelling until you realize that most of them subscribe to an ideology that preaches that the human assaults on the earth's biosphere are either grossly overblown, quickly neutralized by technological innovation, or of little consequence due to the resiliency of nature.

They therefore have no qualms about undermining environmental regulation, because they fervently believe market incentives can much more effectively persuade people to curb pollution and reverse ecological degradation. It never seems to have occurred to them why regulation became necessary in the first place, a convenient lapse that winks at the damaging excesses of unrestrained laissez faire.

Finally, the casual acquaintance that many of these environmental skeptics have with their subject matter helps to ease any pangs of conscience. Such ignorance is made even more blissful by the added complexity that renders contemporary ecological threats less visible to the naked eye than the pollution insults predating the 1970s.

Green Scam

There are times when the deception totally lacks sophistication. For example, some organizations intent on rolling back environmental laws simply assign themselves an environmentally friendly-sounding name and count on public apathy (and perhaps naivete) to sustain their masquerade.

Brazenness aside, there is a confessional aspect to these organizations seeking to disguise their true intentions with euphemisms. They appear to think they are doing something wrong or fear that, no matter what they say, no one is going to believe they are doing something right. The former motivation is ethically indefensible. The latter is tantamount to an admission of a lack of conviction in the correctness of their cause.

One of the most blatant examples of attempted camouflage of a horrendous environmental record was the GOP House Task Force's 1996 campaign instructions to its members. Lawmakers were counseled to participate in highly visible environmentally oriented ceremonies within their respective districts in order to project a "green" image—in stark contrast to their legislative performances.

Having It Both Ways

Environmental detractors often attempt to have it both ways. They are more interested in making a point than proving one, and in creating straw men that will corroborate their ideological convictions. Look at the way they manipulate epidemiology: They label scientific studies in that field as meaningful if the studies bolster their arguments, meaningless if the studies do not.[16]

Usually it's the latter, since epidemiologically derived clusters (i.e., geographically concentrated outbreaks of disease) often are used in building a case for promulgating the environmental regulations that the detractors so passionately despise. When clusters tilt the scales towards regulation, polemicists such as Michael Fumento belittle the epidemiological data as too small a sampling, or one collected over too short a period of time. If these two alleged deficiencies aren't convincing enough, the validity of epidemiology itself is disparaged by dismissing the cluster phenomenon as more often than not a natural fluctuation.[17]

Still, Fumento and other bashers always leave the door slightly ajar for epidemiology in the event it can buttress their case. And although they frequently characterize the science as a crude tool, they grant it the dubious distinction (at least in their minds) of being more accurate than animal laboratory tests. With this back-handed compliment, they trash in one fell swoop the two basic methodologies used to formulate pollution regulation.

What's the real scoop on epidemiology? Clusters of disease that raise suspicion of environmental pollution may be random quirks of fate. Then again, they may not. In a society where public health concerns are supposed to receive highest priority, the clusters constitute sufficient circumstantial evidence of a possible problem serious enough to warrant at least some investigation. The more life-threatening the malady of those in the cluster, the more resources should be devoted to the research effort, and the more consideration should be given to taking precautionary regulatory action.

Tweedle Dum and Tweedle Dee

Anti-environmental polemicists often use specious analogies in attempts to win public support. These analogies have little staying power once you exercise common sense or a rudimentary knowledge of environmental science. Consider the following: To demonstrate that private land managers are superior to their public counterparts, the authors of *Eco-Sanity* note that "while some species of wildlife have been hunted to extinction, no farm animal ever has suffered the same fate."[18]

This is a preposterous comparison, in both a literal and figurative sense. The relationship of wildlife and farm animals to modern society is—with rare exceptions—totally different. Farm animals are a major food source. Wildlife (excluding commercial fish species) is deemed more of an aesthetic adornment, so its extinction would not represent to the average Joe the catastrophe that, say, the eradication of chickens or cows would.

If the suggestion is that private landowners are more humane than public land managers toward undomesticated critters, remember that the individual landowners who constitute the majority of sports hunters—at least in our country—account for much of the wildlife mortality in the public domain. It should be added that raising domesticated stock in protective custody prior to systematic slaughter or maintaining an affectionate relationship with a pet hardly qualify property owners as more beneficent caretakers of the animal world.

If we're talking about the destruction of lower life forms in terms of absolute numbers, public lands are a virtual oasis from human-generated carnage when compared to the nation's barn-yards.

Universal Poison

Few disparagers are more clever purveyors of specious analogies than Gregg Easterbrook. As a self-anointed gadfly of the national environmental movement, he constantly seeks to make the case that the Greens favor abandoning the industrial age for a return to a primitive pastoral state. He then chimes in that "what's most natural may not be what's most beneficial for the environment."

Certainly, the immediate impact of natural disasters is likely to be grievous environmental damage. But that's not the nature-induced environmental damage that Easterbrook is talking about. He tries to make his point by illustrating how "natural" deteriora-tion over a protracted period of time is more pernicious than human impact on the earth. Easterbrook does this by comparing New York City with the southeast Asian nation of Bangladesh, asserting that the former has higher population density and a more materialistic lifestyle, yet the air and water are getting cleaner and migratory fowl have returned.[19] By contrast, he makes much of the fact that Bangladesh's natural environment is declining despite its predominantly rural character.

The Asian ecological degradation that Easterbrook identifies is, for the most part, the result of environmentally unsound human activity, not natural evolution, so Manhattan and Bangladesh afford no true comparison between man and nature. Rather, we have one situation where humans have upgraded their surround-ings from a decrepit condition they created in the first place, and another where they are responsible for an ecological decline. Further undermining the analogy is the folly of comparing an entire nation to a city. They have about as much in common as an ocean liner and a rowboat.

Implicit in Easterbrook's analogy is that the latest technologies are generally superior to simpler, less mechanized processes. Sometimes, maybe even most of the time, that's true. But both modern farming and subsistence agriculture can be environmentally friendly or destructive. It all depends on how they are practiced.

Bangladesh's environment has been degraded not because of its people's primitive methodology but primarily because of population pressures that have forced Nepalese farmers to deforest upstream mountain slopes in order to cultivate marginal land. Rivers that flow into Bangladesh originate at high altitudes, and their flood impact during the monsoon season is magnified by the loss of alpine woodlands' absorptive capacity, causing increased siltation and erosion downstream. In other parts of Bangladesh, desertification has spread due to neighboring India's diversion of some rivers for its own use.[20]

Smoke and Mirrors

Another sophistic analogy that bashers frequently flaunt is the following: Urbanization does not foster poverty. It systemically brings about prosperity.

The proof? In wealthy nations such as the United States and Japan, three-fourths of the population lives in cities, whereas in Third World nations, such as China and India, only one-fourth does.[21] If that's not convincing enough, Hong Kong and Singapore are the richest nations in Asia and just happen to be city-states, so there!

Let's cut through this gobbledygook. While China and India may have only one-quarter of their citizens living in cities, their overall populations are so enormous that their urban dwellers far exceed those of other countries in absolute numbers. These two sovereign states also lack the infrastructure to serve residents as effectively as affluent, industrialized nations do. Many of their cities are little more than a collection of hovels.

In regard to Hong Kong and Singapore, they possess a unique commercial-middleman status. That enables them to accumulate large amounts of capital, which they use to attain vast amounts of natural resources (including food) from other countries, resources their own tiny land base could never provide. How can you compare these artificially carved-out city-states with full-blown nations in which cities are only one component in the demographic, geological, and environmental mix?

Undoubtedly the most deleterious comparison of all is one that, if accepted at face value, would sanction unfettered environmental degradation.

It is a comparison that developing nations repeatedly made during the 1970s and '80s to justify politically their poor environmental track records. When they recognized the errors in their thinking and began to back off, anti-environmental polemicists in the industrial world stepped into the breach and subjected us to the same old saw. It goes as follows: *There's nothing wrong with environmental protection. Indeed, it's commendable, but it is a luxury only wealthy nations can afford. When daily survival is at stake in poor nations, a little pollution and the fate of future generations seem inconsequential.*[22]

The fundamental flaw in the "environmental protection is a luxury" argument is that it fails to recognize the synergistic relationship between a healthy environment and a healthy, prosperous populace. Ignored is the linkage between good health and productivity, efficient resource use and job opportunity, and sustainable environmental practices and secure employment.

Maintaining clean air and water, adequate green space, and a sustainable use of natural resources may temporarily demand more sacrifice and regimentation—economic and otherwise—in the developing world than in those more advanced countries with a substantial head start. But the arduousness of the task is a prerequisite, not an obstacle, to survival and an enhanced quality of life. Furthermore, even the most impoverished countries with proper guidance could afford many fundamental environmental improvements. These improvements require some basic behavioral changes and introduction of simple, inexpensive technology, rather than massive capital infusions. The strategies range from boiling water to kill pathogens to adopting low-cost solar energy technology that reduces air pollution and deforestation. One of the most recently developed of these technologies is a table-top water purification system invented by a physicist at Lawrence Berkeley National Laboratory in California. It uses mercury vapor lamps to kill pathogens at a rate of 15 gallons per minute and a cost of two cents per metric ton of water. In addition, it weighs a mere 15 pounds, is priced under $300, and can be operated with solar cells.

Name Calling

Detractors of the environmental movement tend to demonize their foes through unrelenting name-calling in which the latter are stereotyped as implacable enemies of modern civilization. It's a technique that House Speaker Newt Gingrich has developed into an art form and manifested through a steady stream of invective against environmentalists and other critics.

Gingrich places those who agree and disagree with him into two distinct camps. Individuals who oppose his environmental views are dismissed as "extremists." He automatically classifies all of his critics, regardless of the issue, as "liberals," the ultimate mark of shame by his reckoning. People who embrace his vision are patriots committed to progressive change, with the clearcut implication that those who defy him are not.

This hard-edged, rigid approach is self-defeating. To make sweeping generalizations about individuals' character on the basis of their particular viewpoint concerning a specific issue offends most people, potential supporters included. No one likes to be dismissed as incapable of independent thinking and intellectual flexibility. Nor do people take kindly to seeing their dissenting opinions branded as heresy. An honest difference of opinion is more in the American tradition than an absolute, autocratic posture. Americans are not enamored with ideological warfare, preferring accommodation to confrontation. Nor are we inclined to lose sleep over manic reports of ongoing Machiavellian plots that are insidiously subverting our society.

You might think Gingrich would eventually figure out that placing people into neat cubbyholes is a tortured exercise in demagoguery that turns off voters. Yet he has been slow to learn from his rebuff at the hands of the general public, and other environmental detractors who have dutifully emulated his combative style have been even more resistant—with the same negative results.

Hyper Hyperbole

Hyperbole is the name of the bashers' game in stereotyping adversaries. Environmental activists are excoriated for being doom-and-gloom soothsayers who warn that the human race will inevitably reduce the earth to a moonscape.

Following are other examples of horrific hyperbole cooked up to tarnish the Greens:

> • "Behind environmentalists' call for energy con-
> servation lies a professional hatred of the pri-
> vately owned auto—and of the individuality
> and freedom it represents."[23]

Get serious! Environmentalists cherish mobility as much as the next person. Campaigning for automobile fuel efficiency hardly constitutes an appeal for banning privately owned motor vehicles.

> • Then there's the mantra: "Environmental groups
> have effectively scared many Americans away
> from fresh produce" (through their pitch for
> natural foods).[24]

What a ludicrous charge! How many Americans have ceased purchasing produce because of environmentalists' eminently sensible admonition to wash fresh fruits and vegetables thoroughly to get rid of lingering pesticide residues? Or because "eco-warriors" express a preference for organically grown foods?

Since no one is immune to the full range of environmental threats, the bashers' hyperbolic stereotyping eventually alienates just about all, save their own kind.

No Shame

Throughout history, many a rogue caught redhanded has sought to escape punishment through a brazen diversionary tactic that creates confusion. Instead of pleading guilty, the accused—without offering any supporting evidence—straightfacedly claims his misdeeds were perpetrated by his accuser.

Incredibly, this shameless turning of the tables sometimes works. When you have enough moxie, there's always a chance of bluffing your way out of just about any incriminating situation, especially if your audience is uninformed or naive enough to be seduced by the power of suggestion.

The saving grace is that a modicum of reflection is usually all that is necessary to expose this perversion of the venerable maxim, "the best defense is a good offense."

Consider the spectacle of denigrators of the Green movement chastising environmentalists for "twisting information so that it confirms to their views."[25] I won't tell you that environmental activists have never been guilty of distortion, but they certainly don't integrate it into their daily routine. It takes a lot of gall for the bashers to condemn others, without supporting documentation, for the deceitful methodology that is their own stock in trade.

Anti-environmental polemicists complain that the eco-doomsdayers "consistently cite each other's work as evidence of the truth."[26] Sure, environmentalists exchange data. We all invoke precedent to prove a point. What counts is if the numbers stand up to scrutiny, and the environmentalists' generally do. Their critics' recycled material generally doesn't.

"Character assassination and charges of guilt by association have been the weapons of choice among Washington's vested green professionals," writes anti-environmental polemicist Alston Chase.[27]

It's true that environmentalists regard with suspicion the conservation credentials of critics who rely on hefty grants from corporate polluters. They also consider it an atrocious conflict of interest when Congress allows industries to participate in the drafting of environmental regulations that would govern commercial activity.

To their credit, the environmentalists at least offer hard evidence to substantiate their criticism of professional linkups they consider highly suspect. By comparison, Chase and the contrarian school he typifies seek to debase environmentalists' public image with unflattering descriptions grounded in hearsay, myth, and—it appears—wish fulfillment.

PART 4

THE CYNICAL PURSUIT
OF FAME AND FORTUNE

8

THE GREAT MISCOMMUNICATOR: RONALD REAGAN

Detractors of the environmental movement were sounding off long before Ronald Reagan arrived on the scene. But it took the florid anti-environmental rhetoric of the 40th President of the United States to focus the national spotlight on their ideologically driven crusade.

The godfather of flamboyant environment bashing was fond of exercising his script-reading skills to regurgitate the half-baked ideas of such self-anointed ecological iconoclasts of the 1970s as Julian Simon (a University of Maryland economics professor) and Herman Kahn (the Hudson Institute). This particular "cornucopian" duo rejected the existence of any serious natural resource depletion problems, and maintained the principle of the more population growth, the better.

You had to hand it to Reagan. Unlike most politicians, the "Great Miscommunicator" never temporized about where he stood. The former actor always attempted to follow his script to the letter, no matter how obtuse it might be. He was, after all, a product of an industry that judged individuals more on how they read their lines than on what they actually said.

His ultra-right-wing diatribes regularly depicted environmentalists as "extremists" who wanted to burden the American people with regulation, establish a centralized federal government that trampled on states' rights, seal off all public lands to any commercial development, and employ subversive tactics to replace our democracy with a communist or socialist regime.

Those outlandish, undocumented charges made no headway with any but the relative few who regarded them as affirmations of their particular ideological bias.

Fortunately for Reagan, the public tended to separate the messenger from the message. He was rarely held accountable for his anti-environmental invective, undoubtedly due in large part to his disarming, tongue-in-cheek delivery and studied, laid-back personality.

Ignorance is Bliss

Reagan's sporadic, simplistic treatment of environmental issues graphically illustrated his disinterest in and ignorance of the subject matter. His borrowing from so-called environmental experts whose perspectives he found ideologically compatible became a conditioned reflex. It made no difference what their credentials were or whether their pronouncements had been subject to scientific peer review, as long as their conclusions adhered to the party line. Because Reagan's political stature invested him with an aura of authority, he quickly became the bashers' leading spokesman. To this day, they dutifully recycle much of his drivel, seemingly oblivious to the damage they are inflicting on their own credibility.

For its part, the American public made a mistake in letting Reagan's environmental balderdash slide. Darned if he didn't try to implement many of his cockamamie ideas when he entered the White House. It took a monumental effort from a Congress energized by a belatedly indignant, vocal electorate to frustrate the president's intentions. Thanks to his Teflon persona, the Great Miscommunicator emerged virtually unscathed, leaving his subordinates to bear the brunt of the ill will.

All of this is not to say we escaped uninjured from the Reagan years. Valuable time was squandered in frequent stalemates between the executive and legislative branches. In most sectors, the national pollution cleanup was put on hold. We lost our claim to environmental leadership in international circles, and with so many federal research and development programs in limbo, we found ourselves playing catch-up in technological fields (e.g., solar energy) where once we were second to none.

Advanced Warning

In the years before his successful presidential run, Reagan conveyed his views on environmental issues through syndicated radio broadcasts from the West Coast. One of candidate Reagan's favorite themes was questioning the imposition of tougher regulatory restraints upon many of his pals in the corporate world. He argued that pollution from American industries should be treated with a high degree of tolerance, not only because it was an inevitable byproduct of a healthy economy but also because it was relatively inconsequential in comparison to the damage caused by natural processes.

This "nature is a villain" theory is a favorite of environmental bashers, but it has gained scant credence in scientific circles. Reagan could not have cared less. His radio commentaries weren't aimed at the National Academy of Science, but at unsuspecting laymen at the grassroots level. The ex-actor downplayed the need to circumscribe industrial polluters through national ambient air quality standards, given the damage allegedly being inflicted by nature.

"Suspended particulates [one of the most common air pollutants] can be dirt, swamp gas and other of nature's wonders," he informed his listeners. Later, in a further attempt to rationalize away air pollution fears, he exclaimed: "A buffalo herd would kick up enough dust to violate the ambient air standard."

As an unabashed apologist for nuclear power, commentator Reagan sought to quell public concerns by asserting that "natural radiation is 10 to 20 times greater than that from nuclear power plants." It was a comment worthy of the late Dixy Lee Ray, former head of the Atomic Energy Commission, who was Reagan's pronuclear guru and remains the principle scientific authority for many contemporary environmental bashers.

If Reagan were president today, his beatification of nuclear energy's safety record would be a major source of embarrassment, considering the scandalous disclosures that the federal government conducted radioactive exposure experiments on unwitting human subjects who subsequently fell ill.

Nature's Villainy

One of Reagan's most egregious examples of scapegoating nature involved a broadcast appeal for more timber cutting of old-growth trees on public lands. In an ill-informed swipe at nature's reproductive efficacy, he counseled his audience that "dead trees are pure waste and are harmful to the forest."

Any basic high school biology text will tell you that dead trees are a vital component of the forest's regenerative cycle. As they decay, they return essential nutrients to the soil, providing irreplaceable habitat and forage for many species that roam the forest floor and functioning as important housekeepers of the woodland ecosystem.

Perhaps candidate Reagan's most infamous vilification of nature was his public assertion (which he steadfastly refused to retract) that trees were more to blame for air pollution problems than human beings were. He quoted an American Petroleum Institute study that proclaimed "80 percent of air pollution comes not from chimneys and exhaust pipes, but from plants and trees."

The conclusion of the oil companies' study was so self-serving, and its implications so absurd, that even some of Reagan's own staff could not keep a straight face. Several days after the infamous "trees" remark had surfaced in headlines around the country, Reagan's droll press secretary, James Brady, assured his boss a measure of immortality. Sitting in front of newsmen on the campaign press plane, Brady suddenly glanced out the window at the forest below and blurted in mock horror, loud enough for all to hear: "Look, killer trees!"

Reagan was not allowed to forget his arboreal gaff for the rest of his political career. It made fine fodder for the monologues of late-night talk show hosts, as well as Ted Kennedy's roasting of the former California governor at the 1980 Democratic presidential convention.

For those who find Reagan's description of trees as earth's primary polluters a ludicrous characterization but don't know how best to refute it, keep in mind the following basic principles. A tree emits pollutants, but they are released gradually into the atmosphere from many point sources in a large area, and then are widely dispersed. The incremental pollution they generate has been a fact of life for eons, giving all species plenty of time to adapt to the exposures. Just as importantly, the discharges never attain the lethal concentrations of manmade emissions, which possess the potential to undermine the immune systems of human beings and other living organisms.

Finally, so-called "natural" pollution plays some sort of beneficial role in environmental evolution. For example, the carbon dioxide emitted by dead vegetation and marshlands is absorbed by living plants and is essential for their health. We might regard lava from a volcanic eruption as an unwelcome natural pollutant, yet its ash residue contributes mightily to soil regeneration. Excessive exposure to solar radiation can trigger cancer in human beings, but moderate absorption of sunlight provides us with Vitamin D, which promotes healthy bone structure and kills skin pathogens.

Nuclear Knight

Reagan's broadcasts on nuclear power were veritable commercials for the industry. He asserted that the fear for public safety was exaggerated and had hindered the spread of nuclear power generation. Reagan's declaration that "natural radiation is 10 to 20 times greater than that from nuclear power plants" is irrelevant for public health purposes. Obviously, in the area near a nuclear facility, that ratio heads in the opposite direction when an accident occurs.

But even where there is no mishap, the kind of radiation discrepancy described by Reagan offers meager comfort. While our bodies have adapted to natural levels of radiation, our tolerance level may not extend much beyond that amount, in which case even small increments of additional exposure from the routine operation of a nearby power plant could put us at risk.

Undaunted, Reagan boasted over the airwaves that "since the first nuclear plant went on line 20 years ago, there has not been a single nuclear injury." Not too long after this rosy pronounce-ment, the Soviet Union's Chernobyl nuclear reactor was the scene of a meltdown in which reportedly 31 to several thousand people were killed, depending on whose version you accept.

Don't get the impression, however, that evidence contradicting Reagan's safety claims didn't exist when he stepped up to the microphone to ease listeners' concerns. The Three Mile Island (TMI) nuclear plant mishap near Harrisburg, Pennsylvania, was already history, having occurred on March 28, 1979. Reagan down-played TMI by assuring his radio audience that "no one was killed, no one injured, and there will probably not be a single addi-tional death from cancer among the two million people living within a 50-mile radius of the plant." It turned out he was a worse prophet than a president. Fourteen years after the accident, researchers found distinct cancer "hot spots" within a six-mile radius of TMI.

One really can't blame Reagan for predictions gone awry. After all, it takes foresight to be forewarned. But it is unconscionable that in the immediate aftermath of the TMI mishap, he would contend there were no adverse impacts — even as residents in the vicinity of the plant were losing their hair and developing body sores.

The Pennsylvania Gas & Electric Company has insisted that the amount of radiation released in the nuclear accident was equiva-lent to no more than a chest x-ray and that no adverse medical effects were observed. Yet the company quietly agreed to out-of-court cash settlements—some as high as a million dollars—to a number of the power plant's neighbors claiming TMI-related injuries.

There is further evidence that the very industry for which Reagan was shilling isn't as benign as its top executives suggest. Pressured by Congress in the mid-1980s, the Nuclear Regulatory Commission (NRC) launched an investigation of safety condi-tions. It ultimately concluded that the risk of a severe core melt-down in the United States was approximately 45 percent over a 20-year period, not exactly a fail-safe scenario.[1]

What of the lingering, stubbornly intractable problem of assur-ing safe disposal of long-lived radioactive waste? No problem, declared Reagan. "All of the nuclear waste now on hand and yet to be accumulated between now and the year 2000 could be stacked on a single football field, and the stack would be only six feet high."

According to his math, that pile would amount to 288,000 cubic feet of nuclear waste, a calculation which assures that the Great Communicator will never be remembered as the Great Tabulator. By the end of 1990, the volume of high-level radioactive waste in this country from nuclear weapon production alone amounted to 1.4 million cubic feet.[2]

His careless utilization of numbers is also evident in his defense of the economics of nuclear power. "True," Reagan declared, "nuclear plants cost more to build, but from then on, they run more economically than oil, gas, or coal-fired plants." Although the nuclear industry applauded his words, it knew better. Keep in mind that 1974 was the last time the U.S. industry received an order for construction of a new power plant. One-fourth of the 109 remaining nuclear plants in the United States will close over the next decade because of increasing operation and maintenance expenditures, including $100 billion in cost overruns recorded during the past 20 years. Another dagger in the industry's economic heart is the enormous expense of decommissioning worn-out facilities, a procedure involving millions of dollars but rarely mentioned in corporate financial projections.

The bashers' claims notwithstanding, nuclear power is far more expensive than coal. An extensive comparative evaluation by Charles Comanoff, a nationally renowned energy analyst, demonstrates that reality.[3]

Reagan's kneejerk platitudes on behalf of the nuclear power industry coincide with his disparagement of wind power, despite more than 16,000 wind turbines generating 2.7 billion kilowatt hours of electricity in his home state of California at a cost comparable to other fuels (including nuclear) that are much more heavily subsidized by the federal government.

Shortchanging Renewables

The mention of wind brings us to renewable energy, which Reagan treated as an exotic option more in tune with science fiction than Main Street USA. In his broadcast harangues, he repeatedly charged that solar power and other renewables were technologically incapable of making a major contribution to national energy needs. "The simple truth is that solar and wind power are not practical alternatives for providing the increased electrical power we'll need by the year 2000," he declared.

By 1993, however, renewables were responsible for 12 percent of the nation's total primary energy production (already surpassing nuclear, which provided just 8 percent). Moreover, those most knowledgeable about the capabilities of this "clean" energy source note that renewables could satisfy half of the U.S. energy demands by 2030 with presently available technologies. All that is required, they say, is to give renewables a level playing field on which to compete with fossil fuels and nuclear power, both of which continue to be far more generously endowed by Washington. The need for more federal aid for renewables at a time when Reagan wanted to downsize government plus the rivalry between alternative and nuclear energy sources were the main reasons the former California governor chose to scoff at clean energy's practical potential.

Redbaiting

Reagan was also deeply suspicious of the motivations of those critical of the nuclear power industry. Leveling charges reminiscent of the McCarthy era, he used the microphone to rail against "Machiavellian" forces seeking to undermine nuclear power generation—and the country. According to Reagan, nuclear energy was being sabotaged by a long-haired, rag-tag rabble of anti-American radicals who opposed economic growth, the Vietnam War, and masculinity, not necessarily in that order.

True to his Cold War orientation, Reagan also considered the anti-nuke crowd to be in league with the Kremlin and, as such, a national security threat. It must have been awkward for him when some of the anti-nuclear demonstrators turned out to be diehard Republicans with blue-blood pedigrees. But embarrassment in these situations was always transitory. As I have noted, his Hollywood training endowed Reagan with an extraordinary ability to block out reality when it clashed with a scenario that suited him or others to whom he was beholden.

Copy Cats

If imitation is the sincerest form of flattery, Reagan should be preening at the tribute paid to him by environmental bashers. They have dutifully retained his suspicion of nuclear foes' ulterior motives, and broadened it for good measure.

With the collapse of the Soviet Union, the refrain is no longer that environmental "extremists" want to turn us over to Moscow; it is that they seek to establish in our midst their own variation of a socialist state.

No Kidding Around

After his inauguration, Reagan quickly sought to implement a regressive environmental philosophy that all but a prescient few had thought was nothing more than campaign rhetoric. Nowhere was this more evident than in the energy field. One of the president's first moves was to appoint James Edwards, a onetime dentist and former governor of South Carolina, as secretary of energy. Edwards knew more about electric drills than electric power, was enamored of the nuclear industry, and was skeptical of conservation's potential.

If that weren't enough of a resume to clinch the job, Edwards' behavior in the statehouse erased all doubts. While serving as chief executive, he declared that South Carolina didn't need environmental laws because the prevailing winds carried pollutants out to sea. With that kind of insight, there was no better man to preside over the dismantling of the agency he was appointed to oversee.

The Reagan White House laid out the scenario for Edwards: fold the Energy Department into the Commerce and Interior departments, where it would then fade into bureaucratic oblivion. Congress got wind of the plan, but an unruffled Edwards denied at his January 1981 confirmation hearing that his true mission was to phase out the agency. Some 11 months later, however, Reagan announced his intention to do just that as a cost-saving measure, reflecting the low priority he assigned to the federal government's leadership in producing a national energy policy.

Naturally, Edwards rose to the defense of his boss, asserting to Congress that the breakup was essential to prevent the Energy Department from "growing like Topsy." He predicted, "Congress probably will debate it rather vigorously for two or three months and then vote sometime in April or May. Then we can carry out the administrative chores of dismantling it, and I can be fishing down on the beaches of South Carolina in June or July."

Reagan's reorganization proposal did not produce the result that Edwards had anticipated. Rep. Richard Ottinger, D-N.Y., chairman of the House Energy and Commerce Subcommittee on Energy Conservation and Power, called the intended dissolution "short-sighted and ill-conceived." He was further irked at the administration for "secretly attempting to dismantle the Energy Department by ignoring congressional mandates." With the Democrats in control of Congress, Reagan's planned euthanasia of the Energy Department was doomed.

A year later, Edwards did end up on the South Carolina beaches, but it was because he, rather than the Energy Department, was scuttled.[4]

Lost Ground

Despite being thwarted in his plan to dissolve the Energy Department, Reagan was successful in squelching any progress in developing an energy policy to carry the nation into the twenty-first century and beyond.[5] Funding for energy conservation was slashed by more than 70 percent, contributing to the deterioration of energy efficiency in the mid-1980s after impressive gains in the late 1970s. Reagan reduced federal financial assistance for research and development of renewable energy resources by more than 85 percent. He also eliminated the tax incentives for development and use of solar energy and conservation in the residential sector. Not surprisingly, during Reagan's tenure in office, the United States lost its lead in the development and commercialization of advanced solar technology to Japan—a nation whose government heavily subsidized renewable energy research in the private sector.

Reagan sought to eliminate auto fuel efficiency standards altogether. He contended that they put American-made vehicles at a competitive price disadvantage to European and Japanese imports (even though many low-cost foreign models already offered superior fuel economy). While his abolition campaign did not succeed, it did manage to reduce fuel efficiency standards from 27.5 miles to 26 miles per gallon.

Woe to Regulation

This myopic disdain for conservation reflects one of the trademark characteristics of Reagan and the bashers who have followed in his wake: an intense distrust of regulations and the federal government that promulgated them. "I would do away with regulations that not only hamstring resources but tie industry down," Reagan vowed while campaigning in Alaska for his first term as president. "I think there has been some environmental extremism dictating policy from Washington for the last couple of years... people are ecology also."

Reagan's war on excessive regulation did strike a responsive chord in the American people during that campaign. Unfortunately, the public failed to notice or chose to suppress that the candidate was not making the same distinctions they were making between environmental protection rules and the red tape involved in paying taxes or obtaining a permit to start a business.

Reagan delegated the responsibility for scaling back pollution controls to his ideologically driven Environmental Agency administrator, Anne Gorsuch. But he discovered soon after taking office that public enthusiasm for deregulation did not extend to environmental safeguards. Americans associated environmental regulation with protection of public health. As such, they preferred to err on the side of caution, and their influence ultimately relegated Gorsuch's "reform" initiatives to the dust bin.

Yet Reagan was not completely ineffectual. While his discredited policies became the butt of jokes, there was nothing amusing about the slowdown he caused in efforts to upgrade environmental protection.

Cost-Benefit

A disadvantage that environmentalists constantly face, and bashers perpetually seek to exploit, is the difficulty in quantifying the benefits versus the costs of anti-pollution regulations. Benefits are often diffuse. Costs can usually be tabulated in neat numerical tables for all to see. That has made it easier for Reagan and his successors to dramatize the expense of pollution control while playing down or ignoring its virtues. It's a very one-sided presentation, but how do you pin down benefits based on injury that would occur if regulation were not in place?

Although we can't measure environmental protection rewards with precision, we know through anecdotal evidence and extrapolation that significant benefits do accrue. Environmentalists also have leverage in a society where personal and environmental health take precedence over short-term monetary profit. Ironclad proof of a pollution threat is not necessary to justify establishment of safeguards. Reasonable concern based on the weight of evidence prevails until and unless those being regulated can convincingly demonstrate a case for relaxing protections.

While the relative clarity of costs gives foes of regulation an initial advantage, their edge is ephemeral. It dissipates rapidly with the spread of education, and even faster if the regulation they decry fails to curtail serious pollution.

The Technological Fix

For Reagan and those who have followed in his footsteps, environmental salvation rests in tapping the creativity of the free marketplace. That is inherently a polluter-friendly philosophy. No one need worry about civilization mucking up the environment, because human beings' superior brain power will combine with the profit motive to create technology that repairs whatever wounds are inflicted upon the earth. Is it any wonder that this creed plays so well in so many corporate boardrooms?

Reagan's blind faith in the invincibility of technology was graphically illustrated in his opposition to the federal government's 1972 ban on DDT. "California is being eaten alive because the U.S. Fish and Wildlife Service refuses to allow the spraying of the swampy Tijuana River estuary," he told his radio audience seven years later. During another broadcast, he asserted that "DDT is harmless to human beings and poses no threat to animal, bird, or marine life. Yet it is banned on the theoretical grounds that it might, under some circumstances, some day, harm someone or something."

Actually, the pesticide's toxicity is highly persistent in the environment, posing a major threat to non-target creatures such as aquatic species and "good" insects whose predatory feasts are important natural controls on pest populations. DDT has also been conclusively linked to the thinning of waterfowl's eggshells as well as to cancerous growths in laboratory mice. Although no irrefutable connection has been established between DDT and human cancer, suspicions are mounting.[5] The Rohn and Haas Company in 1990 disclosed a troubling pattern of pancreatic cancer among employees who produced DDT at its Philadelphia plant from 1948 to 1973. You might have expected Reagan to be disturbed by the rising level of toxic DDT residue in human mothers' milk, even if uncertainty shrouded just how health-threatening the phenomenon actually was.

It may be difficult to document any direct human health benefit derived from the DDT ban. But there has been a conspicuous recovery of bald eagle and brown pelican populations, two species hard hit by toxic pesticide residue accumulated from the ingestion of contaminated fish and other prey. For the many scientists who consider these birds' fate an environmental harbinger of how *Homo sapiens* will fare, the winged creatures' comeback is a powerful vindication of the DDT prohibition.

Wealth Without Health

Reagan's unqualified endorsement of pesticides was a reflection of his ignorance of fundamental ecological principles, as well as evidence of his disturbing predilection to put public health at risk for the sake of commerce. Like most bashers, he never seemed to consider the ramifications of possessing wealth without health. In the case of synthetic chemical sprays, he did not appear to understand that insect pests' short life span accelerates the natural selection process, enabling a species constantly exposed to pesticides to develop immunity through mutation within the span of relatively few generations. Pests' growing resistance to chemical controls has led frustrated applicators to increase the concentrations they spread. While those dosages have a steadily diminishing effect on target species, that is unfortunately not the case for the rest of the ecosystem.

The pro-mercantile bias deeply ingrained in Reagan and most other bashers has led them to advocate that the individual consumer be required to show that a product with potentially lethal ingredients is dangerous before it can be removed from the marketplace. Forget about the manufacturer having to demonstrate beyond a reasonable doubt the item's safety before it can be placed on the shelves.

That outlook elevates balance sheets ahead of the balance of nature and plays to the illusory notion among many in affluent circles that they can buy their way out of the ubiquitous path of unregulated industrial pollution.

Holy Rollers

Reagan's obsessive contempt for the Endangered Species Act (ESA) is typical of the debunkers. Back in 1979, Reagan denounced the ESA as an "absurdity which gives priority to fish, weeds, and spiders regardless of the merits of any proposed project." To this day, critics of the law berate its neglect of the human condition and economic reality, and they are just as much out of sync with the facts.

The ESA does provide for consideration of economic concerns, but they are just one of a number of factors involved in the law's application. It is a statute whose consultation mechanism has worked well. In more than 99 percent of cases, federal authorities have averted conflicts between endangered species protection and the plans of private property owners at an early stage.

Implicit in Reagan's endangered species recriminations was a premise that has often been stated explicitly by the bashers: animal and plant species have no intrinsic worth; their value is calculated by their usefulness to human beings, and if this characteristic is not discernible, the species are deemed expendable.

This squares nicely with a view the vast majority of bashers have always held, namely that human beings are apart from the natural world rather than a part of it. The thinking reflects the influence of a literal interpretation of the Scriptures, an interpretation holding that the earth is an evil place that must be subdued and used for profitable purposes en route to eternal salvation.[6] Reagan's born-again Christian Interior Secretary, James Watt, was a leading proponent of this doctrine, which attracts ideological foes of the national environmental community like flies.

Among those who reject the doctrine are people familiar with elementary ecology and individuals who support the constitutional provision mandating separation of church and state.

As for the bashers who consider nature an extraneous force solely meant to be conquered, where were they when their high school biology teacher explained that *Homo sapiens* was part of a highly interdependent ecosystem? Why didn't they learn that every creature has a purpose, a niche? If an organism is suddenly eradicated, the loss will probably produce an adverse chain reaction within the ecosystem. Only if some other species can immediately fill the void will the disruption go relatively unnoticed.

By viewing people as part of nature rather than distinct from it, environmentalists are not denying the human race its cognitive superiority over other life forms. Indeed, that intellectual dominance combines with a sense of ethics to instill in humanity a special custodial responsibility to help other species on the planet survive as best they can. Rather than sacrilegious, the philosophy of inclusion is a profoundly spiritual response.

Bigger is Better

In his radio commentaries, Reagan sought to popularize another fallacy that remains an elementary part of the contemporary bashers' case against the Endangered Species Act. He made a distinction between preservation of large, well-known mammals and obscure species, the latter being dismissed as too insignificant to warrant our attention (or taxpayers' dollars). Reagan and company also complained about extending the ESA safety net to relatively plentiful similar sub-species of an animal or plant in danger of extinction.

These objections also reflect an appalling ignorance of basic biology. The tiny creatures and plants that bashers hold in such contempt actually form part of the foundation of the food chain on which we depend. Invertebrates, a frequent object of basher scorn, comprise approximately 90 percent of the estimated 10 million animal species on the planet.[7] Those repelled by the thought that we are a tiny minority on a planet swarming with bugs should think again. Virtually none of our crops will grow without the pollination and soil conditioning carried out by those invertebrates, primarily insects. If we really want to be cut down to proper size, we should keep in mind that all life on earth depends on millions of microscopic organisms known as bacteria to perform functions necessary for survival.

Bacteria and insects keep us from being inundated by our own waste. In the United States, where humans generate annually 130 million tons of organic waste and livestock contributes 12 million tons of manure, it's the smallest organisms of our planet that break down and eliminate virtually all of our excremental residue.[8]

Hence, tiny organisms at the bottom of the food chain merit our respect, not disdain. They have proved for millions of years that they can get along just fine without us, an independence that is not reciprocal. Every time we get hung up on size, we should remember that we could survive the extinction of the grizzly but not the demise of the earthworm.

Regarding the complaints about extending protection to sub-species when they are so similar to the main species in jeopardy, what about the urgent need to preserve genetic diversity? Differences in genetic makeup—even minor ones—provide some protection against an infectious disease wiping out an entire genus.

The Great Lockout

Reagan strove throughout his political career to provide the private sector with greater opportunity to exploit public lands. He bitterly complained about extractive industries being "locked out" of federally owned acreage by excessive regulation, even though his lament was not borne out by the facts. More than 80 percent of federal lands are accessible to industrial activities in varying degrees.

Unimpressed with Washington's generous dispensation, Reagan campaigned vigorously to increase offshore oil drilling, expand mining activity on federal tracts, and open up Alaskan wilderness to far more development than existing law allowed. The approach was consistent with his view that undeveloped land had no intrinsic worth and could only be valued by how much of its raw materials were subject to exploitation.

Happily, his ideas were not shared by most of the nation or by Congress, which stubbornly resisted his grandiose plans. Yet Reagan's legislative defeats did not mute his outbursts or discourage the disparagers who followed in his tracks. They continued to demand that the federal government strike "a better balance" between the environment and the economy in its management of public lands.

Reaganites were correct that a "better balance" was needed. The only problem was that they had the tilt wrong. Although bashers insist that economic development is not receiving its due, the industry-generated environmental degradation of federal lands suggests otherwise. It is environmental protection, not the economy, that needs to be elevated to achieve an equilibrium.

Perverse Privatization

Beyond Reagan's dissatisfaction with government management was an even more fundamental objection. He was upset that Washington was the landlord of public lands in the first place. His preferred alternative was privatization or, failing that, state and municipal ownership. "I think the federal government is land greedy and is hanging onto land it was never intended to hold onto," the presidential candidate told his radio audience. He made it sound as though the owners of federal property were not the American public but some faceless bureaucrats on the fifth floor of the Interior Department building in the nation's capital.

A nagging question arises from such federalphobia: If the private sector assumed management of public lands, what would happen to officially designated wilderness areas when money could only be made by changing the character of the region?

No Digging, No Value

"Putting timber into wilderness preservation," proclaimed radio commentator Reagan, "results in it being lost forever to productive use."

Bashers measure the physical value of any open space devoid of development only in terms of the potential for extraction of raw materials. Reagan and his ilk have difficulty ascribing any intrinsic worth to tranquility, aesthetics, or wildlife. That's why they don't regard non-consumptive uses of public lands—hiking, camping, bird watching, and the like—as reasons enough to keep terrain off-limits to development. This brings us back to their strict interpretation of the Scriptures. Earth is an entity to be conquered, not accommodated—a reading of the Bible that encourages exploitation of the planet with minimal restraint.

I noted previously that candidate Reagan did not conceal his intended environmental policy. It was just that no one took him seriously when he declared that, if elected president, he would "invite the coal and steel industry in to rewrite the Clean Air Act."

In the aftermath of victory, Reagan attempted to fulfill his pledge and undoubtedly would have succeeded if the national environmental movement and its allies hadn't successfully exposed his contemplated capitulation to industry. When widespread public and congressional condemnation followed, the administration was forced to pull back from its brazen collaborative effort with corporate polluters.

While the Reagan administration still managed to play havoc with the nation's environmental policy, the damage was not nearly so great as it would have been if the president had been given carte blanche.

Rose Garden Hypocrisy

Because Reagan did not initially pull any punches doesn't mean that he and those who subsequently adopted him as a role model were free of hypocrisy. He railed against big government encroaching on people's lives, yet he stood squarely for an abortion ban. What greater governmental invasion of an individual's privacy is there than for authorities to exert control over a woman's reproductive choices?

Moreover, while many bashers demand that, as a matter of conscience, the government enter the picture to save a fetus, they lose interest in officialdom playing any role once the birth occurs— even for an infant born to a household in desperate straits and needing outside assistance to survive.

Off the Deep End

You would think that some of Reagan's more bizarre environmental ramblings would give his heirs apparent pause. But rarely does one encounter bashers contradicting or disavowing the former president, an exercise in loyalty that may reinforce their sense of ideological purity but dramatically undermines their credibility.

How convincing can one be who links his or her destiny to an individual who, at one point in his presidential campaign, actually proclaimed pollution to be a form of therapy? "North Carolina's Great Smoky Mountains' haze comes from nitrogen oxide," Reagan announced one day to his radio listeners, "and some doctors think the air up there benefits tubercular patients."

Not content with casting nitrogen oxide as a respiratory palliative, Reagan asserted on another occasion that "natural oil off the Santa Barbara, California, coast also cures. The city used to advocate that winds blowing across oil slick water purified the air and prevented the spread of infectious disease." Maybe Reagan was just spoofing the environmental movement. He certainly was aware that there was no mad scramble to erect health spas on the summit of the Great Smokies or along the Santa Barbara coast.

Whatever the case, it was no laughing matter once he assumed office. Much to the delight of his *Fortune* 500 pals, he treated pollution, if not as a beneficial phenomenon, at least as a benign one.

Today's bashers have derived their inspiration from a political figure who transported the nation from the forefront to the back benches of global environmental activism and temporarily reversed anti-pollution progress in many domestic sectors. Their hero was responsible for the unconscionable blocking of legislation mandating the placement of warning labels on our exports of domestically banned toxic substances. He withheld funding for national park expansion and maintenance, and saw to it that the nation dragged its feet on strengthening acid rain controls. He drove dedicated and talented career public servants out of environmental agencies with his ideological war against the federal bureaucracy he was elected to administer.

In short, their idol was so environmentally destructive that, nearly a decade after his departure, the nation still hasn't fully recovered from his two-term reign.

9

THE MADAME OF MENDACITY: DIXY LEE RAY

While Ronald Reagan has provided the emotional inspiration for many contemporary environmental bashers, the late Dixy Lee Ray is their principal intellectual frame of reference.

In 1990 and 1993, Ray, former chairwoman of the Atomic Energy Commission, who also had been governor of the state of Washington and a college zoology professor, wrote heavily annotated books lambasting the national environmental movement for grossly exaggerating the ecological threats to humanity. A dominant theme was that environmentalists were relying on hysterical scare tactics rather than sound science to gain public support. Ray's texts fluctuate between straightforward factual examination of the better known environmental controversies and strident ideological advocacy in which she misrepresents her opponents to advance her agenda.

There is nothing wrong with scientists being advocates. They are simply expressing a viewpoint formed from the information accumulated in the course of their work. The only prerequisite is that they make clear when they are acting in that capacity, so there is no confusion between fact and opinion.

In her second book, *Environmental Overkill*, Dixy referred to the importance of scientists separating these two roles: "The rational assembling of evidence is the responsibility and business of science. But where the evidence warrants action plans, it's up to elected officials. This distinction is too seldom appreciated"[1] (especially, and ironically, by Dixy herself). After noting the difference between science and actual policymaking, she declared shortly thereafter that "politicians should only proceed on the basis of proven science ... and when scientists disagree, it's best to withhold judgment and avoid precipitous action."[2]

That is a prescription for "paralysis by analysis." It would reduce governments to virtual rigor mortis, since it's possible for politicians to find scientists on opposing sides of nearly every controversy. The prospect of bureaucratic gridlocks didn't particularly faze Ray because she—and most other environmental bashers—are suspicious of big government and would prefer to see its scope greatly diminished. The flagrant inconsistencies in her work did not seem to bother her either. Indeed, she appeared oblivious to the havoc they played with her credibility. Ray thus ended up presenting herself as either unwilling or unable to recognize the frequent conflict between the scientific objectivity she revered and her ideological correctness.

For example, in *Environmental Overkill* she wrote that "no one really knows if the world is warming up, and hence, it is best to withhold judgment...." Yet several pages later, there was Dixy declaring that no one disputes that "an increase in the concentration of greenhouse gasses will lead to increased warming."[3] She also asserted that "there is sufficient reason to protect much of the remaining swampy and estuarine areas...."[4] A noble but short-lived thought. Within three pages, she proclaimed that a choice must be made "either to preserve wetlands or protect public health. We can't have it both ways."

Why did Ray suddenly reverse field and decide that wetlands and public health were antithetical? She concluded that because wetlands were breeding grounds for mosquitoes and there were strict prohibitions on pesticides in the wild, the swamps must be drained if we were all not to fall victim to malaria, encephalitis and yellow fever. Funny, our nation still has a substantial number of wetlands, and DDT has been banned for 22 years, yet I don't recall any insect-transmitted epidemics ravaging our population in recent decades. That holds true even in the southernmost portion of our nation, where mosquitoes are a perennial presence. Could it be that effective sanitation and insect repellent are able to neutralize the threat of serious illness being transmitted by the bite of those ubiquitous blood suckers?

Whatever the answer, wetlands' positives overwhelm the negatives. Once scorned as dank, fetid pest holes, marshlands are now recognized as a treasure trove of important public health benefits, ranging from water purification and flood control to spawning grounds for the fisheries that contribute significantly to our diet.

That Ol' Debil Nature

Because Dixy was uncomfortable incriminating industry or any other source of manmade emissions as polluters, she conjured up a villainous natural resource on which to blame urban smog: "In places like Atlanta, Baton Rouge, Tampa, and Los Angeles, the natural production of hydrocarbons from trees and other vegetation far exceeds what we humans can be held responsible for."[5] (Now we see where Ronald Reagan was coming from!)

It's a specious argument that Ray and other environmental bashers raise time and again: ease off on criticizing human beings because their contamination of the planet is dwarfed by that of Mother Nature. If we accept that premise, are massive deregulation and unchecked laissez-faire far behind?

Dixy's vendetta against nature also triggered her schizophrenia. Only a few pages after identifying vegetation as primarily responsible for our smog-bound cities, she wrote "by planting lots of green growing plants downtown, we could bring to cities a breath of fresh air."[6]

Vacillation

Other examples of Ray's inconsistency permeate throughout her writings, but I shall limit myself to just a few of the most egregious examples. The historic international Earth Summit, held in Rio de Janeiro in June 1992, stuck in Ray's craw. This historic gathering, she declared, "operated on the premise that nature has been irreparably changed by industrialization ... and the only remedy is to reduce progress and economic growth in the industrialized world."[7]

If you think that she is ascribing an unduly misanthropic tone to the summit, you ain't heard nothin' yet. What of her assertion that the conference's overall goal was to "save the planet ... from human beings"? According to Ray, the diplomats from 174 countries who gathered in Rio were more interested in preserving trees and lower animal forms than mankind. Yet she dutifully deferred to the summit's final official declarations, of which the very first was "Human beings are at the center of concerns for sustainable development."

Although Dixy professed supreme confidence in human beings' technological prowess, her faith abruptly evaporated when solar power was at issue. She swiftly dismissed the idea of any breakthroughs to make solar energy cost-competitive with other energy alternatives.

Why was she so negative when she normally rhapsodized about the unlimited potential of human ingenuity? Her grossly inflated cost projections for solar photovoltaic cells suggested we were encountering a bias against any alternative that might eclipse nuclear energy, the technology with which she was most familiar and on whose viability she staked much of her professional reputation.

She was also conspicuously erratic on the acid rain issue. First, she cited approvingly a federal study that concluded "acid rain should be viewed as a long term problem requiring pollution controls."[8] Yet on the very next page, she attributed to the study director the response that no harm would come to lake and stream water quality if nothing were done to curb the phenomenon. Indeed, she declared, the facts show that regulations to reduce acid rain are "totally unnecessary and a waste of money."[9] If that were not enough exoneration, she claimed the study showed that acid rain actually benefited trees by adding nutrients to the soil.[10] Just when she would have us believe we should be turning our eyes heavenward in supplication to acid rain, she reported that the very same study director maintained that acid rain had a negative environmental effect.

We are witnessing ideological imperatives intruding upon rational thought processes and creating inconsistency that devolves into utter incoherence.

Federal Demons

As with most environmental bashers, Dixy was convinced that the federal government was more the source than the solution of society's woes. She loathed command and control regulations (as opposed to free market incentives), perceived raw nature as a frequent impediment to—rather than a building block of— economic growth, and maintained (in selective fashion) unswerving confidence in the supremacy of technology. She questioned why we should risk dampening the creativity of our producers by forcing them to provide assurance their merchandise was environmentally benign prior to its introduction in the marketplace. Better for the sake of industrial progress to require the public to demonstrate any suspected hazards of new products before such items are removed from the shelves. Sounds very much like the refrain of an unabashed shill for industry.

Ray's objectivity was also fatally compromised by an obsessive fear that world government would rob the United States of its sovereignty.

Straw Men

A favorite technique of Dixy's, and one constantly utilized by her successors, is to create straw men. All adversaries are depicted as holding extremist views that, in fact, only a tiny radical fringe espouses. If the bashers can succeed in linking mainstream opponents to viewpoints repugnant to virtually everyone, victory is a foregone conclusion.

In this vein, Dixy described the modern national environmental movement as "anti-development, anti-progress, anti-technology, anti-business, anti-established institutions, and above all, anti-capitalism."[11] About the only thing missing in this impassioned indictment was "pro-concentration camp."

None of those allegations were accompanied by corroborating documentation, because there isn't any. Sure, environmentalists often blame industrial activities for "fouling" the earth; but that is a far cry from maintaining that industrial progress must grind to a halt, which was the demand Dixy attributed to the Greens.[12]

One hates to disappoint Dixy and her disciples, but capitalism is very much a part of the environmentalists' game plan. The environmental community is relying heavily on industry's technological prowess to remedy much of the ecological mess produced by civilization's darker side.

Distortion A La Dixy

Ultimately viewing everything through an ideological prism, Ray becomes incapable of maintaining objectivity and treats as gospel every statement that coincides with her views. For instance, in her zeal to absolve industrial polluters from any disease-causing culpability, she asserted that "aside from a sharp increase in lung cancer caused by cigarette smoking, there have been no significant increases in the rate at which people die from any of the common forms of cancer over the last 50 years."[13]

This is just plain wrong, illustrating the pitfalls of trying to fit the facts to a premise rather than the other way around. The reality is that skin, breast, and colon cancer are all on the rise, with environmental factors, including some of industrial origin, considered prime suspects.

Back on the Farm

Ray denounced "organic farming" as a primitive technique, especially when compared to conventional, modern-day agriculture (which requires large infusions of synthetic pesticides and fertilizers). This badmouthing of organic farming is typical of the knee-jerk antagonism and suspicion that bashers display towards any lifestyle alternative championed by the environmentalists. Dixy falsely implied that organic farming eschews modern machinery, a slur in keeping with saying whatever it took to depict her target group as so hopelessly out of kilter that she would win her argument by default.

Just as misleading was her contention that organic agriculture was much less productive than its conventional counterpart. Consumed by ideological venom, there was no reason why she would pay heed to, much less inquire about, any late-breaking research. A pity, because in New Zealand, scientists contrasted seven organic farms' performance with that of nine nearby conventional farms between 1988 and 1992. The results: the organic farms not only were able to maintain their soils in better condition but were also usually more cost-efficient. Their higher labor costs were almost always offset by savings from not having to purchase expensive synthetic fertilizers, pesticides, and herbicides.

Hence, as a scientist who constantly admonished against making rash judgments, Dixie embarrassed herself by expressing the unqualified opinion that organic farming was incapable of meeting modern needs. Her rejection of this "natural" methodology seemed even more uninformed in the aftermath of a 1989 National Academy of Sciences report. It concluded that "well-managed organic farming reduces production costs and the risks of environmental and health damage without necessarily decreasing per acre crop yields, and in some cases, actually increasing them."

Oceanic Muddle

Despite Ray's degree in marine biology, her dissertation on oceanography was as flawed as her evaluation of agriculture. In *Trashing the Planet*, her first anti-environmental tome, she described the deep sea beds as deserts devoid of life.[14]

This was a desperate attempt to set the stage for a solution to the as-yet-insoluble problem of safely disposing of nuclear waste. She was trying to build a case that burial of wastes in the deep ocean floor would put all our worries to rest. In her haste to achieve her goal, she ran roughshod over scientific reality. Exploration with special cameras and sensing equipment has shown that there is an active biological community of worms and other microorganisms inhabiting the deep ocean floor.

Furthermore, the deep ocean bottom is not as stable as she would have us believe. It is subject to shifting as a result of currents and geological disturbances.

Asbestos

In a surge of anti-regulatory fervor, she attempted to persuade us that the hazards of airborne asbestos had been blown out of proportion. She argued that the soft asbestos known as chrysotile, which accounts for 95 percent of all the asbestos used in the United States, is "generally benign ... and not of itself, very dangerous."[15] This exoneration of asbestos as a health hazard has been recycled by many subsequent environmental detractors, eager to demonstrate how oppressive and unduly costly federal government regulation can be.

There's only one catch. Dixy's analysis was inaccurate. While the Environmental Protection Agency acknowledges some differences in toxicity of various asbestos fiber types, it notes that the data are inconclusive, and that there is no evidence whatsoever that chrysotile is harmless. On the contrary, indications are that chrysotile is less lethal than other types of asbestos only in cases of mesothelioma (chest tumors).

When it comes to lung cancer and asbestosis, there is little empirical difference between chrysotile and other asbestos fibers as causative factors. A 1990 study conducted for the U.S. Public Health Service is even more incriminating. It states: "statistically significant increases in lung cancer mortality have been reported in workers exposed primarily to chrysotile."[16]

In the Eye of the Beholder

As we have seen, the moment Dixy encounters statements, data, or conclusions that coincide with her ideological viewpoint, she accepts them as unassailable truths. Hence, in a tirade against environmentalists' opposition to runaway population growth, she treated as gospel some scandalous rumors that came her way. She accused environmental activists of trying to ruthlessly impose de facto birth control by seeking bans on various pesticides that would normally curb fatal insect-borne diseases.

To back up her charges, Ray alleged that Dr. Charles Wurster, chief scientist for the Environmental Defense Fund (EDF) in

1971, declared that there were too many people on earth and that a DDT ban was "as good a way as any to get rid of them."[17] She even claimed he made similar remarks while testifying in Congress before the House Agriculture Committee that same year.

Alas, Wurster never uttered those words. Nor did he appear before the House Agriculture Committee. If Ray had taken the trouble to investigate, she would have discovered that the quote she attributed to Wurster was actually the words of Victor Yannacone. He was a disgruntled individual who had been dismissed from EDF's board of trustees and, in a fit of pique against the organization, held a press conference where he attributed those scurrilous remarks to Wurster. Yannacone's accusation was picked up by several local newspapers and, despite Wurster's subsequent denial, took on a life of its own, becoming part and parcel of the environmental bashers' folklore.

The Sorcerer's Apprentice

A Gallup Poll conducted for the Center for Science, Technology and Media in November 1991 is another example of environmental bashers' penchant for recycling misinformation to bolster their ideological crusade.[18] In an essay trashing Vice President Gore, columnist George Will cited the poll as evidence that a majority of the world's climatologists doubted the validity of the global warming theory and thus disagreed with the vice president. Gore, after all, insists that an overwhelming scientific consensus subscribes to the presence of the greenhouse effect.

Will most likely learned of this poll through the assertions of Ray, Rush Limbaugh, and other bashers who made the survey a cause celebre in their debunking of the threat of global warming. Yet in examining the precise language of the poll, one finds that the environmental bashers are severely distorting the survey's results. In actuality, the poll reveals that scientists are uncertain about the extent, but not the existence, of the problem. Approximately two-thirds of the 400 respondents did believe that the greenhouse effect was occurring, and 90 percent answered that human-induced global warming was under way.

One final note relating to that poll: While not all the 400 Gallup respondents were climatologists, the several hundred members of the Inter-Governmental Panel on Climate Change are. They represent a collection of the top weather scientists in the world, and in that capacity, they have concluded that the greenhouse effect is real enough to warrant some precautionary remedial action.

Dixy's proclivity towards overstating her case was not restricted to polling results. She warned that, without human intercession, nature would soon cripple the world's food-producing capacity.[19] One wonders how she would explain the era when humans were essentially hunters and gatherers. Despite little in the way of human intervention, the planet's crop-producing capacity did not wither.

Ray's supposed culprit in this instance was no culprit at all. On the contrary, natural processes are the cornerstone of the world's entire food supply. She would have been on firmer ground if she had maintained that, without a boost from technology, it would be difficult for the natural resource base that underwrites modern food production to keep pace with a burgeoning humanity's nutritional needs.

The Art of Malignment

Ray and her disciples revel in character assassination of their opposition. "Activist environmentalists are mostly white, middle-to-upper income, and predominantly college-educated," she declared. "They are distinguished by a vocal do-good mentality that sometimes successfully cloaks their strong streak of elitism, which is often coupled with a belief that the end justifies the means and that violence and coercion are appropriate tactics ... They also tend to believe that nature is sacred and technology is sacrilege."[20]

This characterization is a grotesque misrepresentation, designed to turn mainstream America against the environmental movement. To begin with, Dixy's clock evidently stopped ticking back in the early 1970s, when middle-class Caucasians probably did constitute a majority of environmental activists. In the last decade, a massive grass-roots environmental movement has emerged, encompassing many people from economically depressed communities, which tend to be most exposed to serious pollution threats. One would have to be wearing thick ideological blinders not to recognize the spread of environmental activism to all strata of society.

Turn the Other Cheek

Ray's assertion that environmentalists "often sanction violence and coercion as appropriate tactics" is defamatory poppycock. The environmental movement evolved from the same non-violent tradition as the civil rights movement and, with rare exceptions, has limited its expressions of protest to peaceful demonstrations and courtroom challenges. Dixy sought to confer guilt through association by contending that the organization Earth First, which she labeled an "ecology terrorist group," was representative of the vast majority of environmental activists. Earth First's aim, she warned, "is coercive and its recommended actions subversive."

Dixy was disingenuous in lumping this fringe group with the environmental mainstream. Furthermore, she overstated the radical nature of the organization. Civil disobedience, not bloodletting, remained its tactic of last resort. Earth First founder Dave Foreman, whom Dixy excoriated for allegedly encouraging sabotage of roads, pipelines, and just about anything else to do with civilization, scoffed at the oft-repeated charge that the organization advocates reverting to a primitive existence. "I like my wine, good books, and symphony," he confided.[21]

What Earth First does preach, Foreman contended, is living in harmony with natural systems, a lifestyle that doesn't entail rubbing sticks together to start a fire or taking up residence in caverns. It's a blueprint in which modern cities have a place alongside restored and preserved ecosystems, with buffer zones to halt any advance by the urbanized edges of civilization. For many, that is hardly a radical notion.

Ray's accusation that Earth Firsters (and other environmentalists) are anti-technology is another bum rap. It prompted

Foreman to note, "there's good technology and bad technology." The trick is to differentiate between the two.

Blood and Tears

Environmentalism has been notable for its pacifist orientation. Unfortunately, the same cannot be said of at least some who count themselves as its enemy. A recent survey conducted by the San Francisco-based Center for Investigative Reporting found that, from 1988 to 1992, there were 100 acts of violence and/or harassment perpetrated against environmentalists throughout the nation. The attacks included shootings, stabbings, fire bombings, and muggings. Although no Greens were killed, the incidents far exceeded in numbers and severity the handful of militant acts committed against polluters and other debasers of nature by a few unbalanced eco-extremists.

One explanation for that huge disparity: The violent reaction that environmentalists sometimes provoke often stems from their campaigns against corporate polluters that are major employers in the surrounding community. Few things can set off an individual more than the perception that his or her livelihood is being placed in jeopardy because of someone else's quixotic whims.

Don't mistake environmentalists' crusade against pollution as opposition to modern technology. Technological progress is a cornerstone of mainstream environmentalism's utopian vision, as long as the progress is ecologically benign, reliant on the sustainable use of natural resources, and consistent with qualitative rather than quantitative values.

Nature in the Raw

Dixy's and her acolytes' opportunistic habit of shifting back and forth on issues when it suits their purpose is reflected in how they relate to nature. On one hand, the natural world is a phenomenon subordinate to humanity, an entity without intrinsic value; its worth can only be measured by the amount of benefits *Homo sapiens* derives from harnessing it.

On the other, there are times when Ray and her crowd conclude that it is to their advantage to depict nature as omnipotent, far beyond the control of humanity, and comprised of violent forces whose impacts greatly eclipse any environmental damage inflicted by mankind.

This perspective also serves as a rationale for laissez-faire. If our planet has survived the enormous pollution of Mother Nature this long, how can our relatively minor disruption of the environment be cause for alarm? It's the dream argument for any chief executive officer of a corporate polluter: regulation should be relaxed because pollutants emitted are too minuscule in the scheme of things to make any difference. No wonder environmental bashers receive a far warmer reception from the *Fortune* 500 than from the general public.

Dixy defended timber harvesting in old growth forests by declaring that trees go through "a life cycle of growth, maturity, old age and death ... whether humans are present or not."[22] In other words, the timber is going to be harvestable at some point no matter what we do, so why let it go to waste?

To appreciate the bashers' hemming and hawing in this area, consider the following. In the very next paragraph, she reversed her field and argued that much of the natural forest would never reach maturity *without* human intervention (i.e., chopping down trees). "Management by neglect has brought our national forests to a condition where vast areas are being destroyed by bugs and disease."[23] Either way, harvesting would be a blessing. As usual, Dixy tried to have it both ways.

Counter Balance

When public concern arose over the pervasive use of highly poisonous and persistent synthetic pesticides, Governor Ray countered that we were ingesting many more natural toxins in our food without noticeable injury.[24] Here she borrowed from the highly controversial, and I might add dubious, theories of Dr. Bruce Ames, whose outlook has made him the authoritative source for the chemical industry crowd and their supporters. Ames contends that since the human body has been able to absorb natural toxins without evidence of any direct harm over the ages, exposure to a little more of the same sorts of poison, albeit of a synthetic kind, won't make much of a difference.

Yet the argument can be turned against Ames and Ray. Evolution has enabled human beings to acquire genetic resistance to natural carcinogens in food. Unfortunately, we haven't had hundreds of thousands of years to build up immunity to the plethora of synthetic pesticide products flooding the market and infiltrating the grocery shelves.

But more than evolution challenges Ames' thesis. Dr. Devra Davis, a noted cancer epidemiologist and senior adviser to the assistant secretary of Health and Human Services, notes that foods containing the natural carcinogens decried by Ames also possess very potent anti-cancer agents that seem to neutralize any toxic effects.

Broccoli is a noteworthy example. An extract from the vegetable has been found to reduce tumors in laboratory rats. Davis cites other empirical evidence of nature's success in warding off its own poisons. She points out that vegetarians have below-average cancer rates, smokers who eat vegetables have lower rates of cancer than smokers who don't, and a study undertaken in China has found that people who consume a lot of garlic and onions have less incidence of stomach cancer.

Evolution can also be a palliative on a far grander scale. Note, for example, how the earth's ecosystems have adapted to natural pollution over the ages. Beyond the threshold created by evolution, however, the margin of safety may be very slight. Even a small increase in manmade pollutants could be enough to throw things out of sync, especially since the change is bound to occur abruptly and in relatively concentrated form. Hence, we should derive no solace from Dixy's scoffing at the relatively modest degree of radiation, greenhouse gases, and other pollutants we discharge into the environment compared to what nature herself emits.[25]

Homenis

"Homenis" is the concept that any substance is capable of being lethal if administered in a large enough dose, and Ray seized upon it to promote her point of view. "Even seemingly benign or necessary substances, such as water, can be toxic if taken in large enough doses," Dixy intoned. (Lethal, yes. Toxic, no! It's the quantity of potable water, not the content, that can kill.)

By stressing that everything can be dangerous, Ray hoped to advance the converse hypothesis that, at sufficiently low concentrations, virtually every substance is harmless. If she could have persuaded the public of that rationale, she would have dramatically weakened the underlying premise for what she deemed to be the gallingly excessive regulation of toxic substances. Those rules are based on the principle that prolonged exposure to low levels of highly poisonous substances can have a cumulative adverse effect.

Some denigrators of the environmental movement, eager to make an even more dramatic case that low doses of any substance are non-lethal, try to portray the chemical world as monolithic. They insist that an overdose of even the most innocent substances will cause cancer. In fact, approximately 80 percent of the substances that have so far been tested have proven not to be carcinogens. Ingesting them in excessive amounts may make you sick, but it won't trigger a malignancy.

Nuclear Apologist

As a former chairman of the Atomic Energy Commission (AEC), Ray was partial to the nuclear power industry. Indeed, she staked much of her reputation on nuclear power eventually becoming the foundation of the nation's energy mix.

As you might expect, her assessment of the energy picture was that "by any measure except in public relations, nuclear power is an unparalleled success." With a statement like that, it's hard to imagine how Dixy could retain any credibility whatsoever. She ignored the American business community's complete lack of confidence in the economic future of nuclear power, as evidenced by the absence of orders for new nuclear generating facilities since 1973.[26] How could she be oblivious to the meltdown of Russia's Chernobyl plant and the suffering it spawned? What possessed her to dismiss the Three Mile Island accident in this country as an incident "in which escaped radioactivity harmed no living creature and caused no environmental damage?"[27] Surely she was well aware of the adverse symptoms experienced by individuals in the vicinity of the nuclear facility shortly after the accident.

The fact is she could not resist exploiting a phenomenon that plays to environmental bashers' temporary advantage, especially in the eyes of the gullible and uninformed. Cancer resulting from exposure to radioactive and other toxic pollutants usually has a lengthy latency period (anywhere from 10 to 30 years). During that time, critics such as Dixy could thus cite the absence of the disease as "proof" that environmentalists' warnings were overblown.

Reviling Renewables

Complementing Ray's advocacy of nuclear power was her dismissal of the idea that renewables could make any meaningful contribution to the nation's overall energy picture. She contended that solar, wind, geothermal, biomass, and the like supplied less than one percent of the nation's electricity (conveniently excluding from the renewable mix our country's hydropower, which she admitted contributed about 4 percent to the total picture). That, according to Ray, left nuclear responsible for 20 percent and fossil fuel for 75 percent of our electricity. Her numbers were incorrect. If hydro is included, renewables are currently providing eight percent of our country's electricity.

The demeaning of renewables didn't stop there. For one who put so much stock in the technological genius of *Homo sapiens*, Dixy was curiously downbeat about the prospects for wind power. She perceived "significant problems" associated with wind and expressed doubt that it would ever produce substantial amounts of electricity.[28] This despite global wind energy potential amounting to roughly five times current world electricity use (and that's without locating such facilities in environmentally sensitive areas).[29] As of 1994, the U.S. wind industry was already generating approximately 3 billion kilowatt hours annually, enough power to satisfy the electricity demand of a million Americans.[30]

Ray was also pessimistic about solar power.[31] "Solar generated electricity is not a practical alternative for producing large amounts of electricity" she proclaimed. Yet even now, all of our nation's electricity needs could be met by solar plants spread over 20,000 square kilometers, an area roughly one-tenth the size of that occupied by all our domestic military bases.[32] Might not technological refinements reduce even that modest space requirement? Of course! And what of the growing commercialization of photovoltaic solar cells over the past decade? It's not even mentioned by Ray.

Perhaps most spurious of all, she played a semantic shell game in her discussion of energy policy. By referring only to electricity, she made nuclear power seem as though it had greatly surpassed renewables in our energy brew. But electricity comprises only about 43 percent of the nation's energy picture. Heating, cooling and horsepower directly from fossil fuels and renewables constitute the remainder.

Indeed, if we look at the total picture of energy production, the roles of nuclear and renewables are just the reverse of Ray's description of them. The renewables that Dixy deemed too exotic to exploit in any significant manner provide about 12 percent of the nation's energy, compared to nuclear with less than an eight percent share.

Dixy also neglected to mention the following: If national policy were more supportive of development of the alternative energy industry, renewables technology could provide at least 25 percent of new or replacement electric and thermal capacity and transportation fuels by the year 2005, according to Dr. Donald Aiken, Chairman of the American Solar Energy Society.[33]

Benefit of the Doubt

Nowhere are Dixy and her environment-bashing cohorts more obviously apologists for industry than when they argue against taking action to remedy pollution hazards until every last nuance of a highly suspect situation is understood. "Whenever there is a clear difference of opinion among scientific experts, the conclusion must be that no one really knows. And when no one knows, it is best to withhold judgment and avoid precipitous action," Dixy counseled.[34] In plain language, she would procrastinate even in the face of a public health situation in which the threat was palpable and the weight of evidence gave reason not to tarry.

To require that people be dropping in their tracks and that their demise be linked conclusively to an environmental hazard before mandating any mitigation on the polluter's part would certainly appeal to an unscrupulous business executive. It would give suspected corporate polluters the benefit of the doubt. Companies would be able to defer pollution abatement expenditures, thereby enhancing their profit margins, quite possibly at the expense of public health. We would face virtual abandonment of pollution prevention at the source and spiral toward anarchy in the marketplace.

Most Americans, I believe, reject such a policy on principle. If anything is going to be put at risk in their scheme of things, let it be dollars rather than lives.

Of course, if you can minimize the environmental risk with little or no economic penalty, all the better. But protection of public health and the biosphere takes precedence. That's where the "precautionary principle," a basic tenet of environmentalism, comes into play. It goes like this: Faced with an unproven environmental threat that possesses catastrophic potential, it's better to err on the side of caution, especially when the preventive strategy makes good sense in its own right. The precautionary principle is ready-made for the global warming controversy, which is why the environmental bashers' plea to temporize our response to climate change draws scant public attention and even less public support.

Since when is preventive medicine a scourge? What are the basic steps being advocated to minimize a precipitous rise in global average temperature and its potentially calamitous impacts on the earth's weather patterns and ecosystems?

Two basic strategies are being advocated to moderate climate change: utilizing energy far more efficiently in both the industrial and residential sectors, and engaging in a massive reforestation effort. Add energy efficiency's cost-effectiveness to reforestation's benefits of improved soil conditioning, air and water quality, enhanced recreational opportunities, timber availability, and aesthetic backdrops—and we can't go wrong. That holds, even if fears of global warming ultimately prove unfounded.

Yet environmental bashers maintain that economic growth would be stifled by streamlining manufacturers' operations and recalibrating our energy usage to obtain more with less. Their deductive reasoning defies logic, but logic never was their forte anyway.

Diddling with Dioxin

Dixy's view that we overreacted to the potential threat of highly toxic dioxins was another of her crapshoots with public health. She asserted that the forced evacuations of the dioxin contaminated communities of Love Canal and Times Beach were driven by hysteria—because "no deaths or serious harm to humans can be attributed to dioxin."[35] If that were the case, why did Occidental Petroleum Corporation agree to pay New York state $98 million to settle a lawsuit regarding contamination at Love Canal? No one, including the chemical companies charged with responsibility for the canal pollution, disputed that there were at least acute short-term health effects, such as severe skin rashes and bruises, resulting from excessive exposure to dioxin.

Secondly, there is enough circumstantial evidence to classify dioxin as a suspected carcinogen and justify the cleanup of contaminated sites, such as Love Canal. Among the evidentiary findings: A 1991 National Institute of Occupational Safety and Health study of more than 5000 U.S. workers exposed daily to dioxin found a 50 percent higher incidence of lung cancer and soft-tissue sarcoma than in the general population.

The dioxin controversy affirms the wisdom of the precautionary approach. In the early summer of 1994, less than a year after Ray's last skeptical tract was published, the U.S. EPA released a comprehensive study indicating that even low-dose dioxin was much more of a significant causative factor of cancer, reproductive failure, and weakened immune systems than originally thought.

Penny Wise, Pound Foolish

Environmental bashers routinely cite the imposition of allegedly prohibitive costs on business as justification for their anti-regulatory posture. Whether it's dioxin, asbestos, radon, acid rain—you name it—the message is that the expense of curbing these pollutants far outweighs the benefits. Trouble is, the bashers have a nasty habit of inflating the costs and either understating or ignoring the benefits altogether.

Ray quoted a "world-famous" economist, Wayne Gray, as declaring that 30 percent of the drop in industrial productivity in the 1970s and 1980s was due to the regulatory costs imposed by EPA and Occupational Safety and Health Administration (OSHA) rules. Gray's credibility—and by extension Dixy's—suffer grievously with the disclosure that industrial productivity actually rose during those two decades. Even more damaging are statistics showing that, over a period of time, environmental regulation actually improve industrial productivity and competitiveness, according to a U.S. Commerce Department-commissioned study.[36]

The environmental bashers' panacea for industrial pollution is the technological fix. If we're mucking up the planet, not to worry: our scientific genius will extricate us by finding a way to clean up and reinvent what was destroyed. That, in turn, provides a rationale for being more tolerant of industrial operations that are rough on the ecosystem, especially if they turn a handsome profit and create jobs.

The fundamental flaw in this technological-fix nostrum is that it does not possess the infallibility that bashers attribute to it. Scientists, inventors, and technicians can work wonders, but they are ultimately subject to limits imposed by the finite nature of the world's natural resources (even though, happily, some of these resources are renewable).

Technological advances can also sometimes produce unforeseen secondary consequences that are not only undesirable but may ultimately dwarf or even nullify the primary benefits.

Too Good Nature(d)?

Dixy revealed the chief bane of her professional existence two-thirds of the way through her tome *Environmental Overkill*, when she described "government by regulation" as the embodiment of "tyranny" and the "essence of environmental overkill."[37] That's pretty strong language, considering that regulation is the means by which the government enforces the laws of the land. What alternative to rulemaking would the bashers suggest? Flowery proclamations pleading for cooperation? Exhortations appealing to our nobler instincts? Non-binding recommendations relying on good will and voluntary compliance? Human nature being what it is, there are simply times we can't control our baser instincts without external constraints.

The bashers' wrath is not so much directed at Congress, which is constitutionally mandated to write laws. Rather, it is aimed at the executive branch, which is charged with upholding them.

Ray often made it sound as though unelected federal regulators have no right to promulgate rules. But the Constitution and Congress have vested in the executive branch the authority to issue regulations implementing the various statutes. Lawmakers recognized they could not micro-manage federal agencies.

Just so the executive branch won't become too autocratic, the federal bureaucracy's rules are subject to public review, congressional modification, and legal challenge by affected parties. Nonetheless, the way bashers often tell it, the White House is an omnipotent potentate acting in a vacuum. Such incendiary rhetoric stems from Dixy and Company's dissatisfaction with government's role in shaping our lives. In their view, we would be far better off guided by the ebb and flow of the marketplace.

What's Good for the Goose...

Governor Ray was so obsessed with discrediting big government and its regulatory infrastructure that she succumbed to the very shortcomings she imputed to her adversaries. "Scientists who value their standing in their peer community will be cautious not to overstate, and they feel compelled to provide context for what they say," she preached.[38] "Discount any unsupported assertions, even if they come from an environmental authority."[39] Good advice, but contrary to her own modus operandi, which usually accepted as gospel any undocumented allegations consistent with her ideology.

Her prose is also riddled with name-calling unaccompanied by any supporting evidence. Ray dismissed environmental activists as alarmists who shouted "cover-up" or "whitewash" at the first signs of any dispassionate peer review of their claims. She also complained that environmental activists employed political pressure to keep their work from undergoing exhaustive scrutiny but, again, examples were conspicuously lacking.

If environmental lawyers and lobbyists were operating from such a flimsy scientific base, how did Dixy explain their astonishing record of success against batteries of high-priced industry attorneys and influence peddlers in arguments before the courts and Congress? Was she suggesting that our judicial and legislative branches were on the take or victims of a massive Ponzi scheme?

The former scenario seems laughable; if officials were seeking under-the-table payoffs, they'd be largely wasting their time with environmental organizations, which operate on shoestring budgets. A far more likely source of graft would be the corporate world, which has the resources to buy and sell the environmental movement a thousand times over.

Acceptance of the latter scenario would be tantamount to alleging that our political system lacks the capability to weigh the evidence and then act in a prudent and equitable manner. In essence, Ray would be contending that our democratic form of government was dysfunctional.

Media Bias

Dixy also railed against the media, denouncing them for citing environmental experts as authorities without identifying precisely what their credentials were. Obviously, every time a person is quoted, there is not enough space to print his or her curriculum vitae. Furthermore, in most cases, the environmental authority is so well known that further elaboration is unnecessary.

The same could not be said for Dixy's sources, many of whom were dredged up from well-deserved anonymity to embroider her ideological party line.

Even more bizarre was her summation of environmentalism. The movement is not, she exclaimed, "about facts and logic. ... No amount of scientific proof, however decisive it may seem to a scientist, will influence or change the minds of those [environmentalists] who hold deeply felt beliefs."[40]

The Greens, in her view, operated from emotionalism, spreading misinformation through "self-appointed experts" and "spokesmen." Ray then proceeded to lay out an incriminating bill of particulars that any impartial observer would find far more applicable to her own behavior than that of her adversaries.

Beloved DDT

Dixy was insistent that "science must persist in its constant research for the truth, without itself falling victim to the convictions that arise from preconceived beliefs."[41]

Yet preconceived beliefs are what she is all about, her debunking of the United States' 22-year-old DDT ban being a case in point. To Ray, the ban was a manifestation of bureaucratic overkill from the start. "DDT was the first, best, and most remarkable of modern pesticides," she proclaimed. "Its history is a tale of triumph that ended in tragedy.[42]

This "miraculous" pesticide that, according to Dixy, had "never been demonstrated to harm a soul,"[43] was banned in 1972 throughout the United States except in cases of extreme emergency. The restraints also had a chilling effect on DDT use in certain other parts of the world, especially those that relied heavily on the United States for financial assistance.

That was more than Dixy could bear. She asserted that because of DDT's demise, a massive resurgence of malaria occurred overseas. Moreover, she predicted that significant outbreaks would ultimately erupt in this country's southern tier, where the climate permits mosquitoes to breed virtually year-round.

Well, malaria did make a comeback overseas, and it happened in the presence of DDT. As for our own country, four years after

Ray's prediction that malaria would sweep across a DDT-deprived southland (and 22 years since the ban went into effect), all's quiet on the southern front.

If she had bothered to check her facts as thoroughly as she demanded that other scientists do, Ray would have discovered that malaria was rebounding in many places despite DDT, thanks to a buildup of resistance to the toxin among disease-transmitting mosquitoes. In fact, 51 out of 60 malaria-carrying mosquito species throughout the world had developed varying degrees of immunity to the pesticide by 1985. Some of the little devils even began to alter their behavior so as to land on the underside of leaves, where pesticide applications rarely penetrated.

One deleterious consequence of DDT losing its effectiveness was that frustrated applicators began increasing the amount they introduced into the environment. All that accomplished, however, was contamination of the ecosystem with a pesticide that was causing ever-decreasing disruption to target species and increasing damage to birds, fish, and beneficial insects.

How could there have been so many adverse consequences when Dixy had assured us that DDT had never caused any harm? Even if one attributed her choice of words to poetic license, scientists are supposed to deal in hard facts in making their case. As far back as 1975, scientists found DDT to be highly toxic to most aquatic life, even at low concentrations.[44]

Contrary to Governor Ray dismissing the thinning of birds' eggshells and subsequent reproductive failure as a natural phenomenon, researchers have detected a distinct connection between exposure to the insecticide and breeding disruption. Museum shells and collected bird eggshells have displayed a marked thickness decline corresponding with the 30-year period of DDT usage in this country. There is also a correlation between the degree of shell thinning and the amount of DDT residues in eggs and birds. In addition, shells have begun returning to normal thickness since the suspension of virtually all DDT applications.[45]

Dixy's misguided gilding of the DDT lily persisted nonetheless. Her contention that DDT did not linger in the environment was belied by the fact that the compound's degradation in soil was typically very slow, with half-life values of 10 years or more not uncommon. In fact, DDT and its derivatives still survive in some of our nation's soils, waters, and wildlife, as well as in human tissue, 22 years after the ban went into effect.[46]

Although such persistence alone would seem cause for concern, Dixy still maintained that the DDT threat was grossly inflated. She chose to ignore that the chemical compound had been found to cause tumors in laboratory testing of mice. Most unsettling of all, where the presence of the insecticide's long-lasting derivative DDE had been detected at high levels in women's blood, a statistically significant link to breast cancer was discovered.

Just the Facts, Ma'am

All Dixy's causes celebres contained flat-out errors of commission as well as omission. Whether a deliberate distortion or the result of sloppy research, it was a harsh indictment of her scientific competence and veracity.

DDT serves as an excellent illustration. Dixy accused the EPA of imposing a total ban in 1972. Wrong! Domestic usage was allowed in emergency public health situations, and export of the pesticide was—and is—still permitted. EPA administrator Bill Ruckelshaus's decision to remove DDT from most sectors of the market was not a snap judgment.[47] After he and his staff reviewed reams of documentation and testimony for several months, the administrator concluded that Americans would be better off without DDT because of its "persistence, transport, biomagnification, toxic effects, and absence of benefit in relation to availability of effective and less environmentally harmful substitutes."

Those were not sufficient motives for banning DDT, as far as Dixy was concerned. She speculated that it was all a diabolical plot by environmentalists to curb population growth: no DDT, more mosquitoes, more malaria, more deaths, fewer people.

A simple fact eluded her: There is no linear relationship between DDT use and a decrease of mosquitoes, once the insects acquire immunity. How paranoid could she get?

Maligning Science

Taking their cue from Ray, contemporary bashers constantly misrepresent environmental activists as being "anti-technology." But it's not technology per se that environmentalists oppose (indeed, they stake much of the future upon it), it's the abuse of technology.

The bashers portray environmental activists as doomsdayers. In fact, it's the activists who are the optimists and visionaries. They believe in the human potential to create a better, biologically sustainable world, and they offer a sweeping, detailed blueprint for achieving that goal. It's really the bashers who are a depressing, pessimistic lot, downplaying the existence of problems that—left to their own devices—could become not only monumental in scope but irreversible in character.

10

THE PRINCE OF PONTIFICATION: RUSH LIMBAUGH

On the book jacket of Dixy Lee Ray's 1993 anti-Green diatribe *Environmental Overkill* is a revealing testimonial from conservative radio talk-show host Rush Limbaugh: "A way must be found to get this book into the hands of as many Americans as possible. The myths promulgated by militant environmentalists are now accepted as fact by far too many who are ripe for a cure for this so-called crisis—a 'cure' which will actually rob them of much of their economic and political freedom. Dixy Lee Ray challenges the environmental prophets of doom and gloom with penetrating, searing truth. *Environmental Overkill* is a bright light that exposes the fraud and deceit being perpetrated against an unknowing public."

Clearly, Dixy and Rush deserve each other, and the American people deserve neither. After wading through only a few pages of Limbaugh's environmental writings, one can't help thinking that Rush should drop whatever he is doing and head straight to the nearest junior high school for crash courses in elementary biology and environmental science. The guy is essentially clueless about the subject matter he is addressing, and on the occasions when common sense alone should carry the day, he is too ideologically driven to pay heed to logic.

It's actually easier to dispense with him than with some less recognizable environmental bashers whose basic understanding of ecology at least initially lends some credence to their assertions, even to an informed audience. One usually finds factual errors "liberally" sprinkled throughout conservative Limbaugh's environmental essays, often as a result of his blindly resurrecting discredited arguments of fellow ideologues. No matter how sullied the credentials of self-styled experts, if their conclusions reinforce Limbaugh's intransigent right-wing philosophy, they become an unimpeachable source for his broadcasts and books. Rather hypocritical for someone who berates much of the mainstream media for not thoroughly checking the facts before publishing them.

Fair Weather Friend

If further evidence is required that Limbaugh is no beacon of consistency, when the "liberal" media produce a story that he deems useful for furthering his cause, he treats it as indisputable fact. Under his manipulative approach, *The New York Times* can change in a split second from a mouthpiece for bleeding heart liberals to the voice of authority.

None of this should come as a surprise from a professional polemicist with a penchant for environmental half-truths and innuendo. Ideologues such as Limbaugh are more interested in extracting a sharply etched, self-serving moral from an environmental controversy than verifying whether the message is grounded in fact. They start from a preconceived notion and then seek (or twist) facts to substantiate it, as opposed to the far more arduous and honest process of gathering data and then drawing a conclusion. Keep in mind that when the solution precedes the problem, a simplistic and thus misleading interpretation of complex events is often the result.

No Middle Ground

Given the ideological glue that binds environmental bashers together, it's no small wonder that they feed off each others' straw men, gross exaggerations, false dichotomies, and blatant misrepresentations. Because environmental deterioration can be an insidiously slow process not readily visible to the naked eye, it plays right into Limbaugh's overly simplistic view of the issues. He can scan a deceptively placid horizon and crow, "See, I told you so." The ecological rube generates a certain appeal by adopting an all-or-nothing stance. An environmental threat exists only if it's obvious and unequivocally proven. Otherwise, stop fussing over some extremists' delusion, roll back the regulation, and dispense with expensive compliance expenditures. Such a tack can be irresistible to uninformed individuals with little patience for complexity and a modicum of concern about the future.

Even the more contemplative among us find it hard at times to resist the temptation of simplistic answers in a complex world, so we shouldn't be shocked that Limbaugh's pitch evokes an initial sympathetic response in many quarters. The good news is that this response is not a deeply ingrained one, nor does it bear up well when subjected to extended scrutiny and reflection.

True Lies

It's obviously much easier to belittle Limbaugh when his statistics are flat out contradicted by existing conditions.

In his first "masterpiece," *The Way Things Ought To Be*, he declares that he "doesn't believe that the earth and her ecosystem are fragile, as many radical environmentalists do."[1] He later goes on to say "the earth is a remarkable creation and is capable of great rejuvenation. We can't destroy it. It can fix itself."[2] Remarkable creation? Without a doubt. Capable of dramatic recovery? Certainly. We can't destroy it? Nonsense. It can fix itself? Sometimes, but in many instances the process will take centuries.

One wonders whether Limbaugh, on his recent trip to Israel, had an opportunity to visit the Negev and Sinai deserts, which were reduced to their barren state by poor agricultural practices in Biblical times. As we have seen from Dixy's machinations, Rush is setting the stage for the contention that anti-pollution regulations can be relaxed to reduce industry's overhead without any appreciable adverse environmental consequences.

But there is a limit to the punishment that any ecosystem, no matter how resilient, can take from humanity. One of the most perilous aspects of this limit is that scientists often cannot determine how close civilization is to crossing an ecological point of no return. By the time the alarm bells have sounded in some instances, it is too late. Given that uncertainty, caution would seem the better part of valor.

Not for Rush, however. He expresses disbelief at the idea "that after hundreds of millions of years, the last two generations of human existence might be capable of destroying the planet." Limbaugh berates environmentalists for promoting this premise, which of course they don't in any literal sense. The environmental mainstream holds that humanity possesses the potential to destroy life on earth as we know it, but not life itself. Cockroaches and hardy microorganisms at the very least are thought to possess the capacity to survive a full-scale thermonuclear war.

Of course, that doesn't provide much solace for the human race, but environmentalists don't have time to brood. They must concentrate their energies on heightening the public's vigilance against ecological threats, and on making certain that the unadulterated pap expounded by Limbaugh and like-minded individuals is recognized for what it is.

Limbaugh relishes depicting environmentalists as "radical" throngs who "paint humans almost as an aberration, as the natural enemy of nature; and who are unalterably opposed to our way of life—capitalism."[3] Naturally, he never specifically identifies who they are, and with good reason: He can't. They don't exist. Environmentalists as a class are not into self-abnegation any more than the rest of us. They put a premium on human life, especially their own.

Another favorite Limbaugh target is environmentalists' alleged anti-capitalism. In fact, virtually every major reform advanced by the mainstream environmental community in the past 25 years has relied heavily on the entrepreneurial creativity of private enterprise.

Why the wild accusations? For this reason: If Limbaugh can make these generalizations stick, he will ostracize many of his detractors and co-opt their followers.

Animal Infatuation

Limbaugh also is fond of gratuitously deprecating animal rights groups (again without identifying the specific objects of his scorn). "The animal rights crowd," he proclaims, think that all animal life-forms other than humans peacefully co-exist."[4] They think no such thing. Even the most simple-minded, marshmallow-hearted activist recognizes that animal life unfolds in a violent world where tranquility is a fleeting moment between meals.

My suspicion is that even Limbaugh knows better in this instance, but he is so determined to crucify animal rights activists that he won't hesitate to say whatever it takes to achieve his objective.

Superiority Complex

In celebrating the human race's superiority to other life forms on our planet, Rush boasts that "humans are the only creatures capable of cleaning up the messes made by themselves and all other creatures." He should have conferred with a microbiologist and an entomologist before making such an all-encompassing generalization. If he had done so, he would have discovered that bacteria and insects decompose virtually all of the world's waste. Without them, all the modern sanitation complexes, incinerators, and septic tanks on earth wouldn't spare us from ultimately being buried up to our eyeballs in excrement.[5]

Many of these organisms also play critical roles in pollinating plants, transferring nutrients, maintaining soil fertility, and recycling organic wastes, all prerequisites for a sufficient food supply to sustain the human race.

For his curtain call in biological ignorance, Limbaugh describes an "environmental wacko" with whom he once had an encounter as a "long-haired, maggot-infested FM type."[6] Come on, Rush, a maggot is larva and does not colonize people who are alive, however scraggly their appearance. The insects only take up residence in corpses. You were either communing with the dead or engaging in a poetic license that never should have been issued.

Radio Rodomontade

The airwaves are a major arena for Limbaugh's environmental rantings. Take his 1994 broadcast in which he delivered a tirade against what he considered to be "junk science," that is, science that incriminates corporate polluters. Rush sought to trivialize experiments identifying certain manmade chemicals as carcinogenic. He noted that ingestion of large doses of saccharin had been found to cause bladder cancer in laboratory rats and quipped that if you overloaded rats with water, they would get cancer too.[7]

Talk about "junk science"! Overdoses of any concoction are likely to make a living organism sick to its stomach. But only a relatively few substances have been found to have cancer-producing properties, and purified drinking water is not one of them.

When Limbaugh makes an inane, environmental-oriented remark over the airwaves, it's usually a variation on one of the themes in his books. In another monologue, he tells us not to worry about any loss of tropical rain forest to human depredation because nature, in its compensatory wisdom, is offsetting the shrinkage with an increase of greenery in Europe. Rush should also seek immediate tutorial help in rudimentary math. Between 1980 and 1990, Europe did expand its wooded area by approximately two million hectares (1.4 million acres).[8] But during that same period, 154 million hectares of tropical rain forest were lost, a land mass about three times the size of France.[9] Hardly a quid quo pro.

Moreover, even if the gains and losses had somehow been offset, the world would still have been far poorer. Tropical rain forests are much richer in biological diversity than temperate woodlands, and as such, possess greater potential to enrich our lives with "miracle" chemical compounds.

Rush also commented during a broadcast that food shortages in Africa were not due to a harvest shortfall or environmental degradation but to communists and other nasty types making a shambles of the distribution system. Darned if Rush is going to accept an explanation offered by the liberals when he can contrive a version soothing to right-wing sensibilities.

If he were not so caught up in ideological polemics, he would concede that the food shortage problem in much of sub-Saharan

Africa is not because of bad people, but too many people. Increased food production in the region has been unable to keep pace with population growth, and per-capita caloric consumption has been steadily decreasing. In some of the most hard-pressed African nations, attempts to catch up with the population explosion have forced farmers to cultivate marginal land and accelerate erosion, thereby compromising further the fate of future generations.

An expert on the Dark Continent, Rush is not.

Monkey Business

On November 2, 1994, Limbaugh opened his three-hour broadcast by boasting that he had news that would blow "environmental wackos" out of the water. What, pray tell, was his environmental bombshell? He triumphantly announced that a University of Wisconsin anthropologist had just released a report proving beyond a shadow of a doubt that endangered species benefit from the chopping down of forests. Hence, Rush gloated, all those environmental wackos urging preservation of the rain forest to save endangered species were "flat, dead wrong."

Of course, the study concluded nothing of the sort. That was quickly confirmed by its author, Dr. Karen Strier, who expressed outrage at the misrepresentation of her work. Strier had found that, in the coastal forests of Southeastern Brazil, the birthrates of rare muriqui monkeys actually increased in a wooded area disturbed by human beings.

But to deduce from that scenario that more logging is better was a mindless leap of logic. Strier herself made clear that the study applied only to the small colony of monkeys she had been observing for a dozen years in a slightly disturbed (not clear-cut, mind you) forest. She stressed that the study shed no light on the fate of the many plant and animal species that shared the woodland habitat with the muriqui simians, and was in no way a recommendation for harvesting pristine forests to improve conservation. It was still preferable to keep undisturbed habitats intact wherever possible.

Limbaugh seized on this study and distorted its findings because he saw an opportunity to dramatize his view that the earth has the capacity to rebound from any abuse we inflict. In actuality, far from saving endangered species, razing of tropical rain forests (which is taking place worldwide at the rate of 100 acres a minute) is rendering them extinct. And since the population density and diversity of rare plant and animal species are by far the greatest in these forests, biologists fear we may be losing as many as 50,000 species a year to bulldozers and chain saws.

Nor should Limbaugh get his—and our—hopes up about the rain forest's regenerative powers. Were he better informed, he would know that the nutrients responsible for the lush foliage reside in the roots of the plants rather than the soil, which is surprisingly infertile. Within 3 to 10 years after being leveled, most tropical rain forest sites are little more than wastelands.

Just Kidding

When he is confronted with facts that indisputably refute one of his statements, the talk show blowhard's typical response is to beat a hasty retreat, an approach he would undoubtedly employ if he encountered Dr. Strier. To save face in these situations, Limbaugh usually tries to palm off slander as slapstick humor, exclaiming apologetically that he was "just kidding."

The trouble is that all too many uninformed people ignore his belated disclaimer and continue to take him seriously. As long as they do, it ain't funny.

Only nine days after the Brazilian monkey business, Limbaugh again displayed his ignorance of fundamental environmental principles and his penchant for distorting the facts. The stimulus for this "buffoon" eruption was the tragic situation in the strife-torn central African nation of Rwanda.

Limbaugh complained that environmental wackos cared more about trees and animals than desperate, starving human beings in that unfortunate country. He was reacting to a non-African conservation expert's criticism of impoverished Rwandan refugees cutting down trees in the famous Three Volcano National Park and selling the timber. The expert indicated that he could sympathize with the refugees if they had harvested the firewood for their own heating and cooking needs, even though he thought that too was ultimately a self-defeating strategy. What really appalled the expert was that Rwandans were leveling part of a forest that is home to the last remnants of the Mountain Gorilla as well as thousands of animal and plant species found nowhere else, just in order to earn some spare change.

That was the last straw for Limbaugh. An assault on free enterprise! "Environmentalists want to protect the trees and the animals and to hell with mankind," he shrieked. As usual, Limbaugh got it wrong. Environmentalists want to protect the trees and the animals *for the sake of* mankind.

To generate sympathy for his position, the radio talk show host asserted that the park the refugees were pillaging had previously been closed to human intrusion. In fact, the park was the nation's major tourist attraction and thereby a primary source of foreign exchange and a cornerstone of its domestic economy.

The environmental objective Limbaugh was vilifying was an appeal for the Rwandans not to kill the goose that laid the golden eggs. While it's sometimes tempting to excuse desperate people for desperate acts, especially to attain short-term relief, there's no future in applauding such behavior.

If the refugees were allowed to proceed until the entire park's original growth had been decimated, what then? Their future might be compromised solely for an ephemeral gain. They would be eradicating rare, irreplaceable species that could contain chemical compounds capable of working medical miracles. They would be diminishing a valuable renewable resource, an act that in turn would jeopardize the lands surrounding the park. With fewer roots to absorb the rainfall, water pouring down the mountain slopes would flood and erode the countryside and Rwanda's agricultural productivity. Last but not least, they would be trashing their country's chief tourist attraction and losing the sorely needed hard currency brought in by foreign visitors.

The solution for these refugees is not to destroy their country for a quick fix. Somehow, their government and the international community must help them build an economic infrastructure without devastating the natural resource base in the process.

All such concerns are irrelevant to Limbaugh, who on environmental matters tailors his narrowly focused appeal to the moment. It can be an effective ploy, because rare is the individual who at first blush is more preoccupied with the future than the present.

Let's Pretend

Limbaugh has the nasty habit of trying to transform his ideological foes into pariahs by misquoting them in the most atrocious ways imaginable. We have him asserting that the Sierra Club "wants to limit the number of kids you can have to two."[10] Even if Sierra Club members believed that we should be compelled to restrict family size to two children (and they don't), they would be irrevocably ostracized from American society if they openly advocated such a draconian course. Environmental groups do not represent—as Limbaugh suggests—the second coming of the Third Reich and its mandatory sterilization policies. Environmentalists are campaigning to persuade couples to *voluntarily* limit offspring to no more than two. In a free society, integrating small family size into the national psyche will never be accomplished through a rule of law, only by a rule of thumb.

Limbaugh's slipshod modus operandi is again on display when he classifies the Audubon Society as "decent" while denouncing the Sierra Club as a bunch of "doomsday fanatics."[11] Audubon ingratiated itself with Rush by allowing an oil rig to operate on a wildlife refuge the organization owns in Louisiana. Limbaugh should not be faulted for his admiration of the venerable Audubon Society. However, he should be held accountable for his inconsistency, since Audubon and the Sierra Club are in agreement on virtually every major environmental issue.

Deforestation Mirage

To paper over humans' destructive environmental impacts, Limbaugh often dredges up shibboleths popularized by other environmental bashers. One of his favorites is tree cover. Contrary to "wackos" hand-wringing about deforestation, Limbaugh asserts, "we have more trees in this country today than when the Declaration of Independence was written."[12]

In absolute numbers, that may be true in the lower 48 states, because a lot of land cleared at that time for farming was subsequently abandoned and has been occupied by secondary stage growth. However, most of the eighteenth century woodlands, filled with mature trees and rich in biodiversity, are no longer with us; they have been leveled by human beings. What now stands in their place are frequently low-grade shrubs, saplings, vulnerable-to-disease timber industry monocultures, or relatively sterile, semi-mature forests.

Limbaugh has repeatedly stated on his radio program that "trees' worth is measured only by what we do with them ... Sometimes, that includes doing nothing."

Rush doesn't grasp his contradiction. That we can derive passive, abstract enjoyment from observing a tree (as opposed to extracting material benefits from it) suggests that the foliage around us indeed possesses intrinsic value.

Man and Nature

All of this *Sturm und Drang* is linked to Limbaugh's discomfort at humanity placing nature on any sort of pedestal. It doesn't mesh smoothly with his anthropocentric view that "animals and everything else are subspecies whose position on the planet is subordinate to that of humans."[13]

Indeed, he revels in censuring animal rights groups for "believing animals are superior to human beings."[14]

No matter that animal rights groups believe no such thing. Limbaugh's strategy is to make his adversary an object of total revulsion, incapable of attracting any sympathy—even pity—from society at large. His animal rights-inspired harangue against nature worship evolves into a broad indictment of environmentalists. He accuses them of being "religious fanatics" who believe "God is nothing more than the earth."[15]

With that outburst of demagoguery, Limbaugh has managed to misrepresent the world's major religions, all of which have numerous followers participating in the global environmental movement. To set the record straight, the overwhelming majority of environmental activists, grounded in many different religious backgrounds and reflecting the teachings of their respective faiths, view our planet as a work of God, not in itself the Almighty.

Property Righteousness

Rush also condemns environmentalists for wanting to "severely" curb private property rights (without citing any specific examples). The hyperbolic word here is "severely." A fundamental tenet of our common law is that property rights are not absolute, which is why zoning ordinances are an established part of the nation's legal infrastructure.

Environmentalists are not "hostile" to private property rights.[16] After all, many of them are landowners themselves. What they advocate (and our laws mandate) is that titleholders not be permitted to use their property in a manner that violates the rights or physically harms the well-being of others. In fact, contemporary society doesn't look kindly upon a landowner who arbitrarily destroys natural resources on his or her property, natural resources that are important in the aggregate to the nation's long-term health yet have been alarmingly depleted. That's why people can no longer at their whim eradicate wetlands or endangered species located on their property.

Mankind's relatively recent recognition of the finite nature of the earth's natural resources goes hand in hand with the growing realization that we are custodians, not absolute rulers, of our private domains.

A Question of Labor

Limbaugh maintains that "most people running environmental groups don't work. What they do is persuade other people to donate to their cause."[17] Since when has fundraising been excluded from the realm of honest labor? Limbaugh himself spends a goodly percentage of his radio program urging the public to donate to his cause, primarily through the purchase of his newsletter, books, line of neckties, and other wares.

Environmental organizations are not immune from the exigencies of meeting a payroll. But their fundraising is usually successful because of strong public support for their positions. Rush goes badly astray when he brands the leaders as sluggards. They work very hard at their proselytizing mission, putting in hours that certainly rival those of Limbaugh himself. Environmentalists are only attempting to do the same thing Limbaugh does—compete for public backing in the arena of ideas. (Rush is far ahead in salary; the environmentalists have a decided edge in converts.)

Semantic Sophistry

Limbaugh uses the venerable "straw man" and "vague generalities" techniques to malign animal rights groups. As we have noted, he claims they "believe animals are superior to human beings and have rights the equal of ours."[18]

While you can always find a few individuals who would subscribe to the aforementioned views, it is lunacy to contend, as Limbaugh does, that animal rights activists en masse elevate creatures of the forest above human beings, or assign rights to these lower life forms in a constitutional sense. His literal interpretation of animal lovers' use of the term "rights" is semantic sophistry. What the humane societies of the world are talking about is the "right" of animals not to be needlessly brutalized or slaughtered by human beings. Recognition of this "right" would seem imperative not only in an ethical but environmental sense, since the massive devastation that indiscriminate use of modern firearms can wreak upon animal populations could easily throw ecosystems out of whack.

Limbaugh momentarily acknowledges this imperative.[19] But he cannot sustain for long a recognition of animals as entities entitled to a distinct existence in their own right. His strident, egocentric view of planet Earth soon gets the best of him, and he bridles at the thought that animals have any rights whatsoever.

It's touching to hear Limbaugh say he has nothing against animals per se and "even melts around little dogs."[20] Very touching, indeed, until he admonishes us that protection of animals is somehow a "leftist" plot to promote a radical socialist agenda. This sort of compartmentalization evokes images of Adolf Hitler dissolving into tears when a crippled baby bird fluttered across his path.

Skewering Gore

No single environmentalist provokes more hostility in Limbaugh than Vice President Al Gore.

I don't agree with everything Gore says, either, but Limbaugh is not interested in honest debate here. He's into character assassination, and he brings to bear every devious technique in his repertoire. Limbaugh asserts that in Gore's *Earth in the Balance*, the vice president claimed that "the automobile is the gravest threat the Earth has ever faced.[21]

The inference is that Gore wants to turn back the clock and remove all automobiles from circulation, a desire that if true and openly professed would get him impeached within a week. What Gore did write was that some aspects of the automobile as currently manufactured—not automobiles per se—are environmentally detrimental. He was advocating development of more environmentally friendly cars, such as solar-powered models free of dependence on fossil fuels that generate greenhouse gas pollutants.

Forever the Optimist

Limbaugh rails that Gore is a "radical doomsday prophet" who opposes technological progress.[22]

Even a casual read of Gore's book discloses that he is an avowed optimist who believes the human race has the expertise and resources to make a better world. Coincidentally, sustainable technology is for Gore the ticket to that desired objective.

Rush asserts that Gore claims American agriculture is in trouble because of topsoil erosion.[23] Gore did write that erosion was occurring. But he added that the process could frequently be reversed, an upbeat view that was a far cry from how Limbaugh characterized the vice president's outlook.

Rush also charges that Gore favors forfeiting our sovereignty to a United Nations tribunal when it comes to administering international environmental agreements.[24] Gore actually says that the idea of a supranational authority "is both politically impossible and practically unworkable ... the idea arouses so much opposition that further debate on the underlying goals come to a halt ... especially in the United States, where we are fiercely protective of our individual freedoms."[25]

The only answer is "to negotiate international agreements that ... are entered into voluntarily ... although they will contain both incentives and legally valid penalties for noncompliance." [26]

Limbaugh assures his readers that he is incapable of telling them "anything but the truth,"[27] whereas *Earth in the Balance* is full of "calculated disinformation."[28] Rush must be counting on his audience not reading Gore's book any more carefully than he has—which would seem to be not at all. Limbaugh certainly never made it to the credits preceding the main text—as evidenced by his assertion that Gore's collaborator in writing *Earth in the Balance* was Environmental Protection Agency chief Carol Browner.[29] In a lengthy introductory acknowledgment, Gore thanks by name the more than 100 persons who assisted him in his endeavor. Browner receives nary a mention.

Galluping to the Rescue

Taking his cue from Dixy Lee Ray, Rush misrepresents the findings of that infamous Gallup Poll on the greenhouse effect. The objective, of course, is to discredit Gore's insistence that there is an overwhelming scientific consensus that global warming is taking place.[30] Limbaugh then accuses Gore of preaching that "doomsday is rapidly approaching" as a result of climate change.

That is quite a stretch from the vice president's actual message, which is that we must pay attention to the warning signals and do something about them, or a global ecological collapse could (as opposed to "would") occur.[31]

According to Rush, Gore's solution is "to launch an assault on Western civilization, capitalism, and our very way of life" through "draconian central planning."[32]

What book was Limbaugh reading? Gore actually writes: "Wherever people at the grass-roots level are deprived of a voice in the decisions that affect their lives, they and the environment suffer. I have therefore come to believe that an essential prerequisite for saving the environment is the spread of democratic government to more nations of the world."[33]

There is nothing wrong with challenging the vice president's ideas. But Limbaugh must feel very insecure if he has to falsify what Gore has said in order to make a point.

Demonizing Wilson

Another target of Rush's shrill invective is noted Harvard biology Professor Edward O. Wilson, who triggered Limbaugh's ire with an article in the May 30, 1993, issue of *The New York Times Magazine* assessing humanity's shortcomings.

An individual of Professor Wilson's academic and intellectual stature doesn't need any outside help in defending himself against the likes of Rush Limbaugh. I intend only to point out the flagrant manner in which Limbaugh manipulates quotations. Once again, it's hard to believe Limbaugh read the work he is critiquing, because his fabrications are so far off the mark that they are an embarrassment, even for him.

He contends that Wilson characterizes humanity as "nothing more than a bunch of boobs bent on self-destruction ... It's just the worst luck for all living things that humans are the ones who took dominion over the world ... Humans are an environmental abnormality."[34] Limbaugh also denounces Wilson for failing "to mention a supreme being or Creator in the story ... illustrating the profound gulf between people of theology and those like Wilson in the scientific community. No allowances are made at all for God."

There is no question that Wilson does dwell on humanity's deficiencies and past mistakes at length. But he certainly doesn't reach the definitive conclusion attributed to him by Limbaugh. "Are we racing to the brink of an abyss, or are we just gathering speed for a takeoff to a wonderful future?" Wilson writes. His agnostic answer: "The crystal ball is clouded."

Limbaugh also forgot to mention that, though Wilson admits to being an avid environmentalist, the professor declares that he is "not so radical as to wish a turning back of the clock, not given to driving spikes into Douglas firs to prevent logging, and distinctly uneasy with such hybrid movements as ecofeminism, which holds that Mother Earth is a nurturing home for all life...."

Most important of all is Wilson's ultimate assessment of the human condition. Limbaugh makes an issue out of the title of the article, "Is Humanity Suicidal?" and would have us believe the professor answers his own question in the affirmative. For the record, Wilson concludes that "humanity is not suicidal ... We are smart enough and have time enough to avoid an environmental catastrophe of civilization-threatening dimensions. But the technical problems are sufficiently formidable to require a redirection of much of science and technology, and the ethical issues are so basic as to force a reconsideration of our self-image as a species."

Wilson goes on to say that "there are reasons for optimism," and cites the 1992 Earth Summit at Rio de Janeiro, an international scientific declaration that same year expressing awareness of global ecological problems, and—surprise, surprise—"the greening of religion."

He applauds theologians and religious leaders from around the world for "addressing environmental problems as a moral issue" and meeting with scientists under the auspices of the U.S. Senate to produce a "joint appeal by religion and science for the environment." Wilson's dream: "preserving the surviving ecosystems, micromanaging them only enough to save the biodiversity they contain, until such time as they can be understood and employed in the fullest sense for human benefit."

Although this doesn't sound wildly radical to me, one obviously doesn't have to accept Wilson's vision. But it does behoove his critics not to misrepresent what they are responding to. If they do, the falsification will obscure any honest disagreements they might have with the professor.

It's quite possible that Limbaugh is often aware he is overstating the case on environmental issues but rationalizes (ironically, for a rabid anti-Marxist) that the end justifies the means, and that science is too complicated for the general public to call him to task. A slightly less cynical interpretation is that he is intellectually lazy, mindlessly repeating what he has heard other bashers say, in which case, his behavior is more irresponsible than deceitful.

Self-Verification

Our walking conduit of calumny opens the environmental update chapter of his second "classic" work, *See, I Told You So*, by boasting how uncannily correct he has been in his predictions concerning environmental trends.[35] He invites us to accompany him in "counting the ways" his brilliance has been corroborated by events.

> LIMBAUGH: Despite the hysterics of a few pseudo-scientists, there is no reason to believe in global warming.

> REALITY: The overwhelming preponderance of the world's climatologists concur that global warming is underway. Even the Gallup Poll that Limbaugh cites to illustrate the uncertainty in the scientific community shows that a majority of experts agree temperatures are rising. Scientists are just not sure about the timing, degree, and ramifications of the phenomenon.

> LIMBAUGH: Mankind is not responsible for depleting the ozone layer.

> REALITY: There's a major problem with the notion that it's not human activity but nature that is at fault. Chlorine rising from the sea and volcanoes is soluble, so most of it is washed out of the lower atmosphere during periods of rainfall.[36] The destructive chlorine found in the upper reaches of the atmosphere has been increasing in tandem with emissions of manmade chlorofluorocarbons. These

CFCs are insoluble and have little difficulty ascending to the stratosphere, where they release their chlorine.

LIMBAUGH: The earth's ecosystem is not fragile, and humans are not capable of destroying it.

REALITY: Examples contradicting this assertion could fill volumes. For openers, Rush needs to bone up on the history of civilization and then trek across the Levantine's Sinai Desert. Another egregious example involves the 17 major fishing areas of the world. Primarily because of overfishing and coastal pollution, they have either reached or exceeded their natural limits, with nine of them clearly in decline, according to surveys conducted by the United Nations Food and Agriculture Organization.[37] Closer to home, the famed Chesapeake Bay a century ago yielded eight million bushels annually of its fabled oysters; but now, due to pollution, it produces no more than 300,000 bushels. Unless a lengthy hiatus is imposed on the annual harvest in concert with a successful cleanup, how long can even that number be sustained?[38]

LIMBAUGH: The real enemies of the radical environmental leadership are capitalism and the American way of life.

REALITY: This is a red herring that smells from sea to shining sea. Rush can't authenticate this charge, and if he ever legitimately tried, he would become a laughing stock. The truth is that environmental leaders have loudly proclaimed—and championed—capitalism,

provided it is accompanied by greater environmental sensitivity, as the best way of achieving
sustainable prosperity.

LIMBAUGH: Less-developed cultures are not necessarily more pure or kinder to nature than
technologically sophisticated civilizations.

REALITY: Whoever said they were?

LIMBAUGH: Big-government regulation is not the
best way to protect the environment.

REALITY: Such a sweeping statement is asinine.
History has demonstrated that sometimes federal regulation is the best way to go, sometimes
it's not. To rule it out unequivocally is to deny
the enormous benefits derived from our landmark national environmental and public land
laws over the years. From a practical, daily,
hands-on perspective, pollution often tran-
scends state boundaries, necessitating a
centralized national approach. To rely on a
patchwork regulatory scheme can easily result
in jurisdictions working at cross-purposes
rather than engaging in a coordinated effort to
remediate threats to public health and safety.

LIMBAUGH: Many environmental groups have
adopted their cause with all of the fervor and
enthusiasm of a religious crusade, abandoning
reason and accepting many faulty premises on
faith.

REALITY: This is the ultimate exercise in gall.
Limbaugh can't document this charge, but it
can be turned against him and his compatriot
bashers in excruciating detail.

LIMBAUGH: Mankind is part of nature and not necessarily its enemy.

REALITY: Limbaugh suddenly takes credit for a stance that was adopted in most quarters ages before he arrived on the scene. Environmentalists carry the philosophy a step further. They maintain that mankind not only isn't a foe of nature but ought to—indeed must be—a very good friend.

LIMBAUGH: According to environmentalists, America is the root of all evil in the world.

REALITY: On the contrary, the national environmental movement makes no secret of its abiding faith in America's ability to lead the world in successfully meeting the global environmental challenge of the twenty-first century.

Bioperversity

For a man who professes to champion religious values, Limbaugh is curiously unmoved by—sometimes even disdainful of—the earth's rich biodiversity, a phenomenon of such unimaginable scope and miraculous intricacy that it's hard to believe divine intervention is not at work. He ridicules the need to preserve virgin forests. "What are virgin forests anyway?" he quips. "Are they made up of trees that have never had sex?"[39] He'd be better off not answering his own environmental questions, much less asking them.

Displaying further ecological ignorance, Limbaugh criticizes the Clinton administration for signing the international biodiversity treaty "that is just the latest technique to stop development, halt the timber industry, and surrender our autonomy to a supranational body." In fact, the treaty would expand trade and broaden profit-making vistas for American companies without renouncing our national sovereignty or anybody else's (though we all would be subject to basic international environmental safeguards).

Basic Ignorance

Throughout Limbaugh's so-called environmental writing, nothing is more arresting than how abysmally uninformed he is about the elemental ecological principles underlying his subject matter.

For example, he ridicules environmentalists' concern for the spotted owl in the states of Oregon and Washington, noting that researchers encountered the supposedly scarce creatures in surprising numbers in northern California. Yet even with the inclusion of the California birds, the modest overall population of the spotted owl continues to decline steadily, causing much concern among ornithologists.

Why the fuss over one subspecies of owl? Limbaugh disdainfully snorts. "The spotted differs only slightly from many other types of its breed." See one owl and you've seen them all, right, Rush?

The radio talk-show host displays ignorance of the significance of genetic diversity within species. That qualifies as a serious lapse, because many scientists believe these subtle differences hold the clues to the longevity and resiliency of life itself.

Limbaugh argues that if the spotted owl can't adapt to human beings, then let it perish.[40] That is the harsh reality of life, Rush proclaims, and to illustrate his point, he contends that owls have also been beneficiaries of this "survival of the fittest" environment. A poor mouse has no chance "to evade the attack of an owl," he explains.

But nature is not quite as merciless as Rush suggests. It gives every creature, whether the hunter or hunted, some means to enhance survival prospects. Each animal—even a mouse—is endowed with a weapon or defense whose effectiveness usually correlates to the creature's age and health. That's why it takes some extraordinary event—whether modern technology run amok, or an asteroid strike as some scientists suspect—to bring about a sudden mass extinction.

Farms and Chemicals

Limbaugh mindlessly cribs from other bashers the myth that organic farming falls dramatically short of providing food of sufficient quality and quantity to satisfy our needs. How could he feel otherwise about something environmentalists universally embrace?

But organic farming has more than its Green popularity to send Limbaugh and Company into a tizzy. For that crowd, the very thought that a back-to-nature approach could compete with modern-day technology constitutes a heretical challenge to the dominance—or should I say supremacy—of the human race.

The Old, Old World

Limbaugh's understanding of modern European history is as third-rate as his knowledge of ecology's basic tenets. Again, he seems interested only in fashioning a scenario that complements his ideological mindset. Hence, he cites eastern Europe under Communist rule as an example of why strict national environmental regulation is a disaster:[41] "The key to cleaning up our environment is unfettered free enterprise. When no one owns private property, there is no incentive to keep it clean and pure. Our profit motive has given us the most sophisticated pollution control technology in the world."

No one would dispute that a totalitarian regime is intolerable, and that the competition engendered by free enterprise has played an important role in the development of advanced pollution abatement techniques. But a free market without effective regulation has proved extremely untrustworthy. Sometimes it has performed brilliantly, other times destructively; always it has been responsive to short-term profit opportunities, regardless of whether they were in the best long-term interests of society at large.

The environmental disaster created by eastern European Communist nations resulted neither from a defect in regulations nor the absence of private property ownership. Pollution was rampant because the oppressive regimes chose to pay lip service to some stringent federal environmental laws. Bureaucrats sought to meet or exceed overly ambitious, state-ordained production quotas that involved no consideration of adverse ecological consequences.

As for our own country, Limbaugh states flatly that the concentration of dioxin residues at infamous Times Beach, Missouri, was insufficient to warrant forced evacuation of the town.[42] One marvels at Limbaugh's certitude when—to this day—veteran scientists remain unsure of whether the evacuation was premature in light of cancer's lengthy latency period, renewed concerns about dioxin's toxicity, and a still gaping hole in knowledge of how the substance affects humans.

Bringing us up to date, Limbaugh also declares that "the environment is cleaner than ever."[43] Cleaner than pre-colonial days? Travelers routinely used to drink from streams and lakes along their route. Try that today, and you're a prime candidate for the nearest emergency room.

If Limbaugh had bothered to examine the statistical trends for greenhouse gases and coastal water quality, to name but two major environmental indicators, he would have learned that some pollutants are on the rise, with slim prospects of imminent reversal.

Hollywood Ombudsman

Our conservative radio talk show host berates Tom Cruise and other Hollywood celebrities for campaigning on behalf of the environment when, in Rush's view, they personally don't practice what they preach. Even if Limbaugh's accusations were accurate, why should movie stars be precluded from promoting the proper course of action? Do we disallow people with criminal records from advising others that "crime doesn't pay"? Should clergymen be disqualified from counseling us on how to conduct our lives since they, like all human beings, are imperfect by nature?

If the messenger is constantly permitted to get in the way of the message, we are going to have triflingly little in the way of communication.

Di-Di-Dioxin

Limbaugh's specious logic carries over into his analogy between radon and dioxin. He questions why the former isn't reason enough for people to evacuate their homes the way the latter has been.[44] He then supplies his own tortured explanation. Radon, which is concentrated in the soil in certain areas and can seep up into homes as toxic gas, is a natural phenomenon. By contrast, dioxin, which has forced the abandonment of several communities, is of industrial origin.

The comparison provides a backdrop for Rush's familiar refrain that environmentalists are nature lovers and people-haters. Their response to dioxin was more aggressive, he maintains, because of its identification with the "evil corporate world." The response to radon was more benign because of its "natural" presence in the environment.

Be assured that there is nothing sinister about the different responses to these threats. Congress is in the process of passing legislation that would require the seller of any home to certify to the buyer that the structure is not in violation of existing radon standards.

Evacuation doesn't come into play because, even in the worst-case scenarios, radon gas is easily detectable and can usually be readily—and cheaply—vented.

Dioxin's infiltration into a neighborhood tends to be more pervasive and difficult to reverse. Since it can rarely be neutralized within a brief time frame, situations occasionally arise in which evacuation is deemed necessary for public safety.

True Colors

Limbaugh asserts that "many scientists don't know nearly as much as they pretend about the environmental issues they address."[45] While there are undoubtedly some scientists who fall into this category, one wonders how Limbaugh would be able to recognize them. In a fleeting moment of candor, even Rush will admit on occasion that he is "not an expert on any science."[46]

When caught red-handed regarding some outrageous inaccuracy, Limbaugh will seek refuge in buffoonery. He will impishly justify his faux pas as a deliberate exercise in satiric humor and assure everyone he was "just kidding." But this doesn't fool those who understand the nuances of propaganda. They know that the din created by statements made for sensationalistic effect often drowns out any attempts at retraction.

For individuals who possess a working knowledge of environmental issues, Limbaugh is ludicrously funny when he is trying to be serious and extremely tasteless—even vile—when he is attempting to be irreverent. It's not all that surprising from an author who freely admits that Dixy Lee Ray's books were his major environmental frame of reference and source of inspiration.

PART 5

THE REAL
ENVIRONMENTALISM

11

THE TRUE OPTIMISTS

The allegation that environmentalists are doomsdayers is illogical on its face.

Americans—nay, people in general—are inherent optimists, and the last time I checked, environmentalists were deemed members of the human race. Clearly, if environmentalists were perceived as die-hard harbingers of inexorable calamity, they would never have attracted such a widespread public following or enjoyed such phenomenal success in our legislative and judicial forums. When activists in the national environmental movement express unhappiness with some current conditions, they are not delivering the last rites to modern civilization. Their criticism is almost always accompanied by constructive, practical suggestions to make the world more habitable.

It all boils down to environmentalists acknowledging their victories but not dwelling on them. Too many formidable challenges lie ahead—challenges, however, that can be overcome by human ingenuity.

The gloomiest bunch are the bashers, who in the presence of serious environmental and social degradation insist that we have never had it so good and should savor the status quo rather than concern ourselves about the future. In fact, they often warn that so little pollution remains after our clean-up efforts that the cost of eliminating it would far exceed the benefits and bring our economy to the verge of collapse.

To understate the potential of pollution to diminish our quality of life is unconscionable. Furthermore, rejecting reality in paroxysms of Pollyannaish myopia and denial is abject surrender to immediate gratification regardless of ultimate human costs and a downward spiral that is capable of being averted. What could be more depressing?

Fortunately, an ample body of evidence indicates that, even in the most affluent countries and highest quarters, the future is not being taken for granted. Indeed, the recognition at the uppermost reaches of government is virtually universal. It's decisive action, alas, that all too often has been lacking.

Nevertheless, there is another cause for optimism, apart from the essential first step of acknowledging the problems. Many nations are engaged in cooperative environmental protection efforts that have produced tangible results, modest though they may often be.

On our own shores, Congress (with the aid of presidential vetoes) has resisted ill-conceived legislative attempts to turn back the clock to the good times that never were.

Adjusting to the realities of the fast-approaching twenty-first century, our State Department has officially (and finally) expanded its definition of national security threats beyond the traditional ones of nuclear holocaust and brush-fire conventional wars; provision has been made to include the political ramifications of widespread environmental deterioration.[1] American diplomats have thus begun to worry about the repercussions of water supply shortages, extensive soil erosion, and extreme overcrowding of human populations in the same way they worry about the aggressive maneuvers of some ruthless potentate with expansionist designs.

This newfound enlightenment is a prerequisite to the successful conduct of foreign policy in the years ahead, not only for Washington but for all the sovereign capitals of the world.

Supreme Ironies

If being accused of grim fatalism were not enough, environmentalists are berated for "socialist" tendencies because of their staunch support for anti-pollution regulations and their conviction that Washington must be the final arbiter in ecological controversies with transboundary ramifications.

Free-market buffs usually balk at Washington's mediation of environmental conflicts and other social controversies. Let the marketplace sort it all out and justice will be done, they contend. Yet for all their free enterprise fervor, many of these boosters of capitalism end up as nothing more than "corporate socialists" intent on using the federal treasury to transfer wealth to the business community through massive government subsidies and overly generous tax breaks.

Numerous denigrators of the environmental movement are bedeviled by still another contradiction. They characterize themselves as extremely conservative yet seek to remove government restraints to Darwinian competition in the marketplace. There's nothing conservative about that. Where is the respect for the existing infrastructure and the emphasis on orderly change that are trademarks of conservative ideology? Furthermore, modern-day corporate robber barons often use the free market to target natural resources for exploitation, not conservation. The ultimate irony is that "conservation's" etymology and ethical force spring from the term "conservative" in its purest derivation.

The Good Life

Detractors of the environmental movement depict its proposed reforms as expressions of fabricated desperation that are obstacles to the nation's economic growth, and as vehicles that transform warnings of impending doom into self-fulfilling prophecies.

In fact, while far from perfect, environmental protection initiatives have not only improved our quality of life but also enhanced prospects for the future in a fiscal as well as ecological sense. Estimates of the environmental technology industry's revenues total more than $134 billion, with one million sustainable jobs already created. Conservative estimates are that, by the year 2000, the industry will generate revenues of $200 billion and employ 1.3 million people. Furthermore, deployment of the full range of available cost-effective waste reduction technologies is capable of raising those numbers to $1.9 trillion in revenue and 16 million new positions in the nation's workforce by 2010.[2]

Evidence documenting environmental protection's beneficial economic impacts comes from many quarters. Authors of a report sponsored by the Institute for Southern Studies found that, throughout the nation, the states with the best environmental records invariably had the strongest economies.[3]

"Plants with lower emissions per unit of output are at least as likely, and perhaps somewhat more likely, to achieve higher profits," concluded World Resources Institute researcher Bob Repetto in a comprehensive study of the relationship between industrial activity and environmental regulation.[4]

It has also been demonstrated that environmental protection has a positive effect on revenues from tourism. In Nebraska, for example, bird-watching visitors to sanctuaries created for the protection of sandhill and whooping cranes have contributed an estimated $30 million to $40 million annually to the local economy.[5] A more publicized material benefit: the miracle medicines extracted from rare animals and plants, with the promise of many more cures yet to be discovered, provided we don't waver in our resolve to preserve what remains of Earth's rich biodiversity.

Other Dividends

Environmentalism has produced a formula for halting suburban sprawl, maintaining abundant parkland, reducing traffic congestion, and making life just plain more livable. The prescription consists of clustered, relatively high-density development surrounded by ample open space, with mixed uses that create a self-contained community where virtually everything is within walking distance. It is a blueprint that, on its face, offers a more attractive, commuter-friendly, environmentally sound alternative to the clutter scattered across our landscape. It also happens to be a more economical one. Sprawl stretches public services and transportation infrastructures to their limit and beyond, creating the climate for wasteful duplication, higher taxes, and flat or even falling property values.[6]

Barry Commoner provides us with further environmental dividends. He presides over the Center for the Biology of Natural Systems, which specializes in the development of non-polluting technological alternatives to toxic industrial processes. The center's goals and work are clearly more uplifting than an insistence—in the face of contrary evidence—that some lethal pollution is the price of prosperity and that we've done about as good a job of abatement as could be expected at this point in time.

The Absence of Straitjackets

One of the more distinctive traits of the bashers is their inflexibility. A dogmatic mindset makes them incapable of accepting any solution that doesn't coincide with their ideology, no matter how pressing the need or how practical the cure.

The mainstream environmental movement is not constricted by an ideological straitjacket, so it feels free to expropriate the best ideas of factions with whom it is frequently at odds. This pragmatism is a major reason for environmental activists' dexterity in achieving accommodation, and it explains in part why they are more likely than their detractors to attract the compromise-oriented American public.

In a testament to their open-mindedness, environmentalists do not hesitate to promote solutions combining their regulatory approach and the bashers' market incentives. A good example: the aforementioned study by Bob Repetto of the World Resources Institute. As a charter member of the national environmental movement, WRI strongly supports rigorous anti-pollution regulation. But a majority of the mainstream environmental community is also quite comfortable with Repetto's recommendation of a permit trading system while reducing federal subsidies to industry, thereby enlisting market forces to participate in reversing environmental degradation.

Far from tearing down capitalism, mainstream environmentalists focus on working within the system to make it more responsive to ecological needs.

- The Washington-based Environmental Defense Fund has developed a "safe harbor" strategy for the Interior Department, which adopted it forthwith. Under this scheme, the department solicits the voluntary cooperation of private landowners in preserving endangered species' habitats on their property. In return, the landowners are granted the license to use other, non-strategic parts of their acreage without fear that they will commit a technical violation of the Endangered Species Act.[7]

- The Wilderness Society has devised an approach to preserve biodiversity, dubbing it "Lifelands." Again, this mainstream environmental organization would operate through conventional economic avenues to create a network of public and private lands designed to preserve as many native plants and animals as possible. Tax breaks and other fiscal incentives would encourage private property holders to become involved.[8]

- Conservation International is a nonprofit organization comprised of experts from many different vocations. It seeks to maintain biological diversity by helping indigenous residents of highly coveted, ecologically rich rural areas in developing countries create economically viable alternatives to destruction of ecosystems. Its mission can also be described as making environmentally sustainable development reap immediate financial rewards in the global marketplace.

That's more practical than asking people in desperate economic straits to be good stewards of the earth for the sake of future generations, an objective that they might find difficult to fully appreciate, given their daily trials and tribulations. A classic example: Conservation International has developed overseas markets for Amazonian rain forest products that Brazilian Indians harvest in a "sustainable" manner.

- Founded in 1984, Clean Sites is an alliance of civic, environmental, and business leaders dedicated to creating innovative technologies and partnerships between the public and private sector to improve the disposal process for hazardous waste.

- The American Farmland Trust, a national farmland conservation organization, recently teamed up with industry to preserve agricultural acreage in the leading crop-producing area in the nation, California's Fresno County.[9]

Those are just a few of the many cooperative efforts between the environmental and business communities undertaken *within* the free enterprise system to harness human creativity for the betterment of our planet. You might think the bashers would recognize and applaud at least some of these endeavors, but few—if any—such critics do.

Environmentalists in government also display flexibility, being no less predisposed to interact with entrepreneurs. The Environmental Protection Agency, for example, recently sought to make its regulations more user-friendly to industry by reducing or eliminating penalties for companies that voluntarily disclose and correct their pollution violations. From where I sit, that's indulging capitalism big time.

One other thing: Denigrators of the Greens habitually portray any proposal to tighten environmental safeguards as an erosion of our constitutional freedoms. Most conservation activists I know would argue just the opposite—that stricter environmental safeguards *strengthen* constitutional freedoms. It is difficult, after all, to exercise the full range of rights conferred by our founding fathers when one's health is victimized by pollution.

Contrast these alliances with the unyielding animus of most of the environmental detractors, who by criminalizing opponents have isolated themselves from the vast majority of their countrymen. Even the less fanatic denigrators are prevented by ideology from making concessions, and thus can only enter into coalitions with the "enemy" on those rare occasions when that faction agrees to capitulate without reservations.

Health Over Profits

Some critics characterize the mainstream environmental movement's cardinal sin as "calling for action before sufficient research is available."[10] This is a euphemistic denunciation of a common-sense philosophy: Extend the benefit of the doubt to the prospective victim rather than the potential polluter, when faced with uncertainty about the magnitude of a likely contamination threat. Expenditures for effective abatement procedures are required in these circumstances in order to play it safe.

I don't know about you, but I'm quite content with the way priorities are set in those situations. Health is being placed ahead of profits but, one must quickly add, not instead of them. It's the best of both possible worlds.

Keep It Simple

Mainstream environmentalism's blueprint for the future revolves around adoption of a lifestyle that is often referred to as "voluntary simplicity." Let's begin with what that term is not—a return to the Dark Ages and a monastic existence in which material possessions are forfeited and the quest for the good life is renounced. Rather, voluntary simplicity means placing more emphasis on qualitative than quantitative values. This translates into the pursuit of goals that subordinate financial relationships to human ones, and a lifestyle that is energized more by the acquisition of knowledge than the accumulation of material goods. Conservation becomes the modus vivendi of choice, not desperation. Products are valued for long-lived, high-level performance rather than for simply being in vogue, and planned obsolescence is rendered obsolete.

In a society founded on voluntary simplicity, an individual's character, not his income, defines his identity. Profit remains a driving economic force, but is uncoupled from a linear relationship with consumption so that prosperity can be attained (and sustained) without necessitating the pillage of the earth's natural resources.

If all this sounds hopelessly quixotic, be apprised that a groundswell of public support is building for such behavioral change. In a recent nationwide survey funded by the Merck Foundation, the majority of respondents expressed dismay that material acquisitiveness and plain old avarice were spreading rapidly throughout society at the expense of family values and civic conscientiousness. Just as telling, fewer than half the survey's respondents said they were happier than their less affluent parents.[11]

The Merck survey is not alone in suggesting that the public is primed to embrace the environmentalists' alternate lifestyle. An April 1995 Gallup Poll of working Americans found more than half complaining that they didn't have enough time to do the things they truly wanted to do.[12] Other polls indicate a growing willingness among many Americans to take a pay cut for more quality time with family; for example, a 1994 Gallup Poll disclosed that one-third of respondents would take a 20 percent reduction in salary if they or their spouses could work fewer hours. That sentiment can't help but be bolstered by the recent disclosure that the average couple spends six hours per week shopping and just 40 minutes with their kids.

How about the revelation that there are more shopping centers than high schools in our country? What does that say about our priorities?

No doubt, growing discontent has already driven some Americans towards reduced (not discontinued, mind you) consumption. How many others will follow in an era when crass materialism is celebrated daily in mind-numbing repetition on the ubiquitous television screen? Can mounting concern over the deterioration of traditional values provide a powerful enough catalyst to induce widespread behavioral change?

Plenty of potent stimuli are around to steer Americans in the direction of the behavioral pattern favored by mainstream environmentalism. Our throwaway mentality has entrapped us in an unsustainable (and for many, psychologically unfulfilling) pattern of conspicuous consumption. We have started to grasp the reality that our natural resource base is being depleted faster than we can replace it, and that this situation must be remedied if we wish to avoid presiding over the gradual deterioration of our quality of life.

The environmentalists' cause is further abetted by human beings' propensity to exercise common sense when faced with stressful, unfavorable circumstances. As the ramifications of unsustainable consumption become more widely understood, people are bound to start questioning what's so uplifting about that chosen path, Madison Avenue's entreaties and the plaudits of the environmental movement's critics notwithstanding. In the years ahead, historians are unlikely to treat kindly a lifestyle that opts for immediate material gratification to the detriment of future generations' well-being.

When people who have been entrenched in an unsustainable consumption pattern realize their mistake, don't expect them to display resignation to their fate. The majority of human beings are constitutionally upbeat—enough to make a vigorous effort to turn things around. Environmentalists certainly have great confidence in human resourcefulness when it is exercised in harmony with nature. In their view, achieving that compatibility is a quantum leap towards a lasting prosperity.

Ah, for Sustainability

When environmentalists talk about "sustainability," we should be sure we understand what they mean. To recap, sustainability can be defined as renewable resource use that does not exceed the rate of regeneration, non-renewable resource use that does not exceed the rate at which sustainable, renewable substitutes are developed, and pollution emissions that do not exceed the capacity of the environment to absorb them.[13]

Another succinct description is "the use of goods and services that respond to basic needs and bring a better quality of life, while minimizing the use of natural resources, toxic materials and emissions of waste and pollutants over the life cycle, so as not to jeopardize the needs of future generations."[14]

If the Merck Survey is any indication, many Americans are demonstrating a gradual move towards a sustainable lifestyle. According to that nationwide poll, titled "Yearning for Balance," 86 percent of respondents were concerned about the environment and 88 percent believed environmental protection would require most of us to make major lifestyle changes.[15] The poll also suggested that, at least in principle, many people agree with environmentalists on how we should proceed in purging our malaise. Witness that 82 percent of the respondents declared that most Americans purchase and consume far more than they need (thereby generating enormous waste and, presumably, nagging dissatisfaction in many instances).

If your reaction is that we're hearing plenty of talk but witnessing little action when it comes to exiting the rat race, the Merck Survey refutes that impression to some extent. Twenty-eight percent of those questioned confided that in the past five years, they had voluntarily embraced a tradeoff in which they earned less money in order to lead a more "balanced" life. If "balance" means being less consumed with material acquisition (as it usually does in these cases), the odds that a salary cut would be traumatic are greatly reduced.

The Wall Street Journal recently reported that the "simple life" was becoming a status symbol among the affluent in our society. What the newspaper described is largely a studied, dressed-down chic that still smacks of fealty to materialism but at least is heading in the right direction. Practitioners of the "new" lifestyle are increasingly devaluing acquisition of objects and feverish pursuit of six-figure salaries in favor of meaningful personal relationships, more free time, and vigorous physical activity. It's "cool" to chuck a stressful career, one interviewee told the *Wall Street Journal* reporter.

Children have even replaced fancy homes and cars as the predominant status symbol for many baby boomers, according to the article. Such a shift in values is certainly healthy, provided the child doesn't simply become the latest family bauble. It's a step backwards if the infant is cherished more for what he or she adds to the parents' image than for whom he or she is.

Sustainability does not hold nearly as much of an attraction for many business leaders. As author Harold Crooks wryly puts it: "achieving sustainability inevitably disrupts a waste-based, primary-resource-based economy that is grossly subsidized. Logically, those corporate chieftains with high stakes in virgin-materials production will fight environmentalists' attempts to impose full cost accounting for the ecological impact of their extraction and processing activities. Industries long accustomed to passing along to society responsibility for managing their toxic by-products accept doing so as a natural right."[16]

Sumptuous Simplicity

Engaging in voluntary simplicity is hardly synonymous with abstinence. Only buying what you need in bulk may be frugal, but it's far from ascetic. Taking care of what you own so the product lasts its full lifespan is prudent, not miserly. Obtaining more for less and avoiding interest payments on credit cards are shrewd strategies, not stingy ones.

Still, old habits are not easily jettisoned, and to further compli-cate matters, Americans are an independent lot who don't appre-ciate others dictating how they should lead their lives. While many citizens may be favorably disposed towards directing their priorities away from conspicuous consumption, their actual deci-sion to make this change—if it is to have any permanence—must spring from within, not be imposed from without.

It follows that to expedite the transition to a common sense-based, environmentally sustainable consumption pattern requires that people receive enough information to make informed choices. Toward that end, a course that dispassionately explores the benefits and drawbacks of various lifestyles should be standard fare in the nation's schools, perhaps at the junior high level. What constitutes true happiness should be a subject for freewheeling discussion. Teachers should leave ultimate conclusions to be drawn by students from exchanges of thoughts in the classroom and the home.

Some individuals will undoubtedly decide that ownership of a Porsche or a 24-carat diamond is the best that life has to offer. But a sustainable regimen in which material acquisition is not the determining factor should more than hold its own if its positive ramifications are fully grasped, or so a growing body of empirical evidence suggests.

Positive Thinking

To reiterate, mainstream environmentalists are individuals who are striving to nudge capitalism in the direction of environmentally sustainable activity. Their hopes for a better world rest largely on the widespread application of environmentally friendly, innovative technologies. They are optimistic about humanity's future, envisioning the evolution of a value system that should greatly increase prospects for self-fulfillment through nonmaterial means.

To denounce environmentalists as a bunch of elitists and misanthropes is outright slander. And when you consider from whence the charges originate, it's laughable.

In recent years, the mainstream environmental movement has fought to decrease the exposure of the poor to pollution. That segment of society's need for assistance has been enormous because lack of economic and political clout has frequently transformed low-income communities into toxic dumping grounds for heavily polluting industries. Environmentalists have also been leaders in the struggle to strengthen regulatory safeguards for the elderly, the young, and the infirm, all of whom are much more vulnerable than the general population to pollution.

Contrast the environmentalists' humane response with the stance of their detractors, who advocate rollbacks in anti-pollution regulations and substantial spending cuts in federal programs designed to aid the disadvantaged. Typical of this cavalier deregulatory mentality is the dismissive reaction of auto industry lobbyist Gerald Esper when confronted with scientific evidence supporting tougher proposed air quality standards to curb premature mortality: "... Many of the deaths are of elderly people and others who are sick and who would have died within days anyway."[17]

If detractors' compassion does surface, it's only in response to distress calls from major industries. When this occurs, support is extended for the continuation of corporate welfare in the form of massive government subsidies.

In another ironic twist, many of those who label environmentalists heartless are the same people who insist that our legal system force women to give birth even when they have become pregnant through incest or rape.

Pragmatism Forever

Environmentalists offer a practical blueprint rather than a litany of banal ideological catechisms. Their most far-reaching proposal: Reallocate to environmental cleanup just a fraction of the grossly disproportionate sums devoted to weaponry throughout the world. For example, researchers at the Worldwatch Institute estimate that if the $800 billion that the community of nations spends annually on armaments could be reduced by one-fourth, enough money would be freed up to put an end to the major environmental problems afflicting the human race.

Environmentalists are not merely upbeat about human potential. They draw inspiration from the built-in resilience of nature, which often—if allowed to take its course—makes the necessary adjustments to correct anomalies. There is a practical as well as spiritual side to all this. When we must intervene to prevent imminent destruction to life, limb, or property, the effectiveness of our actions will, in the long run, depend on how harmonious they are with the natural processes.

Strictly Personal

I sometimes think back to that June day in 1958 when I graduated from college. There seemed no limits to the "American

Dream," which at that time was couched in—nay, defined by—material well-being. Three-bedroom, split-level homes with a couple of cars in the driveway were regarded as a God-given right. Since there had never been an oil embargo, no one gave a second thought to our automobiles being gas guzzlers and our domiciles often being grossly energy inefficient. The only liquid cheaper than fuel was drinking water, which at that time appeared—and in most instances probably was—free of contaminants. Mortgages could be obtained for a song. And bigger was invariably perceived as better.

Many Americans' visions of unrestrained bounty have been altered in the course of the past four decades. The 1973 Mideast oil crisis served as a wake-up call that petroleum is a finite fuel source and, as time passes, the substance's diminishing supply will make an ever-increasing dent in our pocketbooks.

Inflation may not have tempered my classmates' ambitions in early adulthood, but it now lurks menacingly in the background for them and the younger generations in their families. We have seen occasional shortages of raw minerals whose infinite supply was always taken for granted. It has begun to hit home that, as global population swells, we will have no choice but to recycle many of our products and rely more heavily on other countries to provide us with some essential raw materials. Energy-efficient cars and compact houses may not yet be widely fashionable, but that is likely to change—if not out of preference, certainly out of necessity.

Yet I don't view these developments in a negative light. They will require us to concentrate our creative genius on the development of non-polluting renewable energy to heat our homes and fuel our transport, making the world a far more livable place in the long run. We should also welcome circumstances that will ultimately compel us to eliminate wasteful practices from our daily routine. That would be a long-overdue response from a throwaway society in the process of exhausting the finite sources of the planet through widespread unsustainable consumption.

While following this script will result in our owning fewer physical possessions, they will be more durable and will perform better overall than our current ones. The world may be less capable of fulfilling the materialistic fantasies so prevalent in the 1950s, but therein lies a valuable corrective: We shall be forced to draw our inspiration more from intrinsic mettle than external trappings. Although it won't always be easy, the necessary turn towards deeper introspection should enhance our ability to cope with the road blocks and abrupt detours that are an inevitable part of the journey of life.

POSTSCRIPT

*"This is not the beginning of the end, but
the end of the beginning."*
— WINSTON CHURCHILL

The environmental picture is fast-moving and ever-changing. Nonetheless, recent events conform to the environmental community's assessment of what ails us and what is needed to effect a cure. Common sense and the inexorable evolution of the laws of nature strongly suggest that environmentalists' diagnoses and antidotes will continue to be on target.

Secondhand Smoke

While skeptics continue to challenge the scientific basis for linking ETS to fatal disease, incriminating evidence builds.

The Harvard University School of Public Health just released a ten-year epidemiological study of 32,000 healthy, non-smoking nurses, which found that the subjects' risk of having a heart attack doubled as a result of exposure to ETS at home or work. It's the most comprehensive study to date, and one no responsible regulator could ignore in determining whether to ban cigarette smoking inside public buildings and other non-residential structures.[1]

Furthermore, the first-ever ETS lawsuit against tobacco manufacturers was recently settled, with the industry agreeing to pay $300 million over three years for research on smoking-related diseases (though admitting no culpability). Filed initially on behalf of a non-smoking stewardess who worked for American Airlines for 14 years and developed lung cancer, the complaint became a springboard for a class action by 60,000 current and former flight attendants seeking $5 billion in damages.

While the settlement required the airline employees to forfeit any right to pursue their class action or seek punitive damages against the tobacco companies, the plaintiffs remained free to initiate individual lawsuits to collect compensatory damages for adverse health impacts. In addition, the burden of proving whether ETS is responsible for a person's sickness shifts from the individual to the industry under the terms of the settlement. That should set the stage for numerous future claims against the cigarette companies, claims whose resolution no doubt will help define ETS's causal relationship to respiratory illness.

Renewables

Even as a West Coast utility made the largest single purchase of solar cells in history, bashers persisted in heaping ridicule on the suggestion that renewables would one day serve as a major energy source for the nation.[2]

The Sacramento, California, Municipal Utility District signed a contract to buy 10 megawatts of solar cells by the year 2002, a move that U.S. Energy Department experts say will create an economy of scale, enabling sun power to be price competitive with traditional sources of energy.

But Sacramento might as well be in another galaxy as far as U.S. Senate Majority Leader Trent Lott is concerned. In the classic basher mold, he told a receptive audience at a convention of the Independent Petroleum Association of America that "solar power is a hippies' program from the seventies, and they're still pushing this stuff."[3] So much for the leadership that is supposed to pilot our nation into a safe and secure harbor at the turn of the century. More perspicacious guidance had better come from the grassroots, or we shall be in for some hard times.

Electric Cars

Progress in the development of the electric car continues, despite bashers' atypical lapse of faith in the capacity of human genius to effect formidable change. Ordinarily, they view technology as the source of salvation, unless of course success doesn't fit neatly into their ideological mold.

One advance in non-polluting automobile technology is the introduction and planned manufacture of lightweight zinc-air batteries that are environmentally safe and possess four to six times the range of lead batteries that power current electric vehicles.

Another breakthrough involves development of a device that takes only ten minutes to recharge the battery of an electric car. Most revolutionary of all is the recent U.S. Energy Department's announcement that researchers have discovered how to use fuel cells instead of batteries to run electric cars. Estimates are the technology won't be ready for mass production until 2010, but when it is, Americans will have at their disposal a non-polluting vehicle that is quickly recharged and capable of twice the gas mileage of current conventional models.

Costs

Earlier in this book, there was a discussion of scientists' attempts to place a dollar value on wetlands. Such computations are proceeding on an even broader scale, with a group of researchers at the University of Maryland's Institute for Ecological Economics responsible for the latest calculations. This team of scientists projected from existing data that global ecosystems provide life-support services worth an average of $33 trillion annually, an amount nearly twice the world's yearly gross national product. Among nature's benefits priced by the researchers were air and water purification, waste decomposition, and crop pollination.[4] These calculations are made in response to contentions by numerous economists that we have imposed an overly stringent environmental protection regime which costs us more than it's worth.

Responding to traditional economists by using their own language is undoubtedly useful in emphasizing the importance of conservation, absent the realization that justifying elemental environmental protection in terms of dollars and cents is ultimately a pointless exercise. That realization is still not widespread enough to prevail in our bottom line-oriented society. Many people have yet to grasp that a price tag can't be placed on natural resources that are essential to our continued existence and cannot be replicated by us if they were ever allowed to disappear. Which leads to a most pressing unresolved question: How long can we ignore this reality without paying a painful price for failing to improve on traditional economists' anachronistic value system?

Prince William Sound

Eight years after the infamous Exxon Valdez oil spill in Alaska's Prince William Sound, the ecosystem has not yet fully recovered.[5] Populations of harbor seals, harlequin ducks, and Pacific herring remain devastated, and sea otters, salmon, and mussels have still not returned to their original numbers, according to the latest official surveys. Alaskans report that on some of Prince William Sound's beaches, the smell of oil persists and, in some instances, one can even uncover petroleum residues by turning over the sand with one's foot.

Oil spill apologists' reassurance that a damaged ecosystem will eventually recover still begs the questions of how long such a process will take, and how complete the rejuvenation will be.

Climate Changes

The bashers continue to use glib distortion in an effort to discredit the global warming threat. Their most recent line is that the earth's overall temperature cooled in 1996, the latest year of record. They further dub that year as "an average one, both climatically and rhetorically."[6]

Once again, bashers employ ellipsis to create a false set of circumstances that support their ideologically driven dismissal of global warming. Yes, the year 1996 was slightly cooler than 1995. What they neglect to point out is that the latest official readings still make 1996 the fifth warmest year our planet has experienced since records of global surface temperatures were first kept in the mid-nineteenth century. It should also be noted that despite the bashers' contention that no significant warming trend has been detected in the past 10 years,[7] the 1990s are already the warmest decade on record. So says the national Aeronautic and Space Administration's Goddard Institute for Space Studies, whose job it is to monitor global climate variability.

Another popular basher theme is that the fiscal burden which greenhouse emission reduction requirements will place on industry will ultimately bankrupt the economy. We've heard the corporate world cry wolf many times in the past when faced with tougher regulations, and then go on to realize record profits. Be apprised there is no reason to believe the scenario would be any different in this case. Indeed, a number of recent studies by public interest groups have exposed the flawed economic models that industry has used to overstate compliance costs and job losses in a self-serving attempt to evade its cleanup responsibilities.[8] Environmentalists' well-documented conclusion, in fact, is that tax reform, elimination of federal fossil fuel subsidies, and improved energy efficiency could meet Greenhouse Treaty emission reduction goals without negative economic impacts, and in all likelihood would spawn positive ones.

Three Mile Island

Uncertainty persists over the health impacts from the 1979 malfunction of the Three Mile Island nuclear power plant. A 1990 Columbia University epidemiological study concluded there was no linkage between the radiation release and cancer rates among people living near the plant. The study is suspect, however, since it monitored residents for only a six-year stretch after the mishap—too short a time for some cancers to emerge from their incubation period. Moreover, a University of North Carolina epidemiological study that used essentially the same data and was released February 24, 1997, did find a correlation between the TMI accident and increased rates of lung cancer and leukemia near the Pennsylvania plant.[9]

While the precise health effects of the nuclear power plant mishap on American soil are still very much in question, the evidence is far clearer in connection with the 1986 Chernobyl nuclear reactor accident in the Ukraine. There were fatalities on site at the time of the Chernobyl meltdown, and in April 1996, Russian researchers released a study of the long-term effects of excessive radiation exposure at Chernobyl. What these researchers found was shocking—the offspring of individuals living in the vicinity of Chernobyl at the time of the disaster had a much higher incidence of genetic damage than children residing elsewhere. So much for the bashers' insistence that nuclear power is as benign an energy alternative as society possesses.

Our life support system's constant evolution guarantees that new environmental challenges will emerge, regardless of how prudently we proceed. What's most comforting is that we are endowed with the intellect to make the necessary adjustments. The only way we can fail is if we allow ourselves to be seduced into inaction—or the wrong actions—by those who would forge ahead without regard to the ebb and flow of nature.

NOTES

ABSURD PROPOSITIONS

1. Joseph L. Bast, Peter J. Hill, and Richard C. Rue, *Eco-Sanity, a Common Sense Guide to Environmentalism* (Lanham, Maryland: Madison Books, 1994), p. 103
2. Executive Summary, Scientific Assessment of Ozone Depletion, World Meteorological Organization, 1994, p. 23
3. Flattau column, December 17, 1994, from conversation with Dr. Devra Davis
4. *Science* magazine, vol. 274, November 15, 1996, p. 1150
5. Dixy Lee Ray article in the *Wall Street Journal*, April 1993
6. Flattau, *New Mexican*, April 22, 1993
7. *New York Times*, January 17, 1995
8. Alston Chase, *Washington Times*, June 9, 1995
9. Michael Fumento, *Science Under Siege* (New York, N.Y.: William Morrow and Co., 1993), p. 359
10. Ibid., p. 42
11. Flattau, *New Mexican*, June 8, 1995
12. Anna Bramwell, *Ecology in the 20th Century* (New Haven, Conn.: Yale University Press, 1989)
13. Ibid., p. 204

FALSE ASSUMPTIONS

1. Environmental Protection Agency statistics
2. *Eco-sanity*, p. 9
3. Ibid., p. 15
4. *Conserving Land*, Population Action International, p. 12
5. Testimony by EPA Administrator Carol Browner before Congress, April 1995
6. *Morbidity and Mortality Weekly Report*, Centers for Disease Control, May 25, 1995
7. Conversation with Devra Davis
8. Health section, *The Washington Post*, February 14, 1995, p. 16
9. *Eco-sanity*, p. 9
10. Ibid., p. 15
11. *Breath Taking*, a Natural Resources Defense Council report, May 18, 1996
12. *1994 Health Update*, American Forests, p. 5
13. *Science Under Siege*, p. 360
14. Per Pinstrup-Andersen, *World Food Trends and How They May be Modified*, International Food Policy Research Institute, October 1993

15. Julian Simon, Earth Day statement, April 22, 1990

16. Letter from Gordon Durnil to Sen. Max Baucus, D-Montana, February 16, 1994

17. *Eco-sanity*, p. 122

18. Ronald Bailey, *Eco-Scam* (New York, N.Y.: St. Martin's Press, 1993), p. xi

19. *Science Under Siege*, p. 369

20. *Jobs and the Environment*, Economic Policy Institute, January 15, 1994

21. *A New Home on the Range*, Wilderness Society, September 12, 1995

22. *Science* magazine, April 28, 1995

23. United Nations Environmental Programme News, September-October 1986, p. 10

24. Worldwatch Institute Paper No. 89, p. 48

25. Ron Arnold and Alan Gottlieb, *Trashing the Economy* (Bellevue, Washington: Free Enterprise Press, 1993), p. 21

26. Ibid., p. 24

27. *National Review*, December 19, 1994, p. 34

28. Glenn Sugameli, *National Wildlife EnviroAction Magazine*, June 1995, p. 11

29. Ibid.

30. Flattau column, August 8, 1993

31. Flattau column, *Wilmington* (Delaware) *Journal*, January 4, 1993

32. Ibid.

33. Ibid.

34. Richard L. Stroup, *Taking the Environment Seriously* (Lanham, Maryland: Rowman and Littlefield, 1993), p. 61

35. William C. Patric, Trust Land Administration in Western States, Public Land Institute, 1981, p. 9

36. *Philadelphia Inquirer*, March 26, 1995, p. E3

37. Ibid.

38. American Geophysical Union press release, May 29, 1995

39. Competitive Enterprise Institute Environmental briefing book, August 1994, p. 3 and 5

40. Ibid.

41. *Sierra Magazine*, November/December 1993, p. 88

42. Ibid.

43. *Population Bulletin*, Vol. 50, No. 1, Population Reference Bureau, March 1995, p. 31

44. *Phantom Risk* (Cambridge, Mass.: MIT Press, 1993), p. 179

45. *Washington Times*, editorial page, May 3, 1994, p. A18

46. Tony Snow, guest hosting for Limbaugh on his radio show, January 3, 1996: "Give lab animals too much of anything, even water, and they get cancer."

47. *The Real Story*, American Health Association and the Environmental Working Group, April 1995, p. 2

48. *Eco-sanity*, p. 99

49. Flattau column, May 26, 1993

50. Ibid.
51. *The Real Story*, p. 9
52. Pimentel et al., *Agriculture Without Pesticides*, Cornell University, November 4, 1977
53. Al Meyerhoff, Natural Resources Defense Council (NRDC), *New York Times*, March 9, 1993
54. *Eco-sanity*, p. 101
55. *The Real Story*, p. 2
56. *New York Times*, October 10, 1993, p. E6
57. *The Washington Post*, May 29, 1996
58. *Investors Business Daily*, July 19, 1993, p. 1
59. Meyerhoff memo, NRDC, March 9, 1993
60. Flattau column, September 21, 1994
61. Greg Millman, op-ed page, *Baltimore Sun*, January 12, 1993
62. Ben Bolch and Harold Lyons, *Apocalypse Not* (Washington, D.C.: Cato Institute, 1993), p. 28
63. Walt Williams, op-ed page, *Washington Times*, February 18, 1995
64. *Eco-scam*, p.62
65. *State of World Population*, UN Population Fund, 1992, p. 7
66. Flattau column, September 21, 1994
67. Nicholas Eberstadt, American Enterprise Institute, *Washington Times*, March 11, 1996, p. A19
68. Memorandum from Sally Eccleston, Population Action International, March 12, 1996
69. Ben Wattenberg, op-ed page, *Washington Times*, March 17, 1994
70. Mattans, *The Washington Post*, September 12, 1994
71. *Eco-scam*, p. 52
72. Ibid.
73. Lindsey Grant, *Focus*, Vol. 3, No. 2, 1993, p. 34
74. David Osterfeld, *Prosperity Vs. Planning* (New York, N.Y.: Oxford University Press, 1992)
75. *Information Please Environmental Almanac*, World Resources Institute, 1993
76. *Prosperity Vs. Planning*, p. 134
77. Competitive Enterprise Institute briefing book, p. 66
78. Flattau column, January 6, 1990
79. *New York Times*, September 18, 1997
80. Charles Cushman, op-ed page, *Washington Times*, July 27, 1995
81. Robert Perciasepe, assistant administrator for water, EPA, letter to the editor, *Washington Times*, August 15, 1995

CAUSES CELEBRES

1. Eric Peters, op-ed page, *Washington Times*, February 21, 1995, p. A11
2. Rush Limbaugh radio broadcast, December 22, 1995
3. *Science* magazine, May 19, 1995
4. Chapman, op-ed page, *Washington Times*, May 31, 1995
5. Electric Vehicle Industry Association fact sheet, November 26, 1994

6. Ibid.

7. Flattau column, November 27, 1994

8. CTA Transportation Technology Review, Vol. 1, No. 1, November 16, 1995

9. Phone conversation with Dave Goldstein, Electric Vehicle Industry Association, December 22, 1995

10. Mona Charen, op-ed page, *Washington Times*, January 24, 1995

11. James DeLong, Competitive Enterprise Institute report, June 1, 1994; *Municipal Solid Waste Report*, May 1994

12. Charen, January 24, 1995

13. *Worldwatch Magazine*, Worldwatch Institute, July/August 1995

14. Ibid.

15. Flattau column, February 23, 1994

16. Flattau, *Santa Fe New Mexican*, April 29, 1993

17. *Science Under Siege*, p. 32-33; *Apocalypse Not*, p. 8 and 39

18. *Apocalypse Not*, p. 40

19. Kenneth Smith, *Alar One Year Later*, American Council on Science and Health special report, March 1990

20. *Apocalypse Not*, p. 43

21. *Environmental Health Threats to Children*, EPA, September 1996

22. *Science Under Siege*, p. 26

23. *Trashing the Economy*, p. 12; *Science Under Siege*, p. 99

24. *Trashing the Economy*, p. 12

25. *Eco-sanity*, p. 168

26. Ibid., p. 176

27. *Science Under Siege*, p. 100

28. Keith Schneider, *New York Times*, August 15, 1991

29. *Apocalypse Not*, p. 59; *Eco-sanity*, p. 166; *Washington Times*, May 12, 1994, p. A18; *Science Under Siege*, p. 123

30. *Apocalypse Not*, p. 58; *Science Under Siege*, p. 112

31. Ibid.

32. *American Journalism Review*, June 1993, p. 231

33. Ellen Silbergeld, Environmental Defense Fund staff scientist, letter to *Baltimore Sun*, November 20, 1993

34. "Rhesus monkey fed low doses of dioxin and develops endometriosis," *Fundamental Applied Toxicology*, 1993; Peter deFuir, EDF, letter to *Washington Times*, March 11, 1994

35. Kathryn Kelly, *Wall Street Journal*, June 29, 1995, p. A16

36. Michael Gaugh, congressional testimony, December 13, 1995

37. *The Washington Post*, June 13, 1994

38. *Apocalypse Not*, p. 59

39. Phone conversation with Dr. Ed Fitzgerald, head of New York State Love Canal study, February 29, 1995

40. Michelle Malkin, Competitive Enterprise Institute, *Washington Times*, December 26, 1995, p. A17

41. Dr. Kelly Brix, New York State Health Department, May 19, 1994

42. *USA Today*, August 17, 1995, p. 10A

43. Telephone conversation with Admiral Elmo Zumwalt, December 26, 1995

44. Ibid.

45. Testimony before House Energy and Environment Science Subcommittee, December 13, 1995
46. *New York Times*, August 15, 1991
47. *American Journalism Review*, June 1993, p. 22
48. *Phantom Risk*, p. 279
49. Ibid.
50. *Atomic Harvest*, p. 34
51. *Phantom Risk*, p. 292
52. Pam Miller, Alaska Coalition, doctorate thesis on media coverage of Exxon
53. Phone conversation with Pam Miller, December 28, 1995
54. *A Moment on the Earth* (New York, N.Y.: Viking Press, 1995), p. 57
55. Ibid., p. 55; Exxon Valdez Oil Spill Trustee Council, 1995
56. Alston Chase, *Washington Times*, May 13, 1995; *Eco-sanity*, p. 154
57. Freeman publication, March 29, 1995, p. 155
58. Trustee Council, p. 10
59. Ibid.
60. Flattau column, *St. Louis Post-Dispatch*, October 23, 1995
61. Ibid.
62. *USA Today*, May 16, 1994, p. 13A
63. Journal of the National Cancer Institute, December 1994
64. Fumento, *Washington Times*, June 27, 1995
65. Journal of NCI, Vol. 86, No. 24, December 21, 1994; Flattau column, January 5, 1995, based on phone conversation with Dr. Michael C.R. Alavanja, one of the authors of the NCI report
66. *Technopolitics* newsletter, November 1993
67. Easterbrook, *New Republic*, April 30, 1990
68. Flattau column, *Santa Fe New Mexican*, November 23, 1993
69. Flattau column, *New Mexican*, September 23, 1993
70. EPA Task Force report, 1992, p. 128
71. David Rothbard and Craig Rucker, Committee For Constructive Tomorrow (a free-market think tank), *Washington Times*, March 28, 1994
72. Alston Chase, *Washington Times*, February 2, 1994
73. Flattau column, March 5, 1994
74. Ibid.
75. *Washington Times*, op-ed page, October 9, 1994
76. *Washington Times*, op-ed page, December 29, 1994
77. Bruce Fein, *Washington Times*, October 11, 1993
78. Advertisement, *The Washington Post*, July 3, 1994
79. *The Washington Post*, June 8, 1994, p. A2
80. *Journal of the American Medical Association*, March 8, 1995
81. Centers for Disease Control; EPA Assessments; *USA Today*, May 14, 1996, p. 10
82. *New York Times*, September 21, 1994
83. *Journal of Tobacco Control*, May 14, 1996
84. Maimonides Medical Center, Brooklyn, New York, study, October 21, 1996
85. *Journal of the American Medical Association*, April 15, 1995
86. *USA Today*, March 19, 1996

87. *The Washington Post*, July 24, 1994

88. Hearing of House Energy and Commerce Subcommittee on Health and Environment, July 21, 1993

89. Letter to the editor, *The Washington Post*, September 1995

90. William Rusher, *Washington Times*, December 29, 1994, p. A17

91. Ibid.; Rusher quoting Forbes senior editor Peter Brimelow in Fall 1994 *American Smokers Journal*.

92. Fax, Office of Smoking and Health, Centers for Disease Control, January 19, 1996

93. *Ecoscam*, p. 142

94. S. Fred Singer, *The Earth Times*, May 31, 1994

95. Dr. James Acker, letter to *Washington Times*, October 8, 1995

96. *New York Times*, January 27, 1995

97. *State of the World 1996*, Worldwatch Institute, p. 23

98. Ibid.

99. *Ecoscam*, p. 147

100. Ibid., p. 150

101. Global Environmental Change Report, Environment Media Services, 1996

102. *Ecoscam*, p. 152

103. Ibid., p. 156

104. Ibid., p. 161

105. Pat Michaels, Competitive Enterprise Institute, "It's Your Business" television program, April 1, 1994

106. *Ecoscam*, p. 161

107. Selinger, Duke University, SEJ conference, October 24, 1993

108. *New York Times*, September 14, 1993

109. "It's Your Business," April 1, 1994

110. Dan Lashof, NRDC memo, May 12, 1995

111. Ibid.

112. Ibid.

113. Warren Leary, *New York Times*, July 16, 1996

114. *Boston Globe*, August 29, 1996, p. A5

115. Letter to the editor, *Washington Times*, June 14, 1995

116. EPA Assistant Administrator Mary Nichols, statement, September 20, 1995

117. Ibid.

118. *Apocalypse Not*, p. 87; Alston Chase, *Washington Times*, August 25, 1994

119. World Climate Organization report, 1994

120. *Science* magazine, June 11, 1993

121. Alston Chase, *Washington Times*, September 4, 1993

122. *Science* magazine, June 11, 1993, p. 1572-73

123. Rothbard, *Washington Times*, May 24, 1994

124. World Climate Organization report, 1994

125. Singer, congressional testimony, September 20, 1995

126. National Weather Service, April 1995

127. Congressional testimony by Albritton, September 20, 1995

128. *Science* magazine, June 11, 1993, p. 1583

129. Singer, congressional hearing, September 20, 1995

130. World Meteorological Organization (WMO) executive summary, 1994

131. Singer, *Washington Times*, September 16, 1995

132. WMO scientific assessment of ozone depletion, 1994 executive summary, produced by 29 of the world's leading experts in atmospheric science

133. Singer, op-ed page, *Washington Times*, February 22, 1994; Alston Chase, op-ed page, *Washington Times*, August 25, 1994

134. Dr. Rex A. Amonette, president, American Academy of Dermatology, House Science Committee Hearing, September 20, 1995

135. Setlow, congressional testimony, September 20, 1995

136. Aaron Wildavsky, *But Is It True?* (Cambridge, Mass.: Harvard University Press, 1995); Science Magazine, June 19, 1993

137. Robert Gordon and James Streeter, National Wilderness Institute, *Washington Times*, February 8, 1994, p. A16

138. Fish and Wildlife Service position paper, December 30, 1993

139. Letter to *Washington Times*, March 21, 1994

140. Beatie speech, May 20, 1995

141. *Wall Street Journal*, December 27, 1993

142. Gordon and Streeter, op-ed page, *Washington Times*, February 8, 1994

143. Yale Professor Steve Kellert, *Defenders Magazine*, Autumn 1993; *New York Times*, December 21, 1993, p. B5

144. Ed Grimsley, op-ed page, *Washington Times*, December 11, 1993

145. MIT Professor Steven Meyer, March 1995 study

146. Glen Spain, Pacific Coast Federation of Fishermen's Associations

147. Massachusetts Audubon Society report, November 1993

148. Julian Simon, Council for Advancement of Science Writing Briefing, St. Louis, Missouri, November 2, 1993

149. 1996 IUCN list of threatened animals

150. Letter to editor, *New York Times*, May 25, 1993

151. GAO report, RCED 94-224, July 8, 1994

152. Defenders of Wildlife fact sheet

153. *New York Times*, February 11, 1996, p. 20

CHARACTER ASSASSINATION

1. *Ecoscam*, p. 43

2. Tony Snow, op-ed page, *Washington Times*, September 9, 1994

3. Paul Ehrlich, *Population Bomb* (New York, N.Y.: Ballantine Books, 1968), p.72

4. Paul Ehrlich, *Our Planet* newsletter, vol. 6, no. 3

5. Carl Haub, demographer for Population Reference Bureau, briefing, February 23, 1996

6. Jacoby, op-ed page, *Baltimore Sun*, February 7, 1995

7. John Walsh, letter to editor, *Wall Street Journal*, June 30, 1995

8. Paul and Anne Ehrlich, *The Population Explosion* (New York, N.Y.: Touchstone, 1990), 1991

9. *Ecoscam*, p. 62

10. Ibid., p. 9

11. Paul Ehrlich, *The Stork and the Plow*, p. 280

12. Michael Renner, Worldwatch Paper no. 89, May 1989, p. 37

13. *The Stork and the Plow*, p. 282
14. *Los Angeles Times*, February 16, 1996
15. Alston Chase, op-ed page, *Washington Times*, January 26, 1996
16. Babbitt speech in Boston to the AAAS and National Religious Partnership
17. Starter kit for Evangelical Church, Evangelical Environmental Network, 1995
18. Walter Truett Anderson, op-ed page, *Baltimore Sun*, February 1, 1995
19. Mark Dowie, *Wall Street Journal* editorial, May 26, 1995
20. Keith Schneider, *New York Times*, December 26, 1993
21. Denis Avery, Hudson Institute, talk at AAAS annual meeting in Baltimore, February 9, 1996
22. Les Brown, *Who Will Feed China*, Worldwatch Institute, 1995, p. 141

SINS OF OMISSION

1. *Ecosanity*, p. 204
2. *Taking the Environment Seriously*, p. 2
3. *State of the Planet* (New York, N.Y.: The Free Press, 1995), p. 5
4. Easterbrook, *Washington Post Magazine*, April 19, 1995, p. 14
5. Ibid., p. 28
6. Sagamore State University Analysis Bulletin
7. Mike McClosky, *Sierra Club Planet Newspaper*, July/August 1995
8. Easterbrook, *Washington Post Magazine*, April 19, 1995, p. 29
9. *Ozone Action News*, June 5, 1995
10. Easterbrook, *Moment on the Earth*, p. 12
11. EDF analysis, April 18, 1995
12. Easterbrook, *Washington Post Magazine*, April 9, 1995, p. 287
13. Ibid., p. 291
14. Ibid., p. 31
15. Ibid., p. 32
16. Easterbrook, *New Yorker*, April 10, 1995, p. 38
17. *Moment on the Earth*, p. 549
18. Ozone Action memo, June 5, 1995
19. *Moment on the Earth*, p. 296
20. EDF Refutation Report, Part One, 1995
21. Ibid., p. 35
22. *Moment on the Earth*, p.481
23. Ibid., p. 482
24. David Western, *Natural Connections* (Washington, D.C.: Island Press, 1994), p. 17
25. Ibid., p. 36
26. Ibid., p. 44
27. Telephone conversation with David Western, March 21, 1996; *New York Times*, March 13, 1996, p. 3
28. *A Moment on Earth*, p. 482
29. *Natural Connections*, p. 31
30. King Mahendra Trust for Nature Conservation and World Wildlife Fund

Biodiversity Conservation Network Project, Technical Report #2, December 30, 1995
31. *Environmental Conservation*, vol. 15, no. 2, Summer 1988
32. Jonathan Adler, *Environmentalism at the Crossroads*
(Washington, D.C.: Capital Research Center, 1995), p. 8
33. *Eco-sanity*, p. 159
34. Ibid., p. 161
35. Ibid., p. 182
36. Ibid., p. 201
37. *Science Under Siege*, p. 359
38. Ibid., p. 368
39. *Phantom Risk*, p. 154
40. Ibid., p. 155
41. Ibid., p. 279
42. *State of the Planet*
43. Ibid., p. 218

IT'S ALL IN THE TECHNIQUE

1. *Eco-scam*, p. 72
2. Ibid., p. 74
3. EPA, 1996
4. *Apocalypse Not*, p. 10
5. *Trashing the Economy*, p. 5
6. Paul Greenberg, op-ed page, *Washington Times*, June 27, 1996
7. Joseph Romm, Special Assistant to Energy Secretary, letter to *Washington Times*, June 4, 1995
8. Ibid.
9. Flattau column, January 11, 1995
10. *Apocalypse Not*, p. 4-5
11. Limbaugh, radio broadcast, April 25, 1996
12. *Eco-sanity*, p. 110
13. *Ecoscam*, p. 189
14. Alston Chase, *Baltimore Sun*, op-ed, January 16, 1996
15. *Ecoscam*, p. 129
16. *Science Under Siege*, p. 94-95
17. Ibid., p. 156
18. *Eco-sanity*, p. 216
19. Easterbrook, *Technopolitics Newsletter*, July 1995
20. *People and the Planet*, published by Planet 21, vol. 5, no. 3, 1996, p. 231
21. Rothbard and Rucker, *Washington Times*, op-ed, June 1, 1996
22. Bruce Fein, *Washington Times* op-ed, June 24, 1996, p. A16
23. Eric Peters, *Washington Times* op-ed, April 22, 1996
24. Fumento, *Washington Times* op-ed February 27, 1996
25. *Ecoscam*, p. 14
26. Ibid., p. 45
27. Alston Chase, *Washington Times* op-ed, July 13, 1995, p. A17

THE GREAT MISCOMMUNICATOR

Most of Reagan's statements in this chapter were derived
from radio scripts that he used on his syndicated series of
broadcasts prior to being elected to the presidency.

1. *Sierra Magazine*, November-December 1993
2. Ibid., p. 103
3. Charles Comanoff, 1978
4. *Environmental Reporter*, December 25, 1981, p. 1034
5. *Baltimore Sun*, commentary page, April 3, 1992
6. *Rocky Mountain Magazine*, March/April 1981
7. Flattau column, May 2, 1992
8. Ibid.

THE MADAME OF MENDACITY

1. Dixy Lee Ray, *Environmental Overkill* (Washington, D.C.: Regnery Gateway, 1993), p. 206
2. Ibid., p. 14
3. Ibid., p. 17
4. Ibid., p. 100
5. Ibid., p. 58
6. Ibid.
7. Ibid., p. 14
8. Ibid., p. 148
9. Ibid., p. 150
10. Ibid., p. 141
11. Dixy Lee Ray, *Trashing the Planet* (Washington, D.C.: Regnery Gateway, 1990), p. 163
12. Ibid., p. 31
13. Ibid., p. 6
14. Ibid., p. 153
15. Ibid., p. 84
16. Flattau, *New Mexican*, September 23, 1993
17. *Environmental Overkill*, p. 76-77
18. *Environmental Overkill*, p. 190
19. *Trashing the Planet*, p. 82
20. Ibid., p. 165
21. Dave Foreman, interview with author, June 28, 1994
22. *Environmental Overkill*, p. 126
23. Ibid., p. 126
24. Ibid., p. 75
25. *Trashing the Planet*, p. 109
26. Ibid., p. 123
27. Ibid., p. 126
28. Ibid., p. 131
29. Worldwatch Institute Paper 119, June 1994, p. 26
30. American Wind Energy Association update, June 1994

31. Ibid., p. 128
32. Worldwatch Institute Paper 119, p. 29
33. Dr. Donald Aiken, chairman of American Solar Energy Society, Renew America Topic Report, 1993, p. 7
34. *Environmental Overkill*, p. 14
35. *Trashing the Planet*, p. 89
36. *Environmental Regulation and Competitiveness* (Cambridge, Mass.: The Economic Resource Group for the U.S. Commerce Department, July 1993), p. 6
37. *Environmental Overkill*, p. 161
38. *Trashing the Planet*, p. 10
39. *Environmental Overkill*, p. 29
40. Ibid., p. 205
41. Ibid., p. 206
42. *Trashing the Planet*, p. 68
43. Ibid., p. 70
44. *Review of Science Justifying DDT Ban*, Environmental Protection Agency, 1975, p. 6
45. Flattau, *Santa Fe New Mexican*, May 12, 1994
46. Ibid.
47. 1975 EPA Report, p. 255

THE PRINCE OF PONTIFICATION

1. Rush Limbaugh, *The Way Things Ought To Be* (New York, N.Y.: Simon and Schuster, 1992), p. 153
2. Ibid., p. 169
3. Ibid., p. 154, 156
4. Ibid., p. 154
5. Stephen Kellert, *Defender* magazine, Defenders of Wildlife, 1993
6. *The Way Things Ought To Be*, p. 161
7. Limbaugh radio broadcast, May 16, 1994
8. World Resources Annual Report 1996-97
9. Ibid.
10. *The Way Things Ought To Be*, p. 165
11. Ibid., p. 166
12. Ibid., p. 166
13. Ibid., p. 106
14. Ibid., p. 103
15. Ibid., p. 167
16. Ibid., p. 168
17. Ibid., p. 169
18. Ibid., p. 105
19. Ibid., p. 107
20. Ibid., p. 108
21. Rush Limbaugh, *See, I Told You So* (New York, N.Y.: Simon and Schuster, 1993), p. 159
22. Ibid., p. 160

23. Ibid., p. 163
24. Ibid., p. 163
25. Al Gore, *Earth in the Balance* (New York, N.Y.: Houghton
Mifflin Co., 1992), p. 301
26. Ibid., p. 302
27. *See, I Told You So*, p. 158
28. Ibid., p. 162
29. Ibid., p. 162
30. Ibid., p. 163
31. *Earth In The Balance*, p. 178
32. *See, I Told You So*, p. 164
33. *Earth In The Balance*, p. 179
34. *See, I Told You So*, p. 173
35. Ibid., p. 171
36. Flattau, *St. Louis Post Dispatch*, June 20, 1994
37. Flattau, *New Mexican*, June 16, 1994
38. Lester Brown and Hal Kane, *Full House* (New York, N.Y.:
Norton, 1994), p. 80
39. *See, I Told You So*, p. 176
40. *The Way Things Ought To Be*, p. 161
41. Ibid., p. 157
42. Ibid., p. 163
43. Ibid., p. 159
44. Ibid., p. 169
45. Ibid., p. 164
46. Ibid., p. 165

THE TRUE OPTIMISTS

1. *New York Times*, October 9, 1995, p. 6
2. White House fact sheet, December 11, 1994
3. Institute for Southern Studies report, October 12, 1994
4. Bob Repetto, World Resources Institute, *Jobs, Competitiveness and Environmental Regulation*, March 15, 1995
5. Environmental Defense Fund press release, May 1, 1995
6. Conservation Fund's *Common Ground*, vol. 8, no. 1,
November/December 1996
7. EDF press release, May 28, 1996
8. Dr. Mark Shaffer, Wilderness Society, *Lifelands*, April 1994
9. American Farmland Trust press release, July 9, 1996
10. *Eco-sanity*, p. 104
11. Tides Foundation conference report, Airlie, Virginia, April 23-25, 1995
12. *Boston Globe Magazine*, August 18, 1996, p. 18
13. Herman Daly, World Bank, Northwest report, January 1996
14. Norway Symposium final statement, 1994
15. Harwood Group Survey, commissioned by the Merck Family Fund, 1995
16. Harold Crooks, author, book review in *Multinational Monitor*,
March 1995
17. *Counterpunch*, January 15, 1997

POSTSCRIPT

1. *Washington Post; New York Times*, May 20, 1997
2. *New York Times*, May 19, 1997, p. 14
3. *Washington Post*, May 23, 1997
4. *U.S. News And World Report*, May 26, 1997, p. 60
5. *New York Times*, March 16, 1997 p. 24
6. Pat Michaels, State of Climate report, 1997, p. 3
7. Ibid.
8. Dr. Fiorentin Krause, International Project for Sustainable Energy Paths, Critical Review of Economic Arguments of Fossil Fuel Industry, May 1997
9. *Washington Post*, February 24, 1997, p. A6

INDEX

To order *Tracking the Charlatans*, please write:

Global Horizons Press
1330 New Hampshire Avenue N.W., Suite 609
Washington, D.C. 20036

Please enclose payment of $15.95 plus $2.05 shipping
and handling per copy. Make checks or money orders
payable to Global Horizons Press.